GOLF AND PHILOSOPHY

The Philosophy of Popular Culture

The books published in the Philosophy of Popular Culture series will illuminate and explore philosophical themes and ideas that occur in popular culture. The goal of this series is to demonstrate how philosophical inquiry has been reinvigorated by increased scholarly interest in the intersection of popular culture and philosophy, as well as to explore through philosophical analysis beloved modes of entertainment, such as movies, TV shows, and music. Philosophical concepts will be made accessible to the general reader through examples in popular culture. This series seeks to publish both established and emerging scholars who will engage a major area of popular culture for philosophical interpretation and examine the philosophical underpinnings of its themes. Eschewing ephemeral trends of philosophical and cultural theory, authors will establish and elaborate on connections between traditional philosophical ideas from important thinkers and the ever-expanding world of popular culture.

Series Editor

Mark T. Conard, Marymount Manhattan College, NY

Books in the Series

The Philosophy of Stanley Kubrick, edited by Jerold J. Abrams
Football and Philosophy, edited by Michael W. Austin
Tennis and Philosophy, edited by David Baggett
The Philosophy of the Coen Brothers, edited by Mark T. Conard
The Philosophy of Film Noir, edited by Mark T. Conard
The Philosophy of Martin Scorsese, edited by Mark T. Conard
The Philosophy of Neo-Noir, edited by Mark T. Conard
The Philosophy of Horror, edited by Thomas Fahy
The Philosophy of The X-Files, edited by Dean A. Kowalski
Steven Spielberg and Philosophy, edited by Dean A. Kowalski
The Philosophy of the Western, edited by Jennifer L. McMahon and B. Steve Csaki
The Philosophy of Science Fiction Film, edited by Steven M. Sanders
The Philosophy of TV Noir, edited by Steven M. Sanders and Aeon J. Skoble
Basketball and Philosophy, edited by Jerry L. Walls and Gregory Bassham

GOLF AND PHILOSOPHY

Lessons from the Links

EDITED BY ANDY WIBLE

THE UNIVERSITY PRESS OF KENTUCKY

Scholarly publisher for the Commonwealth,
serving Bellarmine University, Berea College, Centre College of Kentucky,
Eastern Kentucky University,The Filson Historical Society, Georgetown College,
Kentucky Historical Society, Kentucky State University, Morehead State
University, Murray State University, Northern Kentucky University, Transylvania
University, University of Kentucky, University of Louisville, and Western
Kentucky University.
All rights reserved.

Editorial and Sales Offices: The University Press of Kentucky
663 South Limestone Street, Lexington, Kentucky 40508-4008
www.kentuckypress.com

14 13 12 11 10   5 4 3 2 1

Library of Congress Cataloging-in-Publication Data

Golf and philosophy : lessons from the links / edited by Andy Wible.
    p. cm.
Includes bibliographical references and index.
ISBN 978-0-8131-2594-7 (hardcover : alk. paper)
1. Golf—Philosophy. 2. Sportsmanship. I. Wible, Andy.
GV967.G566 2010
796.35201—dc22   2010024571

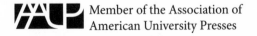

CONTENTS

THE BACK NINE

ACKNOWLEDGMENTS

At age fourteen, I was asked what I wanted to do when I grew up. My response was that I wanted to be a golf pro. I had just fallen in love with the game, and the idea of playing it the rest of my life sounded ideal. I had heard Fuzzy Zoeller once say that he was a lucky man because he never had a job. He simply played golf. Like Fuzzy, I didn't want a "real" job, because most people I knew hated their work. They lived for vacation: they lived to play golf.

Later on, in high school, I realized two important things. First, my skills and mental aptitude for golf were limited. My ability to hit a long, straight drive was suspect, and my talent for choking under pressure was keen. Second, I noticed that teaching golf professionals usually didn't get to play much golf. Though their services are essential to the game, they mainly watched other people practice and play. Such a life seemed more like torture than doing what I loved.

Fortunately, we all have more than one occupational love in life, and I discovered that when I took a philosophy class in college. Philosophy was as mentally stimulating as golf and didn't require the fine motor skills. Twelve short years of college and I do finally have a job that I love. I am lucky to spend my days teaching and writing philosophy. This project has thus been a double joy, bringing together two loves of my life.

Thankfully, many who are attracted to golf are also attracted to philosophy, so I have had an immense amount of help putting this project together. I first want to thank the chapter contributors. They have kindly put up with my timelines and suggestions throughout the process, and their diverse insights and penchant for the game are thoughtfully displayed on every page. I would additionally like to thank Blair Morrissey; Richard Doctor; David Baggett; Tom Maloy; Jim Reynolds; Chris Lubbers; Patrick Lin; Sue Meeuwenburg; Bob Ferrentino; Robert Simon; the series editor, Mark Conard; my brother, Paul; my mother, Nancy; my partner, Oliver Songlingco; the anonymous reviewers of the manuscript; and many others for giving helpful suggestions and encouragement throughout the process. The editing and formatting expertise of Dana Troutman also saved me much agony.

Working with the University Press of Kentucky has been a delight. Anne Dean Watkins in particular has been wonderful, offering suggestions and promptly answering my incessant questions.

A final note of thanks goes to my father, Dan, and my grandfather Harry for introducing me to golf. I will always appreciate their companionship, competition, and lessons on the swing, manners, and life.

WARM-UP

A frequent comment about the eternal issues of philosophy is that everything is a footnote to the ancient philosophers Plato and Aristotle. Subsequent philosophers are simply clarifying and expanding their comprehensive consideration of the ultimate questions of humanity. So why write a book about golf and philosophy? Plato and Aristotle never played golf, so what is there to discuss? The short answer is that if Plato and Aristotle were alive today, they probably would be avid golfers. For at least a few hours a day, they'd change their togas and sandals for knickers and spiked sandals. Lovers of wisdom and the good life are lovers of golf.

In fact, given the chance, what most people really want to do is play golf. When stars retire from basketball, baseball, tennis, football, and other sports, they usually hit the pastures of the world's golf courses. Presidents, physicians, celebrities, CEOs, and philosophers commonly choose golf as their main recreational activity. Yet golf is not simply a sport of the rich, powerful, famous, and tenured. Thousands of public golf courses and driving ranges across the globe allow more than 61 million people to play golf. From Tokyo to Seoul to Sydney to Cape Town to Stockholm to Dubai, golf has emerged from the grazing fields of St. Andrews. The expansion of golf has been the greatest in the United States. The United States contains more than half of all golfers, hosts the most prestigious professional tour, and in the Ryder Cup and the President's Cup takes on much of the rest of the world. With the help of television, the world has watched great American icons like Arnold Palmer and Jack Nicklaus popularize golf for the world's masses, and has seen Tiger Woods reenergize and diversify the sport.

Once people take up this intricate and addictive game, it often consumes them for a lifetime. People don't just play golf; they watch it, they contemplate it, and, most important, they live it: they join golf clubs, vacation at golf resorts, do business on the course, and live in golf communities. Golf becomes intertwined with every aspect of life. More than other sports, playing, watching, and being around golf becomes a large part of who people are.

But why do people choose golf? For some it may be the civility and camaraderie of the game. For others perhaps it is that golf is not as physically demanding as other sports. Almost anyone can play. Ironically, though, the main enduring reason for the attraction is that golf is so challenging. Golf is like a Sudoku that cannot be solved. It seduces one into playing because it looks so easy. The ball is not being hurled at ninety miles an hour, and other players are not throwing themselves in one's way. How hard can it be? The more one plays, however, the more one sees the mental and physical conundrums of the game. Great minds and great athletes are attracted to golf out of a love of a good and consuming puzzle.

Philosophy is similar in many ways. The philosophical questions such as *What is right and wrong, Who am I, What is beauty, Does God exist,* and *Does life have meaning* may at first blush seem easy to answer. Of course, those who have delved into a philosophical analysis of these questions know that they are eternal questions that have perplexed the greatest minds. Answering one philosophical question often creates twenty more. Progress is passionately sought and sometimes achieved, but a wise person learns that these are the most difficult, eternal, and fundamental questions of human existence.

Great thinkers love philosophy for the same reason great and not-so-great golfers love golf, and *Golf and Philosophy* is an effort for the first time to bring these two great cerebral traditions together in a systematic way. This book examines a wide range of ethical, social, and even metaphysical issues that arise around the game itself, and it uses the history and experience of golf as a way to enliven and enrich the enduring questions of philosophy. But don't worry; the book is written for those who love golf, and so, as is true of many good golf courses, every effort has been made to ensure that each hole (chapter) is accessible to all readers while being challenging enough to spur excitement for every handicap.

Some of the wide range of philosophical thoughts and questions explored are: How should we evaluate the aesthetic beauty of golf? Can Ben Hogan and Confucius teach us to live and play better? Does golf teach civility and good character? What can golf teach us about moral theory? Why are amateurs less virtuous than professionals in golf, when it is the other way around in other sports? Does golf adequately value diversity? Is playing golf irrational? Why are golf and mysticism so commonly linked? Can a better understanding of personal identity help overcome midround disasters such as shanks? Can Taoism free our minds to play better golf? What can Plato and Confucius teach us about the real and the ideal in golf and in life? Is the idea of a perfect body and swing in golf a myth? If we better understand the meaning of golf, do we also better understand the meaning of life? Does golf foster and lead to a greater understanding of true friendship? We start each nine with the reflections of two prominent and seasoned philosophers. On the front nine Al Gini begins with the question "Why is play important, especially golf?" And on the back nine Tom Regan's experiences at Pebble Beach start one wondering about the allure and meaning of the game. The final hole is a series of swing thoughts intended to be a catalyst for your own philosophizing when you watch this treasured game and stroll along the world's great courses.

Each hole of the book is written by a person who loves and respects the traditions of both golf and philosophy. As you read and ponder, may your own passion for both traditions grow ever deeper.

THE FRONT NINE

I. The Beauty of the Game

Golf and the Importance of Play

Al Gini

> The true amateur athlete . . . is one who takes up sport for the fun and love of it, and to whom success or defeat is a secondary matter for so long as the play is good. . . . It is from doing the thing well, doing the thing handsomely, doing the thing intelligently that one derives the pleasure which is the essence of sport.
>
> —William James

The statistics are clear. Whether we want to or not, most of us work too much. Sure, we often talk about playing sports like golf, but as adults, there is nothing more we do with our lives than work. We will not sleep as much, spend as much time with our families and friends, eat as much, or recreate and rest as much as we will work. Don't get me wrong; work is important. Our work gives access to salary, stuff, success, and a sense of identity. But just as we all need to work and fulfill ourselves, we also need to play.[1] The joy of picking up the crooked sticks, tackling that dog leg, and beating a friend in a three-dollar Nassau is good for us.

The word *play*, from the Middle English term *plega*, "to leap for joy, to dance, to rejoice, to be glad," is about activity outside the sphere of the customary, the necessary, or the materially useful. According to the poet Diane Ackerman, play "is a refuge from ordinary life, a sanctuary of the mind, where one is exempt from life's customs, methods, and decrees."[2] Her fellow poet Donald Hall suggests that play is about "absorbedness"—"a noun with a lot of verb in it"—which connotes concentration, contentment, loss of self, loss of time, happiness, and joy.[3]

For both children and adults, play is about awe, wonder, rapture, and enthusiasm. Play is something we want to do, something we choose to do that is not work, that we enjoy, and that gives us gratification and fun. In play we drop inhibitions, give ourselves permission to imagine, to be creative, to be curious. Play, like laughter, is an end in itself, something done without any other incentive except for the pleasure involved in the activity itself.[4]

In a cover story in the *Utne Reader,* Mark Harris argues that children are masters of play. They need to play. It's what they do. It's the way they ingest the world. It's the way they learn. By acting out or playing out a situation, they acquire cognitive and motor skills. In play they create a map of reality and come to know and define the other players in the game. Play, says the psychiatrist Lenore Terr, is not frivolous. It is one of the ways we become human. Play, like laughter, says Terr, is crucial at every stage of life. Play, for children and adults alike, helps us unlock the door to the world of ourselves.[5] According to Stuart Brown, president of the National Institute of Play, "Play is part of the developmental sequences of becoming a human primate. If you look at what produces learning and memory and well-being, play is as fundamental as any other aspect of life, including sleep and dreams."[6]

All of us need more play. All of us need to "vacate" ourselves from our jobs and the wear and tear of the "everydayness" of our lives. All of us need to get absorbed in, focused on, something of interest outside ourselves. All of us need to escape, if only for a while, to retain our perspective on *who we are* and *who we don't want to be.*

True play, as it occurs in many sports and particularly in golf, represents a kind of freedom of expression, a chance for openness and creativity. Play is a way of doing something and nothing at the same time. It's a way of both letting go and losing yourself without getting totally lost in the process. It's a way of experimenting with reality. It's an excuse to laugh. It's a catalyst for growth. It's a way of finding balance. Without play, we risk the diminishment of self.

Before turning to the virtues of the "beatific visions" that are possible to achieve while playing golf, allow me to set the stage further with a brief discussion of the nature and purpose of sports in general. Like all forms of play, sports are something we can do or view "for the love of it," "for its own sake alone," "for the joy of the doing." At their best, sports offer a benign distraction, simple entertainment, an escape, or a buffer against the realities of the everyday world. In the words of the philosopher Baruch Spinoza:

"Give men an open field, a ball to catch or kick or something or someone to chase, and they are happy, despite all else."[7]

But besides being fun, sports are supposed to be challenging, expansive, expressive, and encouraging of growth. The ancient philosopher Plato, in his classic works *The Republic* and *The Laws,* argues that the purpose of all individual and team sports is to teach *completion, coordination,* and *cooperation.*

Completion:	The use and testing of one's body
	To extend, expand one's range of physical abilities
	To learn the limits of one's endurance and abilities
	To learn to be comfortable in one's body
Coordination:	Synchronizing body and mind
	To anticipate
	To imagine, to visualize
	To plan, to strategize
Cooperation:	Community effort
	Collective behavior
	Teamwork

There is, of course, one more "C" word to consider, *competition.* The concepts of *completion, coordination, cooperation,* and *competition* in sports are, I think, intimately connected. The Latin root of competition is *competere,* "to seek together," not to "beat" the other. The modern cliché "There is no 'I' in TEAM" is wrong; or, at least, it's true only in the literal sense. There is an "I" in TEAM; in fact, there are many "I's." The trick is to learn how to blend the energy, initiative, and ability of the various "I's" involved in the pursuit of the same goal.

Plato believed that all children, girls and boys alike, must participate in sports. Sports, he argued, are a necessary ingredient in the formation of both the individual person and the collective community. The concepts of self, citizen, and sports participation were, for Plato, conjoined. This is exactly why General Douglas MacArthur, when he was commandant of West Point, required all cadets to participate in a sport. As a student of history, MacArthur was convinced that it was on the playing fields of Eton that the British officer class learned the lessons of *completion, coordination,* and *cooperation,* which ultimately enabled them to defeat Napoleon at Waterloo.[8]

Golf is a sport, a game that can be played in groups (foursomes), in teams (Ryder Cup competition), or, unlike some sports, alone (an option that, for financial reasons, is more and more frowned on by golf course owners). In fact, it can be argued that golf, like running, swimming, skiing, and skating, is one of those sports in which you are basically competing against yourself even when you are playing with others. For many purists (some people refer to them as fans, from the Latin *fanaticus,* fanatic), golf is the ultimate solitary sport because the outcome, no matter what the external variables (course condition, weather), is entirely dependent on the skill of the individual player. So, in essence, each player's chief rivals are his or her best and worst rounds of golf. For the true purist, golf is a John Wayne thing. It's about "true grit," "determination," and "dedication." It's about "commitment," "overcoming mistakes," and "never giving up." It's about "rugged individualism."

My purist father discovered golf during the Eisenhower administration, and his life and the life of our family changed forever. As if he had taken a "non-chemical hallucinogen,"[9] he was immediately addicted. From the beginning, it was always a "game"; it was always about "play," the "pleasure and the joy" of the doing. But for him and for so many others, it was more, much more. It became his avocation, his passion, his raison d'etre. Any time my father was not at work, not involved with a project around the home, or not with the family, he was either playing golf or somehow working on his golf game.

To begin with, my father subscribed to every golf magazine. He read and reread each of them from cover to cover. He would save articles and carefully file them away in two overstuffed filing cabinets he kept in his "golf room" in the basement. He would cut out action shots of famous players and pin them on the wall by his "golf desk." He would often sit for hours listening to golfing records and tapes while staring at the photos. And then there were the books. He bought every book he could find on the subject. Instructional books, novels, picture books, short stories—it didn't matter; if it was about golf, he bought it. As the golf columnist Timothy J. Carroll has pointed out, books give hope to every committed golfer's eternal quest for the "perfect swing" and the "perfect game."[10]

Finally, there was the equipment. Although proper dress and fashion have always been part of the game, this was the one facet of the game in which my father went his own way. As far as he was concerned, most golfers worried too much about clothing and the "right look." He was convinced that excessive concern about one's wardrobe was an affectation as well as a distraction. Khakis or cutoffs were perfect, as long as you were wearing a decent pair of shoes. For him the game came down to the quality of the clubs. He was especially fascinated with putters, and at one point he owned more than a hundred of them. He was also in love with his woods. He collected woods, both for their beauty and for their driving power. He waxed every one of them regularly, and every year he had a few of his favorite clubs professionally sanded, stained, and varnished. Later in his life, I vividly remember the first time he used a titanium "wood." After hitting half a bucket of balls, he sat next to me with tears in his eyes. "God," he said, "I wish I had this club thirty years ago when I could have done something with it. I could have improved my game by four or five strokes. This just isn't fair!"

During the winter months, my father took a one-hour golf lesson every Sunday at the local country club. (He did not have the money to be a member, but lessons were open to nonmembers.) After his lesson, he would come home and do "golf exercises" that he had designed for himself for more than two hours. He would repeat these exercises at least two or three times during the course of a week.

From mid-May until late October, come rain or shine, my father, for more than fifty years, played golf at least twice a week, and at least once a week he went to a "Stop and Sock" to hit three buckets of practice balls. During the winter my father often worked six full days a week and often put in a half day on Sundays, but during the golfing season he took off every Wednesday and Sunday. On Sundays he played thirty-six holes of golf with three other men whom neither my mother nor I ever met, or that he ever talked about. According to my father, the reason for this was quite simple. They were not "family friends"; they were "his golfing buddies." Wednesdays were my father's high holy days. On Wednesdays he regularly golfed thirty-six holes, sometimes fifty-four, and, on occasion, seventy-two, on foot, by himself.

For my father this was golf at its finest. It was all about him and his talents against the game itself. He kept every scorecard, filed by date, and compared his scores from week to week and from year to year. What he was after, I come to realize much later, was not his best score, but his best form and strategy as well as his score. He thought the "how" was just as important as the "count." He was as much or more concerned about what the Italians might call *bella figura*—good form, good figure, good technique—as he was about the final score. He believed that making a great shot by accident meant you missed the shot!

For all of my father's, shall we say, excessive exuberance about golf, and despite his obsession with details and fanaticism about form, he loved golf as a game. He viewed golf as something of beauty and wonder in itself, and playing it gave him a sense of childlike joy. My father was not a happy man by nature, nor was he given to deep philosophical thought. But when he picked up a club and addressed the ball, he was, at least sometimes, poetry in motion. He was taken out of himself. He was lost in the joy of the act. In the words of Thomas à Kempis, "In losing himself, he found himself," at least for the moment. Golf was my father's Zen, his "refuge from ordinary life," and his way to pursue "happiness and joy." Golf made him a better person.

My father didn't know it at the time, but I think he was drawn to the sport of golf and found amusement and pleasure playing golf because sports of all kinds fulfill Johan Huizinga's three criteria of "true play": sports stand outside our mundane day-to-day lives; sports represent a kind of freedom of expression, a chance for openness and creativity; and the rules are clear and self-contained, and winning or losing is obvious.[11]

For the average golfer, golf is a hobby, a social event, a bit of sun, and a little exercise. But for my father and, I venture to guess, hundreds of thousands of other people who play this "ridiculously hard game" (according to Tiger Woods), it teaches them technique, timing, and touch, and it results in a sense of accomplishment (*completion*), self-confidence (*coordination*), and patience with others.

So I say, both philosophically and personally to all people smitten by the game—play on!

Notes

1. Al Gini, *My Job, My Self* (New York: Routledge, 2000).

2. Diane Ackerman, *Deep Play* (New York: Random House, 1999), 6.

3. Donald Hall, *Life Work* (Boston: Beacon Press, 1993), 23.

4. Erich Fromm, *The Sane Society* (New York: Rinehart, 1955), 253.

5. Mark Harris, "The Name of the Game," *Utne Reader,* March–April 2001, 61, 62.

6. Robin Marantz Henig, "Taking Play Seriously," *New York Times Magazine,* February 17, 2008, 40.

7. Al Gini, *The Importance of Being Lazy* (New York: Routledge, 2003), 113.

8. William Manchester, *American Caesar: Douglas MacArthur, 1880–1964* (Little, Brown, 1978).

9. John Updike, "Farrell's Caddie," *New Yorker,* February 25, 1991, 33.

10. Timothy J. Carroll, "Reading about the Green," *Wall Street Journal,* March 22, 23, 2008, W9.

11. Witold Rybczynski, *Waiting for the Weekend* (New York: Viking, 1991), 208.

ON THE BEAUTY AND SUBLIMITY OF GOLF

Robert Fudge and Joseph Ulatowski

Though golf does not require great stamina, the coordination involved in hitting a ball hundreds of yards to a small patch of grass is a testament to human evolution and perseverance. Indeed, given the difficulty of the game and the frustration it engenders, it is not surprising that large numbers of those who try the game quit within a relatively short time.[1] What, then, inspires so many to attempt the game in the first place and breeds such devotion in its long-term players? One reason, we suggest, has to do with the game's aesthetic dimensions—that is, with the game's inherent beauty. More specifically, the environment in which golf is played and the standards of conduct to which its players are expected to adhere are both objects of aesthetic admiration. We consider each of these topics in turn, with the dual goal of explaining golf's aesthetic merits and enhancing the aesthetic appreciation of players and spectators alike.

From the Beauty of Gardens to the Beauty of Golf Courses

One of golf's great attractions is the beautiful setting in which it is played. The rolling green hills, water features, and tree-lined fairways typical of most courses make them objects of aesthetic admiration. Indeed, it is not too much of a stretch to consider a golf course a work of art. But, as is the case with other works of art, a true aesthetic appreciation of golf courses requires a certain level of understanding. A full appreciation of any artwork requires knowledge of the artist's methods, of what the artwork represents, and of how the work fits into the larger context of art as a whole. The same point, we will argue, extends to the aesthetic appreciation of a golf course.

It might seem that we are making a relatively trivial point; why wouldn't increased knowledge of an object enhance our aesthetic appreciation of it? Surprisingly, many philosophers, known as aesthetic formalists, have argued just the opposite. In their view, all that matters aesthetically are the formal, observable qualities of an object, not the cultural or historical context in which it was produced or exists, since these latter properties are supposedly not essential to the object itself. According to formalists, then, the aesthetic appreciation of a golf course should depend only on those features of the course that we can directly perceive through our senses.

Aesthetic formalism suffered a serious setback with the publication of Kendall Walton's highly influential article "Categories of Art."[2] In this work Walton forcefully argues for the position that the historical, cultural, and artistic categories to which an object belongs determine which features of the object are aesthetically relevant. According to this position, it is improper to use the same criteria when evaluating, say, a Michelangelo painting of the Madonna and an abstract painting by Wassily Kandinsky. These paintings share almost nothing in common, except that they are both paintings. So, it would be pointless to argue that Kandinsky's work fails aesthetically just because it does not succeed according to the standards used for evaluating Michelangelo's. To know which standards to apply to the Kandinsky, it is necessary first to know to which category of paintings the Kandinsky belongs. Having established that, we can then proceed to consider such questions as "What ideas was Kandinsky attempting to express through his paintings?" "How did Kandinsky help influence the course of Western art?" "In what ways did Kandinsky's ideas and techniques develop, so that he became the first painter of abstract art?" Situating Kandinsky within the proper cultural, historical, and artistic context thus places us in a much better position to evaluate his work.

If we are to appreciate a golf course aesthetically, we must similarly determine the category under which it ought to be considered. A number of options present themselves. One possibility is to consider golf courses in relation to the category of playing fields. This suggestion is problematic for a number of reasons. First, golf courses differ from most playing fields in that no governing body requires them to be a specific length or width. Many sports, such as baseball, American football, soccer (i.e., football), and cricket are played on rigidly defined fields.[3] The length and width of football fields in the United States are identical at the high school, college, and professional levels (120 yards long by 53.33 yards wide). Golf courses do not have such well-defined dimensions.

Another important feature of many playing fields is a surrounding stadium, especially at the professional level, and this contributes significantly to the fields' aesthetic qualities. By contrast, very few golf courses have grandstands, and these, when present, generally detract from a course's beauty.[4] Much of a golf course's aesthetic appeal derives from its fitting into its surrounding environment, not on how it is separated from it. So, even though golf courses are playing fields, there are enough differences between them and other sports' playing fields to disqualify sports fields as the appropriate category.

As an alternative, we propose that golf courses be considered in relation to the category of gardens. This is not a novel suggestion. The characters Adam and Eve in Michael Murphy's *Golf in the Kingdom* make the connection explicit: "The history of golf and the history of gardens are interlocked," they say. "The golf links here in Burningbush are an exploded garden." Then they explain the relationships between gardens and certain states of mind, how the English made the formal European gardens more like nature, made them gentler and more random.[5] Though we do not go so far as to say that a golf course is a kind of garden, there are enough similarities between them that the comparison is enlightening. To show how, we begin with the aesthetics of gardens, so that we can apply insights in this domain to the golf course.

Despite the wide appeal of gardening—whether of flower gardens, vegetable gardens, or large-scale formal gardens—contemporary philosophers have not paid gardens much attention.[6] Consequently, the aesthetic of gardens has not developed as an independent subdiscipline of philosophy. Rather, as David Cooper notes, the tendency has been to subsume garden appreciation under art or nature appreciation.[7] This tendency is quite understandable. If it is not too much of a stretch to consider golf courses a kind of artwork, then why not gardens as well? Like artworks, golf courses and gardens require planning, creativity, and the application of standardized tools and methods to create an object of aesthetic interest. So it seems not unreasonable to apply the standards of art appreciation to gardens and, by extension, to golf courses.

Cooper warns against making too much of this comparison on the grounds that artworks and gardens differ in many important respects. First, unlike artworks, gardens engage all the senses—flowers are both seen and smelled, birds and insects are heard, berries are tasted, and these all can be touched.[8] A second important difference is that gardens continually change, whereas most artworks are static.[9] Third, there are few artworks that one can literally be immersed in, but this is standard for gardens.[10] Finally, gardens can often be put to practical use in ways that most artworks cannot.[11] To Cooper's reasons we might add that most artworks are about something or are expressive of emotions or feelings in ways that most gardens are not. So there are good reasons not to rely solely on the aesthetics of artworks to understand the aesthetics of gardens.

The reasoning against the treatment of gardens as artworks points instead toward the consideration of them as natural objects. Nature engages all the senses, continually changes, can immerse us, can be used for various purposes, and isn't representational or expressive. Thus, rather than appealing to art aesthetics to explain gardens, it might be more fruitful to appeal to nature aesthetics. To do so, however, would ignore the elements of gardens that are intentionally formed. Or, to put it in Cooper's terms, gardens do not embody the same randomness and indeterminateness found in nature.[12] Nature does sometimes exhibit discernible patterns, but these don't occur with the same regularity and purposefulness found in gardens. Thus, to treat a garden as merely natural is to miss something important about its aesthetic qualities.

Cooper suggests that the proper appreciation of gardens requires that we go beyond both the art and nature models and develop an aesthetic uniquely suited to gardens, at the heart of which is "a sense of the place as a whole that precedes attention to its constituents";[13] in other words, primary to garden aesthetics is the atmosphere that gardens produce. When we are immersed in a garden, and by parity a golf course, we are immediately struck by the overall effect it has on us. The flowering bushes, well-groomed fairways, and water features of a golf course all create an atmosphere that is something more than the sum of its parts and, importantly, affects how we view the parts themselves. Though trees, grass, and water are all natural objects or substances, their presence within an intentionally designed landscape affects how we perceive them and, by extension, their aesthetic qualities. Imagine encountering a single lilac bush during a walk through a grove of pine trees. If the setting is entirely natural, we might wonder how the bush came to be there and appreciate its ability to survive among a wholly different species. Its presence might even evoke a feeling of loneliness, rebellion, or perseverance. Now consider how the aesthetic evaluation of the bush changes if it and the trees that surround it are part of a garden. What a poor choice, we might think, to place a single flowering bush among a group of evergreens. It seems entirely out of place, as if Leonardo had painted a bright yellow streak across the *Mona Lisa*.

Though gardens warrant their own aesthetic, matters are complicated by the fact that there is more than one type of garden. Simplifying greatly, writers often distinguish between English gardens, which have a less cultivated look to them, and formal French gardens, with their well-groomed lawns and trees, water features, and patios.[14] Given the different techniques used to create these gardens and their different styles, a proper appreciation of each type requires different aesthetic criteria. That is, each type of garden warrants its own subcategory in which to be evaluated. This matters for our purposes because the history of golf courses suggests an evolution from those that resemble English gardens to those that resemble French gardens. The criteria for evaluating them have therefore evolved as well.

The earliest golf courses, which belong to the category of linksland courses, were laid out in the land's virgin formation. A linksland golf course does not much change the landscape to meet golfers' needs; it is simply laid out on top of whatever conditions already exist. The Scottish seaside terrain is ideal for this type of course because nothing has to be done to the land to play golf on it. Natural geological features and animal behavior are sufficient to shape the golf course into what it is. The vegetation in Scotland includes broom, gorse, heather, and coarse grasses, interspersed with areas of grazed bent grass and fescues. The broom, gorse, heather, and coarse grasses compose the rough, and the grazed grassy areas form the green and fairway. Because the winds are often gale force and commonly drive livestock to seek shelter behind hillocks, they trample the grass into sandy scars that Scottish farmers call bunkers. These bunkers create hazardous conditions for the golfing experience. There was therefore no need to manipulate the land to create hazards on the first courses; they already existed.

The Royal and Ancient Golf Club of St. Andrews and the Musselburgh Old Course are good examples of linksland courses. Although three or four centuries of golf designers have changed the St. Andrews links—including some changes by the father of golf course architecture, Allan Robertson, whose initial project was St. Andrews' famed "Road Hole" (no. 17), and the golf course designer, greenskeeper, and professional "Old" Tom Morris— its current state is similar to its original one. The Musselburgh Old Course is much the same as it was when it was played in the eighteenth century. According to official club records, two holes were added to the seven original holes—one in 1838 and the other in 1870.[15] Early in the nineteenth century a horse-racing track was built, which surrounds several of the course's holes. Five of the nine holes fall completely within the infield of the track (nos. 2, 3, 7, 8, and 9), and three cross the racetrack (nos. 1, 4, and 6). Only no. 5 falls outside the track. Horse races still take place, and these events require golfers to halt play when the race is on. In spite of this, the track lends itself to the mystique of the ancient club because the course itself hasn't changed, though the racetrack has been added to it. These courses are virtually undisturbed pieces of land on which golf can be played, and they epitomize the linksland course. They are pure and subtle pieces of golf course design that many contemporary golf course architects attempt to imitate in their own creations.

One subcategory of linksland course developed on the public commons: that is, land on which people other than the owner have the right to graze cattle, fish, gather wood, or engage in similar activities. Given its unique development, we dub this category of golf course "public commons linksland."[16] Commons golf does not call for the creation of artificial hazards because it offers an ample variety of preexisting natural and man-made hazards of its own, including ditches and gorse; animals such as ducks, hens, and grazing horses and donkeys; cyclists; clothes drying in the wind; and immovable objects such as lampposts.

The now defunct Blackheath Golf Links is a good example of a public commons linksland golf course. The historian Neil Rhind discusses the design of the Blackheath Links by citing the records of the Knuckle and Winter Golf Clubs: "It will be seen from this plan that the old gravel pits and the existing roads—such roads being mostly one or two feet below the level of the Heath—are taken advantage of as hazards to guard holes and punish a too strongly played approach shot. The fourth and fifth holes are long ones, in a direct line from tee to hole, such line going through a disused gravel pit; when as occasionally happened it is expedient to skirt this pitch in play the distance from tee to hole becomes of course materially increased."[17]

As we see, no attempt was made to modify existing conditions; instead, designers took advantage of the conditions that already existed. Play on the Blackheath Links became exceedingly difficult toward the end of the nineteenth century because foot and animal traffic intensified. This required golfers to adopt rules to accommodate the traffic (for example, "golfers must wait for people and conveyances to pass out of their way before playing"),[18] and another rule indicated what to do if a player's ball became lodged in a gas lamp. Like their linksland cousins, then, public commons linksland courses adapted themselves to preexisting conditions.

When golf began moving inland and crossing "the pond" during the late nineteenth century, golf professionals and greenskeepers began intentionally designing golf courses. For the first time, courses were literally carved out of the English and American landscapes. They were set in suburban areas, not on public commons. So different are these courses from linksland and public commons linksland courses that they warrant their own category, which we will call "built golf courses." Modifying the land for these courses involved cutting down trees, digging artificial bunkers, manipulating these bunkers into various shapes and sizes, and creating elevated plateau greens or elevated plateau tees. The Sunningdale Golf Club and Royal Blackheath Club of Britain (not to be confused with the Blackheath Links) were among the earliest British designed golf courses. A remarkable feature of the Royal Blackheath Club added by its designer is the hedgerow crossing the eighteenth fairway just short of the green. Long-ball hitters may risk losing a ball in the hedge for the greater reward of a lower score. In the United States golf course designers modified the land in many places to create challenging layouts. For example, the team of John Van Kleek and Wayne Styles designed Putterham Meadows Golf Club (now Robert T. Lynch Municipal Golf Course at Putterham Meadows), in Brookline, Massachusetts. The course is representative of a built golf course because it was carved out of the prevailing landscape. The designers and builders worked together to manipulate the land to create a golf course featuring severely sloping, elevated greens. This differs considerably from the grazed areas that constitute greens on traditional links courses.

Linksland courses stateside could be categorized as "links-style" courses because most of them have been intentionally designed and artificially manufactured to be like their British cousins.[19] Further, they have fewer trees than do typical American golf courses, and tall native grasses are allowed to flourish in the rough. Shinnecock Hills Golf Club is a paradigmatic example of a stateside links-style course. Originally designed by Willie Dunn, Shinnecock is dramatically laid out on the outermost edge of Long Island. Another impressive links-style design is Pete Dye's Ocean Course at the Kiawah Island Resort, near Charleston, South Carolina.[20] The Ocean

Course offers majestic panoramic views of the Atlantic Ocean on nearly every one of its eighteen holes. The wind can present a formidable obstacle on both of these links-style courses because of their proximity to the ocean.[21]

A final type of course is the "designer golf course," which follows a preconceived architectural or design plan and is intended to be pristinely groomed. Many courses in the United States, including most private clubs, are designer courses.[22] Perhaps the epitome of this type of course is Augusta National Golf Club, where the Masters Tournament is played each year. Augusta's greens and fairways are always trimmed neatly and shaved to perfection. Other designer courses include the Atlanta Athletic Club (designed by Robert Trent Jones), Pebble Beach Golf Links, in California (designed by Jack Neville and redesigned by, among others, Alister Mackenzie), Tournament Players Club at Sawgrass, in Florida (designed by Pete Dye), Saucon Valley Country Club, in Pennsylvania (Saucon Course designed by Herbert Strong), Pine Valley Golf Club, in New Jersey (codesigned by H. S. Colt and George Crump), and any of the numbered Pinehurst Country Club courses, in North Carolina. Given the category to which these courses belong, players would be thoroughly disappointed to find any of them in less than perfectly groomed condition.

With the evolution of golf courses came a new way of appreciating them aesthetically. Concerning the early period of intentional golf course design, John Lowerson writes: "Playing golf should be an aesthetic as well as a sporting experience. Around the turn of the century there was a clear move toward this, and the grander golf clubs began to develop courses. . . . It could be seen in course layout, especially in the development of bunkers and the intertwining of fairways, rough and trees to combine an adequate golfing challenge with pleasing views. In this sense the very private world of the 'exclusive' golf clubs matched that of the similarly alienated formalized parks of the grander country houses."[23]

Golf, then, has been transformed from a sport initially played on wild seaside terrain to one played within the confines of a designed, groomed, and often exclusive area. As golf courses have evolved, so have the standards of beauty that apply to them. A proper aesthetic appreciation of golf courses requires understanding the categories in which they fall. A golfer most familiar with playing on designed golf courses must learn to shift her aesthetic standards when playing a nondesigned links course for the first time. In many respects, it's like a connoisseur of French gardens having to adapt to the English garden. Great beauty abounds in both, but the beauty takes on a very different character that depends on the type of garden it is.

Naturally, not everyone finds golf courses beautiful. A common objection to them concerns their environmental impact and the destruction of what is natural, a worry that evokes the German philosopher Arthur Schopenhauer's (1788–1860) objection to the French garden, in which "only the will of the possessor is mirrored."[24] In some cases this charge is entirely justified. Courses improperly built in arid climates or that infringe on delicate habitats or environmentally sensitive areas consequently lose a degree of beauty. (The same could be said, incidentally, of gardens or of any other product of human artifice that has the potential for causing a negative environmental effect.) Those courses that are built with environmental considerations in mind, however, can actually be considered more beautiful as a result.[25] In response to concerns about the environment, many golf courses have been built or renovated to reduce their environmental impact. For example, some courses capture runoff water and reuse it in the irrigation of their fairways. Golf courses in St. George, Utah, use nonpotable water rather than culinary water for irrigation. If St. George's golf courses stopped watering their fairways, greens, and rough, there would be no increase in the availability of drinking water to the community. Similarly, 147 acres of Queenstown Harbor Golf Links are built on a fragile wetlands ecosystem. Lindsay Bruce Ervin's design team succeeded in protecting these sensitive habitats through conscientious development of a critical wetlands area. These considerations again show the aesthetic relevance of features of golf courses other than those that are immediately observable.

Our proposed categories of golf courses dovetail nicely with the aesthetics of gardens. Linksland, public commons linksland, and stateside links-style courses resemble English gardens by virtue of their more natural state. An appreciation of these courses must forfeit perfectly manicured greens, fairways, and rough. Built golf courses and designer golf courses are far more well-groomed than their linksland and links-style relatives and more closely resemble French gardens. The standards of beauty that apply to them therefore differ. But despite these differences, all golf courses create an atmosphere that serves as the foundation for the player's aesthetic appreciation and can transform a round of golf into something similar to a garden stroll. The aesthetics of golf, however, is not restricted to the beauty of the course. The conduct of its players is also an object of aesthetic interest and is of vital importance if the game is to be fully enjoyed. It is to this topic that we now turn.

Golf and the Sublimity of Character

Upon addressing his ball in the rough on the eleventh hole of the first round of the 1925 U.S. Open, Bobby Jones inadvertently caused the ball to move by brushing the surrounding grass with his iron. Though no spectators, rules officials, or fellow competitors saw the ball move, and though it provided Jones no advantage in his subsequent shot, he called a penalty on himself, which ultimately cost him the tournament. When praised for his integrity, Jones famously replied, "You might as well praise me for not breaking into banks." This episode deserves comment, first of all because of its contrast with the behavior often exhibited by competitors in other sports. Consider, for example, the routine complaining by professional basketball players when they are called for fouls, no matter how obvious. But second, and perhaps even in part because of the first reason, the expectation that golf players display the utmost integrity when playing contributes to golf's aesthetic character. To explain how this is so, we need to go beyond the beautiful and explore a related aesthetic concept—that of the sublime.

The most philosophically significant treatments of the sublime were written in the eighteenth century by the English philosopher Edmund Burke (1729–1797) and the German philosopher Immanuel Kant (1724–1804). Though Kant is better known for the three great *Critiques* he wrote later in his life, his early writing *Observations on the Feeling of the Beautiful and Sublime* presents a much more accessible introduction to his ideas on aesthetics.[26] Kant's insights on the sublime can help us understand why the comportment and character expected of golfers contribute to the game's aesthetic appeal.

It is first necessary to get a better idea of what Kant meant by the sublime. As is suggested by his work's title, Kant was specifically concerned with the feelings that the beautiful and sublime arouse. Both involve a degree of pleasure, but whereas the beautiful charms us, the sublime has the power to move us.[27] To help explain what he means by this, Kant provides us with myriad examples, as in the following passage:

> The sight of a mountain whose snow-covered peak rises above the clouds, the description of a raging storm, or Milton's portrayal of the infernal kingdom, arouse enjoyment but with horror; on the other hand, the sight of flower-strewn meadows, valleys with wandering brooks and covered with grazing flocks, the description of Elysium, or Homer's portrayal of the girdle of Venus, also occasion

a pleasant sensation but one that is joyous and smiling. In order that the former impression could occur to us in due strength, we must have a *feeling of the sublime,* and, in order to enjoy the latter well, a *feeling of the beautiful.*[28]

We could very well supply examples from golf. Augusta National Golf Club, with its azaleas and dogwoods in bloom, is beautiful; Pebble Beach Golf Links, with its precipitous drops and sound of crashing ocean waves, is sublime. Harbour Town Links at Sea Pines Plantation, in South Carolina, which winds through a resort community, is beautiful; The Royal and Ancient Golf Club at St. Andrews, with its gray skies and forlorn landscape, is sublime.

Though Kant acknowledged a distinction between the beautiful and sublime, he did not think of the sublime as a monolithic type of experience. It also admits of distinctions: "Its feeling is sometimes accompanied with a certain dread, or melancholy; in some cases merely with quiet wonder; and in still others with a beauty completely pervading a sublime plan."[29] Kant terms these feelings the terrifying sublime, noble sublime, and splendid sublime, respectively.[30] The terrifying sublime comes out most clearly on the golf course when an imposing obstacle tests our nerves. Murphy portrays the terrifying sublime when his narrator describes the experience of playing the intimidating thirteenth hole at Burningbush: "It is a par three up a hill, to a pin that stands silhouetted between a pair of twisted cypress trees. Between the tee and the green lies Lucifer's Rug, a field of clotted gorse, 200 yards of it to catch any shot that is less than perfection. Along the left runs a steep ravine, from which several boulders rise. . . . The tee shot had to carry to the green but not roll down the other side, for another ravine dropped off there."[31] The eeriness of the hole is magnified by the character Shivas Irons, who before hitting his shot "cupped his hands to his mouth and gave an incredible cry toward the ravine. It was a long wavering wail, something between a yodel and a cry for the departed dead. It sent a shiver up my back. We could hear its echo from the ravine, bouncing off the rocks."[32] What makes this an experience of the sublime and not simply of terror is that the fear the hole elicits accompanies a feeling of pleasure. Though the experience induces fear, there is no sense that the players are ever in danger. The feelings of fear and pleasure merge into an organic whole that is something more than simply pleasure, simply terror, or simply both feelings occurring at the same time. The terrifying sublime occurs when the terrifying and pleasurable constitute a unified experience.

The sublime does not occur only in the most challenging circumstances. One of golf's greatest joys is to hit a drive that seems to hang in the air for an eternity, framed by trees on both sides, a lush green fairway below, and a clear blue sky above, only to drop down gently near its target. When accompanied by a sense of quiet wonder, such shots produce a sense of the noble sublime; when the beauty of the scene is all-pervasive, the experience is of the splendid sublime. But in each case, what ultimately makes the shot sublime is its fundamental simplicity and the evocation of the eternal.

Perhaps Kant's greatest contribution to the analysis of the sublime—a contribution that will most interest us here—is his application of the concept to persons, especially to their moral qualities. It would be difficult to overstate the importance that Enlightenment thinkers attached to the idea of moral beauty.[33] Yet Kant went beyond typical statements about moral beauty to suggest that human beings, because of their essential dignity, also possess the quality of the sublime. It is here, in the notion of dignity, that the eternal again becomes centrally important. In contrast with Thomas Hobbes (1588–1679), who claimed that our dignity is just the value or price that others place on us, Kant argued that to possess dignity is to be "beyond price." Our value, in other words, is boundless and so, like anything that has no bounds, sublime. But the sublime, as we'll see, has other sources that bear directly on golf.

Golf has a virtually preternatural ability to elicit strong emotional outbursts from its players. The sources of such reactions are seemingly endless—poorly struck golf shots, well-struck shots that career out of bounds or into hazards, playing partners who violate rules of etiquette, and groups who play too slowly all test our patience to the breaking point. But as in life outside golf, our ability to perform well on the golf course requires that we keep our emotions within certain bounds. For Kant the subordination of the emotions to reason is an essential component of moral action. Indeed, he argued that our moral duty is determined by a universal principle termed the categorical imperative. This principle requires that we act according to rules that can consistently be adopted by everyone and that are consistent with each other. This test of consistency is one of reason, not emotion. So if consistency requires that we always tell the truth—as Kant argues we must— then we must tell the truth, even if doing so goes against our inclination to save a loved one's life.

We neither defend nor endorse Kant's absolutist claims about telling the truth, but we raise the issue to note the analogy between Kant's moral theory and the dilemma all golfers face. Like Kant's moral rules, the rules of golf are intended to be adopted and consistently applied by all players, regardless of their inclinations to bend or break them. Whether out of anger, indifference, or competitive zeal, golfers are constantly tempted to improve their lies, help themselves to a mulligan, avoid penalty strokes for infractions of seemingly obscure rules, and the like. Yet, as Kant would insist, the rules are not there to be adhered to or ignored at our convenience; golf is at its best when players respect and enforce the rules, especially when doing so is to the players' own disadvantage. And this brings us to one of the most important claims Kant makes in his *Observations*, especially in the way it prefigures his later moral theory: "Subduing one's passions through principles is sublime."[34] Nothing can better explain why we are so entranced by the integrity Bobby Jones displayed at the 1925 Open.[35] Though Jones was reportedly very angry about his ball's moving, he did not hesitate to assess himself a penalty. To place principle above passion so unreservedly displays strength of character that, no matter how frequently we might encounter it, never fails to grab our attention. The example he presented was an instance of the noble sublime, which added immeasurably to the mystique and aesthetic value of the game.

The sport of golf ranks among the most beautiful of games. The setting in which it is played and the behavior expected of its players are just two of its features—though arguably its two most important features—that are of aesthetic interest. Golf courses are in many respects like gardens, and as we have shown, understanding types of courses can help us considerably in appreciating them. But just as a garden's beauty can be ruined by weeds, so a round of golf can be ruined by poor sportsmanship. It is only appropriate, then, that the rules of golf dictate how its players ought to behave, for when these rules are followed, the result can be an experience that is both beautiful and sublime.

Notes

The authors would like to thank Sylvia Newman, Andy Wible, and Tom Giffin for helpful comments on earlier versions of this essay.

1. Dean Knuth reports: "National Golf Foundation statistics show that participation in the game of golf is relatively flat. NGF President & CEO Joseph Beditz says that

on average over the past decade, two to three million new people try golf every year. 'However, retention efforts have not been as successful as desired. As a result, the number of dropouts remains unacceptably high.' Complaints from those exiting the game are focused around the time that it takes to play, slow play on the course, access issues, cost, and, a common complaint—the difficulty of becoming even good enough to be called a hacker." (Knuth, "Handicapping and Non-Conforming Drivers: High on Technology," February 2002, http://deanknuth.com/handicapping/highontech.html.)

2. Kendall Walton, "Categories of Art," *Philosophical Review* 79 (1970): 334–67.

3. If we interpret "playing field" broadly enough, we could add tennis, hockey, and bowling, among other sports, to this list.

4. An exception to this general principle should be noted. All professional tournaments and opens have grandstands installed temporarily to accommodate the people attending the event. Grandstands and television camera towers, usually an eyesore, make the golf course's aesthetic qualities accessible to the television viewing audience.

5. Michael Murphy, *Golf in the Kingdom* (1972; rept., New York: Viking Penguin, 1994), 60–61.

6. Two notable exceptions are Mara Miller, *The Garden as Art* (Albany: SUNY Press, 1993), and Stephanie Ross, *What Gardens Mean* (Chicago: University of Chicago Press, 1998).

7. David Cooper, *A Philosophy of Gardens* (Oxford: Oxford University Press, 2006).

8. Ibid., 28–29.

9. Ibid., 29.

10. Ibid., 30.

11. Ibid., 31.

12. Ibid., 38.

13. Ibid., 50.

14. For a more in-depth discussion of types of gardens, we especially recommend Ross, *What Gardens Mean.*

15. Early golf courses in Scotland and Britain nearly always had an odd number of holes that were not in multiples of nine, as we see in today's golf courses. For example, the Blackheath Links had seven holes (ca. 1840), and the Royal and Ancient Golf Club of St. Andrews had upwards of twenty-two holes at one time or another.

16. We can compare the sort of play on public commons with a sport that is undergoing a revival: Frisbee golf. Frisbee golf, like its cousin golf, is played on the public commons. Several Frisbee golf courses have been set up in city parks. Avid Frisbee golfers can play these courses at their leisure free of charge.

17. Neil Rhind, *The Heath: A Companion Volume to Blackheath Village and Environs* (Cambridge, U.K.: Burlington Press, 1987), 49–50.

18. Ibid., 50.

19. Links-style courses are popular well inland in higher-altitude cities, such as Den-

ver, Colorado. Murphy Creek Golf Course, in Aurora, is a prairie links-style course, and it has hosted a United States Golf Association event, the 2008 United States Amateur Public Links Championship.

20. Built in 1991, the course played host to a dramatic Ryder Cup match the same year and has made a film appearance in *The Legend of Bagger Vance* (2000).

21. Other manufactured links-style courses are well inland. For example, Rochelle Ranch Golf Course, in Rawlins, Wyoming, is a long (7,900-plus yards) links-style course. The nearly constant high-velocity wind and the complexity of the course's design make Rochelle Ranch a serious test of the best player's golfing ability.

22. Our list of designer private clubs includes Walpole Country Club, in Walpole, Massachusetts, where one author of this piece, Joe Ulatowski, spent many early years either working in the bag room or playing the course. Walpole Country Club was designed by Al Zikouris, who earlier served as a local greenskeeper and apprentice to Orrin Smith. In 1974 the club replaced the original nine-hole course, established in 1927, which was designed by Eugene "Skip" Wogan and located approximately one-half mile from the new course. Some features of Walpole Country Club deserve to be mentioned. The presence of a large pond on the course's first and eighteenth holes tends to intimidate the golfer playing the course for the first time. The seventh green is remarkably fast almost all the time. When the pin is positioned toward the front of the seventh green, it's nearly impossible to hole out a putt from above because of the dramatic slant from back to front and from right to left. The course is always in top condition, and the course's membership and staff take pride in it, a laudable trait of any golf community.

23. John Lowerson, *Sport and the English Middle Classes, 1870–1914* (Manchester, U.K.: Manchester University Press, 1993), 135.

24. Arthur Schopenhauer, *The World as Will and Representation*, trans. E. F. J. Payne (1818; rept., New York: Dover, 1969), 2:404.

25. An enduring debate within philosophical aesthetics concerns whether and to what degree the moral features of an object or artwork bear on its aesthetic qualities. For an excellent introduction to this debate, see Noël Carroll, "Moderate Moralism versus Moderate Autonomism," *British Journal of Aesthetics* 38 (1998): 419–24.

26. Immanuel Kant, *Observations on the Feeling of the Beautiful and Sublime*, trans. John T. Goldthwait (Berkeley: University of California Press, 1960).

27. Ibid., 47.

28. Ibid., emphasis his.

29. Ibid., 47–48. Kant uses the example of St. Peter's basilica to illustrate what he means by a "sublime plan."

30. Ibid., 48.

31. Murphy, *Golf in the Kingdom*, 32.

32. Ibid., 33.

33. For a thorough treatment of this history, see Robert Norton, *The Beautiful Soul: Aesthetic Morality in the Eighteenth Century* (Ithaca: Cornell University Press, 1995).

34. Kant, *Observations on the Feeling of the Beautiful and Sublime,* 57.

35. Jones's action is perhaps the best-known example of this sort of behavior, but it is hardly unique. J. P. Hayes disqualified himself from the 2008 PGA Qualifying Tournament for playing with a nonconforming ball on a single hole.

II. Golf and Moral Character

FINDING THE (FAIR)WAY WITH CONFUCIUS AND BEN HOGAN

Stephen J. Laumakis

A Useful Analogy

Although it may not be obvious to the average hacker or first-year philosophy student, I think a persuasive case can be made that there is a useful and instructive analogy between the best golfer and his pursuit of excellence in the game of golf and the good human person and his pursuit of human flourishing. The key to the effectiveness of the analogy, however, is that we are talking about the really *best* golfers and the truly *best* human beings, because we all know from experience that there are as many ways to swing a golf club and play the game of golf as there are conceptions of how to live a good and successful human life—and not all swings are as good and effective as others in producing the appropriate shot, and not all theories of human flourishing are as easy to realize and unproblematic as others.

Nevertheless, it is also important to keep in mind that there are significant differences—despite their shared excellence—among the best golfers, the best human beings, and the best accounts of how to live a good and successful human life. For example, it is obvious to those who have seen them play that Arnold Palmer did not swing and play like Jack Nicklaus, Tiger Woods does not play and swing like Phil Mickelson, and none of them plays or swings like Annika Sorenstam or Lorena Ochoa. Yet, despite their differences in play, all are, or were, among the best and most successful golfers of all time.

The same kinds of similarities and differences can also be seen in the lives of the very best human beings and among the various accounts of how to live a good and successful human life. For example, Socrates clearly did not live as Jesus lived, and neither lived as the Buddha or Confucius or Mohammed did, and yet each is recognized as a truly virtuous and outstanding human being. Furthermore, as most students of philosophy quickly realize, Aristotle's conception of the good human life is fundamentally different from Plato's, and neither of their conceptions of human flourishing is exactly like Thomas Aquinas's, Immanuel Kant's, or John Stuart Mill's theories. And when we turn our attention to the East, Confucius's understanding of morality and ethical behavior is clearly different from Zhuangzi's and Laozi's, and each of these views is fundamentally different from Siddhattha Gotama's. Yet, despite their differences, each of these philosophers tried to argue for, and presumably live, the kind of life he believed instantiated the best life for human beings.

A Common End and Two Views of It

What sets these good golfers, good human beings, and good philosophers apart from their peers and competitors, I suggest, is their single-minded devotion to the pursuit of excellence as they conceived it and their unrelenting commitment to take the steps necessary to achieve it. So it is plausible to say that each of these golfers was pursuing the same target, that is, success in the game of golf; that each of these human beings was striving for the same goal, that is, living a morally praiseworthy life; and that each of these philosophers was arguing for the same end, that is, a rational and reasoned account of human flourishing. In the broadest sense, all of them were interested in being the best they could be at what they were doing and being (despite their particular differences)—and each found *his own* way to do it and be it. Conceived of in this fashion, then, the pursuit of excellence in golf may be usefully seen as a particular instance of the more general pursuit of excellence in being human and living a morally praiseworthy, successful, and flourishing human life. In short, those who pursue excellence in golf can be seen as models and instances of those who are trying to live a good human life.

To elucidate the proposed analogy between the pursuit of excellence in golf and the pursuit of excellence in living, I will offer a comparison of two distinct conceptions of what one ought to think about while playing golf, and how that thinking serves as a metaphor for how one ought to live one's life. (For the sake of clarity, I am imagining comparing a social conception of the human person and of human flourishing with an individualist account of the same.) The first conception is taken from Confucius by imaginatively extending his thoughts to the practices of golf. The second conception is taken from the instructions of Ben Hogan and creatively extends these instructions to questions about how to live one's life. The texts that form the background of the essay are Confucius's *Great Learning* and his *Analects*, and Ben Hogan's *Five Lessons: The Modern Fundamentals of Golf.*

THE GREAT LEARNING AND GOLF

To get some sense of just what Confucius might say about how one ought to go about playing golf, it is important to have a sense of his basic approach to living or his philosophical outlook. I offer an overview of his philosophy later in this volume,[1] and at this point would simply instruct the reader to think about Confucius's views about philosophy as emerging from the context of the Warring States Period in Chinese history (from roughly the fifth century B.C.E. to 221 C.E.).

As far as Confucius was concerned, the solution to the Warring States chaos was simply to return to the well-ordered days of the past, when citizens cultivated both themselves and their communities by engaging in the appropriate kinds of ritualized practices and following the Tao, or Way, marked out for them by their great moral, social, and political organizers and leaders—the Sage Kings and China's other cultural heroes and icons.

Understood within this historical and cultural context, Confucius's *Great Learning* can be thought of as a programmatic outline of moral advice—from a decidedly theoretical point of view. Its basic teaching is that self-cultivation (i.e., being all that one can be and doing one's best in all situations and circumstances)—in conformity with the rites and rituals (*li*) enacted by the Sage Kings—"the ancients of illustrious virtue and excellence"—is both the foundation of a flourishing and harmonious community and "the root of everything else besides."

The *Great Learning* begins, appropriately enough, with a discussion about ends—or the kinds of things that humans aim at with their thoughts and actions. It announces in its opening line that it teaches a method, or Way, of exemplifying excellence that begins with this goal or target and then specifies the means to that end. According to the *Great Learning,* "Things have their root and their branches. Affairs have their end and their beginning. To know what is first and what is last will lead near to what is taught in the *Great Learning*."[2] It then proceeds to explain precisely how the "ancients" (the Sage Kings and cultural heroes and leaders) of China's past realized their ultimate goal—a well-ordered kingdom—through the intervening steps of ritually organizing and regulating their states, their families, and finally themselves by properly ordering their hearts, their minds, their thoughts, and their knowledge in accordance with *li*. It ends with the simple yet profound observation that everyone from the Son of Heaven (i.e., China's political leader) down to the masses of the people "must consider the cultivation of the person the root of everything else." It also warns, "It cannot be, when the root is neglected, that what should spring from it will be well-ordered." In other words, the state of being appropriately ordered in one's self, one's family, one's state, and one's kingdom is the key to virtue or excellence. These ideas can be extended to how one plays the game of golf.

A rather simple and obvious analogy is to think of one's game, or at least one's above-average round, as one's "well-ordered kingdom"—its excellence is the goal one is trying to cultivate. In this thought experiment, Confucius's *Great Swing* is a programmatic guide to golfing excellence. To be good at something (i.e., golf), Confucius insists that one must first have a clear idea of the goal or target—let's call it a repeating and well-ordered swing that consistently and reliably helps one hit the target of golf—par. Confucius then teaches that this end can be achieved only when its constituent elements or subsidiary parts (i.e., one's long and short games, course management, ball-striking skills, and ability to respond appropriately to the specific outcomes of previous shots) are properly and appropriately practiced and realized. And all this depends, of course, on one's ability to manage oneself—one's thoughts and emotions and the physical stress involved in playing the game—because "the cultivation of ordered thinking and feeling is the root of everything else in golf." In short, we can imagine Confucius advising, "You cannot be thinking of anything other than your swing when you are swinging, or your swing will do anything other than what a well-ordered swing is supposed to do." The *Great Swing* encourages us to recognize the basic truth that ordered practice and execution (i.e., right action) depend on ordered thinking (i.e., right thinking)—and lots of practice too. According to Confucius, then, one simply cannot realize excellence in action without excellence in habit and thinking first. To master this truth in both theory and practice is the key to the *Great Swing* and the game of golf.

THE ANALECTS *AND GOLF*

Confucius's *Analects* is best thought of as an eclectic collection of practical sayings about how he and his followers tried to live out the program outlined in the *Great Learning*. The basic teachings of the *Analects* focus on four key ideas: *xiao, li, yi,* and *ren*. It also offers practical advice about how to realize each of these in practice.

Xiao is the Confucian concept of filial piety or family values. It refers to the fundamental biological fact that the family, a community of at least two persons, gives birth to its offspring and then assumes the job of teaching the child how to go about becoming a good human being. For Confucius the family, and its network of social relationships, is the primary and overriding metaphor and locus for understanding how one is to go about learning the art of self-cultivation or becoming a fully realized human person: it is the family, and the various relationships that constitute it—and not the particular individual—that is the basic unit of a morally good society.

Li, as previously mentioned, is the Chinese term for rites and rituals, and it refers to the patterns of behavior that are called for and enacted as one learns how to participate in the various roles one plays as a member of a family, state, and kingdom. For Confucius *li* refers to the patterned behavior that children learn as they continuously work at cultivating themselves and becoming good sons or daughters. The roots of *li,* as we have seen, go all the way back to the Sage Kings and cultural icons of China's past who first enacted the appropriate forms of living by being moral guides for their people.

Yi is the Confucian term for moral appropriateness or righteousness and is best thought of as the action of doing what is appropriate or called for in any given situation. It refers to something like Aristotle's concept of prudence, whereby the virtuous person learns and knows what is called for in terms of her thoughts and actions in every situation. It is, quite literally, knowing and doing the right thing, at the right time, in the right way, to the right person, for the right reasons, and it is a habit that is acquired only with time and experience and proper training and upbringing—in the context of a morally good family, in Confucius's view.

Ren is perhaps the most difficult and elusive Confucian term to translate. It occurs at least one hundred times in the *Analects,* and it is thought by most scholars to be the single most important Confucian concept because it captures the goal of Confucian ethics—the morally praiseworthy human being or the person of excellence who regularly and unfailingly engages in authoritative conduct and moral action. In essence, *ren* is the fully realized person who has learned and embraced the *li* that characterizes a flourishing family and is taught via *xiao* and instantiated in the *yi* of the morally good person. As the Confucian scholar Roger Ames has said on numerous occasions, a person is *ren* when he or she knows how to get the best and most out of his or her ingredients, whether cooking a meal, living in a family, leading a community, group, or state—or even playing a round of golf.

If we imaginatively apply these key Confucian terms to the playing of golf, I think we get a richer conception of the kinds of advice Confucius has to offer the average golfer. For example, it is not difficult to see how being a fully realized person (*ren*) can also apply to being a good golfer—by being a master of all of the elements of the game. To realize this excellence one must obviously have mastered each of the basic parts of the game in such a way that one may effortlessly do what is appropriate (*yi*) in any given situation during the course of a round. Yet this mastery itself clearly presupposes a basic familiarity not only with the kinds of situations that one typically faces in the course of play, but also with the atypical and extraordinary lies and events that constitute what is traditionally referred to as "the rub of the green." What these peculiar situations call for is a practiced recognition in terms of the pattern of behavior (*li*) that is appropriate (*yi*) to the specific circumstances in which one finds oneself. And I can think of no better way to learn each of these elements of the game of golf than with the ongoing help, guidance, and encouragement of a good teacher or golf pro, who plays a role similar to that of one's parents (*xiao*) in helping one learn how to be the best kind of player one can be.

Additional advice about living a flourishing life that may also be creatively and imaginatively applied to the game of golf can be found throughout the *Analects*.[3] For example, Confucius tells us that the authoritative player (*ren*) alone knows the difference between a good shot and a bad, a smart shot and a dumb shot (4.3). One of his students notes that the Way of the Master is trying one's best and playing the game as the best would play, nothing more and nothing less (4.15). Such players obviously know the difference between what is appropriate (*yi*) and what is just showing off (4.16), and, having found people with a good swing, they imitate them and avoid those with bad swings (4.17), because excellent players always have partners and never play alone (4.25). A little later Confucius admits that there are clearly some players who are better at some particular parts of the game than he is, but that no one loves or studies the game more than he (5.28). In fact, he insists that one can become an authoritative player (*ren*) only by first learning how to deal with difficulties (6.22).

As for the practical kinds of things one needs to do to play the game well, the Master says: correlating one's swing to the particulars of the conditions and lie in which one finds one's ball is the key to excellent play and being an authoritative player (*ren*) (6.30); in strolling in the company of just two other players, one is bound to find a teacher—identifying his strengths, imitating him, recognizing his weaknesses, and reforming one's own game accordingly (7.22); the good player is calm and unperturbed, whereas the hacker is agitated and anxious (7.37); four things are to be avoided at all costs: a hook, a slice, a chili dip, and a whiff (9.4); being an authoritative player (*ren*) depends on oneself and no one else (12.1); one must not rush things—in either thinking or swinging (13.17); the good player usually finds the fairway, but the hacker almost always finds the rough (14.23); the authoritative player (*ren*) is not anxious; the smart player is never in a quandary; and the courageous player is not timid (14.28); most golfers like looking good rather than being good (15.13); truly great players make demands on themselves, whereas hackers are always blaming something for their bad shots and asking for help finding their ball (15.21); in golf as in life, it is not about what you say but about what you do that matters (15.23); it's the golfer who finds the fairway and not the fairway that finds the ball (15.29); to miss the fairway and not return to it immediately is to miss the fairway indeed (15.30); those who play in the fairway (and live in the mean between the extremes of excess and deficiency) and those who play in the rough (and live on the extremes) cannot and do not play together (15.40); golfers are similar in their desires but vary greatly in the excellence of their swings (17.2); hackers tend to be rash, proud, and stupid—and they cannot add or count (17.16); the authoritative player (*ren*) hits the appropriate shot, but the hacker is merely bold (17.23); the exceptional player is aware of what is yet to be learned and never forgets what has already been mastered (19.5); a hacker never knows where his ball is or how many strokes he has taken (19.8); and a good player knows the conditions of his lie, whereas a hacker does not even know where or how to stand at address (20.3).

In addition to these purely imaginative comments, it should be clear from reading the *Analects* that Confucius was very much interested in drawing a sharp distinction and contrast between the good person and the petty person, and by extension and analogy, the good golfer and the hacker. In fact, I argue that one cannot read the *Analects* without noticing this important distinction. Moreover, it would be impossible to deny that Confucius has a very clear understanding and account of the differences between those who follow his Way, or Tao, and those who go some other way. In short, he recognizes and insists that the excellence required to hit the mark he is aiming at is not only of the highest order but also rare indeed (6.29).

BEN HOGAN, THE MAN AND HIS REPUTATION

Though it is clear that Ben Hogan was not a professional philosopher, it does not follow that he did not have thoughts about the game of golf that could be meaningfully applied to questions about how to live a good human life. As my mother likes to say, "We're all philosophers, but not all of us are smart enough to figure out how to get other people to pay us for our thoughts and ideas about life and reality." If she is only partly right, then it ought not be surprising that Ben Hogan had some ideas about living a good, meaningful, and successful human life.

Before turning to the specifics of his ethical views, I think it would be helpful first to say something about the man and his life in order to provide some context for his ideas.[4]

Ben Hogan was the third and youngest child of a blacksmith who committed suicide while Ben was a young boy. To help his family with its financial situation, Ben initially sold newspapers and eventually got a job as a caddy. The rest, as they say, is history: the legendary story of one solitary man's unrelenting effort to become the best golfer he could make himself. In fact, even his harshest critics and greatest competitors admit that his work ethic and determination were second to none. To highlight this point only one example is necessary. When the professional golfer Tommy Bolt was asked to compare Ben Hogan and Jack Nicklaus he said, "I saw Nicklaus watch Hogan practice, but I never saw Hogan watch Nicklaus practice." Jack Nicklaus was and is by most accounts the single greatest golfer of all time, yet even he was smart enough to watch and learn from arguably the single greatest worker at his craft. In fact, Hogan's legendary commitment to his unwavering belief that practice makes perfect is said to have led him to practice until his hands bled. Even if this last point is just an exaggeration, it does not change the fact that his obsessive commitment to the unrelenting pursuit of excellence helped him become the person and great player he was.

THE MODERN FUNDAMENTALS OF GOLF *AND LIVING A GOOD LIFE*

When we turn to Hogan's most famous book, *Five Lessons: The Modern Fundamentals of Golf,* we discover a clear and penetrating account of the basics of golf as he understood and practiced them. We also find, because he was a tireless practitioner of his own teachings, some profound advice about golf that can be applied to questions regarding how one ought to live in order to realize a good and flourishing life.

In *Five Lessons* Ben Hogan, like René Descartes in his *Meditations on First Philosophy,* was seeking a firm foundation of knowledge or the true fundamentals of his life's work. In fact, Hogan tells the reader on a number of occasions that one simply cannot play golf well (and by extension, live a good life) without a repeating swing[5] (or acting in the morally appropriate way), and that he is offering practical lessons (instead of abstract theory) that are based on twenty-five years of his own trial-and-error experiences, as well as what he learned from watching other great players play their games. He also declares that he can be a rather demanding man when it comes to practicing the truths he preaches.[6] He notes that he has little toleration for those fools who, through ignorance of the fundamentals of golf, are happy to console themselves with its exercise and companionship values while simultaneously compounding their frustration by mindlessly ingraining bad habits in fruitless practice sessions. In short, the goal of every golfer (and by extension, every human being), Hogan claims, is to play the game well (or live one's life well), and that end, he says, can be realistically achieved with the appropriate kinds of application, thought, and effort. In essence, he promises that the golfer who goes about it wisely and prudently (i.e., who listens to, understands, and does what he says) will play good golf and should go on to enjoy golf throughout life.

The basic outline of the *Five Lessons* is easy to summarize. According to Hogan, a good golf swing consists of four (or five, depending on how you count them) fundamentals: the grip; the stance and posture; the first part of the swing, the backswing; and the second part of the swing, the downswing. A good golf swing also includes three other "absolute fundamentals" as well: a proper waggle that is suited to each unique and particular shot; a proper turn of the hips; and a proper backswing that stays on plane. Proper execution of each of these fundamentals will, he insists, produce a repeating and grooved swing that can be relied on in any and all circumstances. In fact, Hogan contends that a mere six months of dedicated and wise practice will result in scores at or near 80—so long, of course, as the specified fundamentals have become second nature.[7]

When we creatively translate Hogan's advice about the fundamentals of golf into advice about how to live one's life, we get a remarkably rich and robust (if somewhat mechanical) account of how to achieve one's goal. The two most obvious features of his explanation are its overarching holism and its metronomic precision. With respect to the former, I mean that his account of playing golf, and by extension living a good life, includes both an analysis of its constituent parts or basic building blocks (as in the *Great Learning*), and simultaneously an explanation and consideration of their interconnectedness and roles within the broader context of the bigger picture of his theory (as in the *Analects*). In other words, the parts not only can but ultimately must be understood in relation both to themselves and the greater whole from which they have been abstracted in order for the entire activity (whether golf or living) to make sense and be successful. With respect to the latter, I am referring to the craftsmanlike precision of his deconstruction and reconstruction of the golf swing and how this applies to the "way" one lives one's life.

For example, the observant reader cannot help noticing the drawing and caption that accompany the first chapter, "The Grip."[8] The drawing itself is a side-by-side rendering (by Anthony Ravielli) of Ben Hogan's swing just before impact, and a schematic representation of the same that includes an imbedded generator and the sparks and power that it produces as a result of energy transfer that is likened to "a chain action in physics." Though it is certainly difficult to avoid the drawing's obvious mechanical overtone and its deterministic implications, it seems quite undeniable that in a very real and important way the grip—the part, or basic building block—is the heartbeat of the action of the golf swing—the whole—in precisely the same way that one's brain and conscience are the heartbeat of one's ethical or moral actions throughout one's life.

Moreover, the fundamental distinction between what is purely mechanical and determined—and therefore what is, for at least some philosophers, beyond or outside the sphere of ethical consideration (i.e., one's heartbeat and the chemical processes of one's digestive system)—and what is freely chosen and within one's power to do or omit marks the basic difference between what is amoral and what is ultimately praiseworthy or blameworthy in terms of one's moral character. According to Hogan, it is a proper grip, or an appropriately tuned conscience and brain infused with the appropriate moral principles or fundamentals, that ultimately allows one to hit correctly executed golf shots or perform actions that exhibit real moral character.[9] Both essentially depend on how one goes about things, and neither is merely the result of chemistry or physics.

The chapters on stance, posture, and the first and second parts of the swing simply fill in the remaining details of Hogan's vision of the good human life and how one ought to go about working on the fundamental building blocks of ethics and perfecting one's thoughts, words, and deeds. For example, he insists that two of the most important aspects of one's stance or approach to a specific moral situation are the "feel"[10] and a sense of balance[11] one has as one considers the particular courses of action one might take. He also stresses the interdependence of one's thoughts, words, deeds, feelings, and emotions as one goes about engaging in the appropriate kinds of actions. And, like Aristotle and Confucius, he highlights the development of the right kinds of habit (through continuous practice of the appropriate application, thought, and effort) that will effortlessly allow one to do the right kind of action, at the right time, in the right way, in the right situation and circumstances, and always for the right reason. In fact, he insists that the best way to learn golf is a great deal like learning to play the piano: *one* practices—*by oneself*—a few things daily, arrives at a solid foundation, and then goes on to practice a few more advanced things daily, continually increasing skill.[12] One's aim in both cases, as is the aim in living a morally good life (as Aristotle claims in his *Nicomachean Ethics*), is to properly exercise function (i.e., swing well, play well, and live well) and make the fundamentals second nature. Hogan, unlike Confucius, insists that the key to being a morally good person is *individual* excellence and execution rather than the quality of one's relationships with others.

At the same time, in language and imagery reminiscent of both Plato (i.e., a model or "perfect" swing) and Confucius (i.e., individuals will execute their actions or instantiate precepts or rituals in their own unique and particular ways)—as we shall see later in my "Plato and Confucius on the Form of Golf"—Hogan also points out that there is a basic resemblance among all great golfers, despite their personal differences, because they all do essentially the same things. Moreover, he clearly intends to balance his idealism and universalism with a healthy dose of pragmatic realism by claiming, "When all is said and done, style is function and function is style."[13] One's swing, game, and life may certainly resemble many other swings, games, and lives, but in the final analysis each is *one's own,* and one is completely and solely responsible for their final forms.

Hogan also continues to focus on the significance of particularity in his chapters on the first[14] and second[15] parts of the swing. Like Confucius, he insists that he can work only with a student who is seriously interested in improving his game, and, like the Master, he draws an important distinction between the poor golfer and the good golfer. The latter knows and appreciates how the various elements of the swing are harmoniously linked and come together interdependently, while the former, through both ignorance and bad habits, continues to make last-ditch swing-wrecking efforts and movements that invariably lead to unfortunate outcomes. Unlike the morally praiseworthy person and good golfer who eventually comes to realize that good actions become instinctive and second nature through the acquisition of proper habits, the poor golfer and morally bad person, through his own lack of knowledge about both the fundamentals of the golf swing and moral vice, disrupts the chain of events that would naturally lead to a good golf shot and human flourishing.

Hogan was thoroughly convinced of the soundness of his method, and by extension the truth of his ethical view, because he had used it and it had worked. He practiced the fundamentals with intelligence, and he improved his skills in executing them, in the same way that a good person becomes good precisely by doing the right thing, at the right time, in the right way, in the right situation and circumstances, and for the right reason. Hogan insists that the basic difference between those who succeed and flourish—both morally and in the game of golf—and those who do not is the effort and willpower to do what is called for and the courage to go out and do it. As far as he is concerned, the only thing holding *one* back from succeeding is *oneself,* the only one responsible for that fact. It's not difficult to imagine Ben Hogan's advice to the average golfer and persons intent on improving themselves and their games: "If you want to succeed, do as I and the classic Nike and Avis ads say—'Just do it!'—and—'Try harder!'"

Two Conceptions of the Human Person and Human Flourishing

Confucius and Ben Hogan appear to offer two fundamentally different and distinct approaches to golf and life. For the sake of clarity I shall designate them as the "social conception" and the "rugged individualist account" of playing and living. According to the Confucian understanding, success as a person and player ultimately depends on one's learning how to get along with others in the situations and circumstances in which one finds oneself. In this view the key to being a good human person and good golfer is found in recognizing and realizing the incontrovertible truth and Tao that good people and good players are irreducibly social beings: it is simply a truth of reality that humans are at rock bottom social beings who cannot survive, flourish, or be all that they can be without cultivating ongoing relationships with others. In fact, these very relationships not only form the foundation of their own being, but they also help fulfill their capacity for being excellent human beings. As the Confucian scholar Herbert Fingarette has said, "For Confucius, unless there are at least two human beings, there can be no human beings."[16]

According to the "rugged individualist" or Hogan account, on the other hand, who one is and what one makes of oneself as a person and player are dependent more on natural dispositions and one's own unrelenting efforts to improve oneself than on any other factors. In this view one becomes what *one* makes of oneself as a result of personal choices, decisions, commitments, and efforts. While clearly recognizing that there are certain undeniable physical limitations that are a function of one's biology and physical constitution, this perspective places its focus and consideration on what *one* does with *one's* own determination, resolution, and commitment. The mantras and words of wisdom of this view include: "The only way to make yourself better is practice, practice, practice"; "You and you alone are responsible for what you've done and become"; "Winners never quit; quitters never win"; "Obstacles are what you see when you take your eye off your goal." Thus, the key to success as a person and player depends first, last, and always on *one's* own resources. Such a position is, not surprisingly, perfectly consistent with the American Dream of the solitary individual who pulls himself up by his own bootstraps and makes himself a success through sheer effort and willpower. It was precisely this kind of unwavering commitment that made Ben Hogan the great player he became.

Two obvious questions are: What are the strengths and weaknesses of each view? and, Which is right? A third question I will consider is whether it is possible to join these distinct understandings in a way that preserves the truth of each while simultaneously addressing the shortcomings of each.

FINDING A COMMON "WAY"

I suggest that the two conceptions outlined above form part of a broad spectrum of views that runs from a universal, absolute, and objective communitarian or "social conception" of the person and human flourishing to a particular, relativistic, and subjective "rugged individualist account" of the same. The former position tends to focus on what is common or true for all persons in terms of what they are and what will help them fully realize and actualize their natures and ultimately achieve their aims. The latter position, on the opposite end of the spectrum, includes a cluster of views that tend to focus on what is special and unique about the particular person and the individual context in which she finds herself. The positions we are considering fall somewhere between these extremes, but not in the precise middle. The Confucian view is clearly near what I am calling the "social conception," whereas the view I am ascribing to Ben Hogan is more representative of the "rugged individualist" end of the spectrum.

Among the obvious strengths of the social or Confucian view of things are its basic conformity with the way things are in terms of our biological production and social arrangements (our obvious interrelatedness); its clear recognition of our dependence on others; and its practicality and concreteness. Its apparent weaknesses include its focus on harmony at the expense of truth with respect to individual autonomy and responsibility; its focus on corporate identity and simultaneous failure to recognize individual effort and excellence; and its apparent relativism, subjectivism, and lack of an unchanging, transcendent, absolute—at least from the point of view of those who think there are such abstract objective absolutes.

The strengths of Hogan's "rugged individualist account," on the other hand, are its recognition of and reward for individual effort and excellence; its focus on personal responsibility; and its conformity with the latest psychological studies of motivation and behavior modification. Its prominent weaknesses include its abstraction of the individual from his or her social context and environment; its falsification of biological, psychological, and social facts related to interdependence; and its tendency toward stubborn rigidity in the face of changing circumstances (e.g., its stubborn tendency to believe the proposition "You can do anything if you just put your mind to it," even in the face of overwhelming empirical evidence to the contrary).

Given this mix of strengths and weaknesses of each view (and I am sure that the reader can come up with more of each), it does not seem obvious that either view or approach to life and golf is absolutely and completely right or absolutely and completely wrong. Perhaps that is as it should be, especially if one is committed to the view that the truth of things in ethics is somewhere in the middle (or at least closer to the middle than either Confucius or Hogan suggests). Between the traditional extremes of universal absolutism (the view that all actions of sort X are always and everywhere right or wrong) and individual relativism (the view that whatever you happen to think is right or wrong is right or wrong) is some type of contextual pluralism that simultaneously recognizes both objective guiding principles and their flexible context-dependent application—and consciously tries to harmonize the extremes. In golf terms, I am talking about scenarios in which golf prudence (i.e., objective guiding principles) would suggest or indicate a particular course of action, but one's lie, the stage of the match or round, and one's confidence in one's swing on that particular day at that particular time all help one see (from one's own point of view) that the appropriate shot is that which one actually manages to execute perfectly—despite one's usual tendency to hit a bad shot. Morally we understand the need to recognize personal achievement, but we also acknowledge that we are a success largely because of others. Thus, we attempt to achieve our personal desires to improve, but we also recognize moral obligations to the golfing community with such efforts as volunteering to attract and teach a diverse group of junior golfers.

Such a view would clearly be thought of as misguided by the likes of Plato, Aristotle, Thomas Aquinas, Kant, and Mill because of its lack of a universal, objective, and unchanging standard of good and bad or right and wrong. It would also be rejected by your ordinary, garden-variety subjectivist or relativist for its seeming rigidity, inflexibility, and one-size-fits-all moral questions mentality. The problem with staking out a middle ground, as all philosophers know, is that one has twice as many opponents and enemies as one would have if one were defending one end of the spectrum or the other.

Nevertheless, whether there is in fact a consistent and persuasive case for a middle position that combines the strengths and omits the weaknesses of both Confucius's and Ben Hogan's positions is clearly open for debate. In fact, the real question is whether something like a contextual pluralism can even be coherently conceived. Contextual pluralism has a vision that being both a moral person and a good golfer not only are the kinds of things that one must continually work at on a daily basis (as Hogan insists with his fundamentals)—by cultivating the organic relationships that are essential to each (as Confucius advises with his concepts of *xiao* and *ren*)—but also depend in no small way on one's individual and unique ability to respond in new and creative ways to the ever-changing circumstances in which one may find oneself in life or on the golf course. The answer to whether it is possible is, I think, why thought experiments and arguments by analogy were invented in the first place, and resources for explaining them are what I have tried to provide in this chapter.

Notes

1. See my essay "Plato and Confucius on the Form of Golf: From the Real to the Ideal"—especially the section titled "Confucius's Views about Reality and Golf"—in this volume.

2. I am using the James Legge translation, which may easily and readily be found online at www.sacred-texts.com/cfu/conf2.htm.

3. My "creative translations" are based on the original scholarly translations found in *The Analects of Confucius: A Philosophical Translation,* trans. Roger T. Ames (New York: Ballantine Books, 1999).

4. I recommend two recent biographies, the first by Curt Sampson, *Hogan* (New York: Broadway Books, 1997), and the second by James Dobson, *Ben Hogan: An American Life* (New York: Broadway Books, 2005).

5. It should be obvious to those who have worked their way through Ben Hogan's *Five Lessons* that he is first and foremost concerned with specifying, clarifying, and teaching the fundamentals of the golf swing and that each element must be executed in its appropriate order. In short, a rightly ordered swing (with its grip, stance, posture, backswing, downswing, and follow-through) is the key to success in golf, because a rightly ordered swing is and will be a reliable and repeating swing.

6. Ben Hogan, *Five Lessons: The Modern Fundamentals of Golf* (New York: Cornerstone Library, 1973), 15.

7. Ibid., 126.

8. Ibid., 19.

9. Ibid., 33.

10. Ibid., 40.

11. Ibid., 55.

12. Ibid., 57.

13. Ibid., 60.

14. Ibid., 61–83.

15. Ibid., 84–108.

16. Herbert Fingarette, "The Music of Humanity in the Conversations of Confucius," *Journal of Chinese Philosophy* 10 (1983): 217.

FOURTH HOLE

"QUIET . . . PLEASE!"

Reflections on Golf and Civility

David L. McNaron

Good manners are never a waste of time—civility, madam, always civility.
—Lawrence Tierney, in a line from
Star Trek: The Next Generation, 1988

If asked to name a civil sport or game, many people would no doubt choose golf. Civil people certainly play golf, yet does golf promote civility? I shall defend a qualified "yes" to the question. But as we shall see, answering the question is not as easy or straightforward as one might think. To make my case, I will offer an analysis of the concept of civility; clarify what it means to say that an activity promotes civility; resolve the apparent conflict between civility and competitiveness; argue against the conception of golf etiquette and civility as outdated or suspect; and discuss threats to civility in golf.

My topic is ideally suited for a virtue ethics approach of the sort made famous by Aristotle. Instead of developing principles of right conduct, Aristotle produced a theory of virtues, which he understood as "golden means" between extremes of particular emotions; for example, courage is the mean between cowardice and foolhardiness. Two important points about Aristotle are in order. First, though Aristotle was an ethical objectivist about the good or moral value ("activity of the psyche in accordance with virtue"), he argued that the mean is somewhat relative to individual temperament. He held, in contradistinction to Plato, that the ways we achieve the good are many and vary with individual tendencies. Thus, a person who is naturally bold may attain courage by restraining himself, whereas someone with a timid nature should strive for self-assertion.

Second, ethics for him could not exist independently of politics, since humans are by nature political animals; the good life is possible only within a political community that cultivates the virtues (although, again, he disagreed with Plato and denied there was an ideal type of state). The connection with my thesis is this: civility is necessary for a good society; moreover, community activities that promote civility are themselves morally important.

The official rules of golf, which require players to keep their own scores and call penalty strokes on themselves, place a premium on honesty and integrity, attitudes that form the foundation for civility. Golf *etiquette* even more obviously promotes civility by promoting respect for others. But let's be careful: rules and etiquette are separable. Rules define the game—for example, one *cannot* move a rook diagonally in chess—stipulating what one *must* or *must not* do to play a particular game; etiquette, on the other hand, prescribes *appropriate* conduct. The connection between golf and civility is thus *contingent*, however strong the traditional connection has been. Golf's connection to civility could thus change: the game could jettison its code of conduct in deference to behavior in vogue in other sports, or it could officially sanction breaches of etiquette.

Let's introduce a second complication and distinguish two senses of the word *promote*, the empirical and normative: "to cause" and "to stand for," respectively. The empirical question is whether taking up golf in fact instills civility. Support for this sense is found in the good behavior of most golfers and anecdotal evidence in the literature on golf programs.[1] If golf promotes civility in a normative sense, however, it stands for civility even if players sometimes fail to act civilly. Appealing to the normative sense of *promote* protects my thesis against counterexamples posed by occasional player misbehavior.

The Problem of Incivility

For now I will define civility as considerate conduct, a commodity evidently in short supply. Everywhere complaints are heard about the loss of civility, in transactions of virtually every sort, in American society and beyond. This is a serious problem if civility makes a good society possible. Consider this exchange in *Golf Digest*: "Q: At a local driving range, a man was talking on his hands-free cell phone, hitting balls as he spoke. I asked him if he wouldn't mind taking his conversation someplace else. He responded, 'Yes, I do mind.' Was my request out of line?" In *Golf Digest*'s literate reply, the editor presents a litany of rude, uncivil acts from the contemporary milieu and invokes Sartre's notion that hell is other people. One problem with the reader's predicament is that golf etiquette at the range differs from that on the course:

> There's usually a lot of chatter, often in the form of one terrible golfer giving his even worse golfer friend some instructional advice (as Erasmus says, in the land of the blind, the one-eyed man is king). So maybe talking on a cell phone at a public driving range isn't the worst crime in the world. Inconsiderate? Yes. Unnecessary? Absolutely. In the end, you did all you could. You let your feelings be known, and thus liberated them from deep within your marrow where they would otherwise have festered and rotted and possibly turned into some sort of unseemly tumor. Being civil is so rare these days that it sometimes feels subversive, an act of rebellion. But let's all try to hold ourselves to higher standards—we would never talk loudly on a cell phone in such a public place, would we?—and remain sanguine when nobody else does.[2]

This seems exactly right: one feels subversive—and certainly as going against the grain—when insisting on civil behavior. It seems that incivility reigns—a problem that has come home to golf.

Some academics are addressing the crisis through civility training. Professor Pier M. Forni, who cofounded the Johns Hopkins Civility Project, is a leader in this movement.[3] Forni explains the rise in student incivility: "One [cause] is the continuing erosion of the principle of authority. Then there is the prevailing consumer mentality among students. And the acceleration of informality brought about by digital communication. Finally, I would say the rise in narcissism caused by well-meaning but misguided parental practices."[4] He adds: "We've been doing very well as a society instilling self-esteem in our youngsters. We have not been as good in teaching them self-restraint." He advises instructors to "establish a climate of relaxed formality. With that seriousness of intent but lightness of touch, you play the game of good behavior. And it works." As if speaking uncannily of golf, Forni adds:

> Suppose that instead we fostered among the young the belief that although it is important to win, how we play the game is even more

important. Suppose we tell them that we play the game well when we play it to the best of our abilities, respecting both the rules of the game and our opponents. Imagine the changes the new frame of mind would bring. Here is a new society where we can lose a game and still be happy with what we did. We might not like the final score, but what really matters, the fact that we played the game well, following our heart and our conscience, cannot be taken away from us. Thus defeat becomes bearable, a learning opportunity rather than a crushing blow. We can easily make our peace with it, leave it behind us, and look forward to our next win. But then, in a way, we are already winners. This is civility: the ability to internalize the notion that how you play the game is more important than the final score.[5]

The emphasis on *how* a game is played will be important for the upcoming discussion. It is clear as well that golfers internalize the manner in which they should play, to adhere to both the rules of golf and its etiquette. Aristotle would say that the virtue has been acquired, through habituation, when the person has both attained the right dispositions to behave and formed the right desires: desiring to act in a civil fashion. But let's get clearer on the nature of civility.

What Is Civility?

In discussions of golf, civility is often mentioned along with courtesy, politeness, integrity, honor, honesty, and respect. John Kekes, the author of an important philosophical discussion of civility, arrives at the definition of civility as *conduct according to custom* from a painstaking analysis of Aristotle's views on civic friendship and Hume's notions of sentiment and custom. Aristotle argued that some manner of friendship should obtain among all citizens, even strangers—that we must take an interest in each other's welfare if society is to promote the good life. Kekes finds that Aristotle's account, however,

> did not explain what predisposes people to civility. According to Hume, sympathy does. But how does sympathy, regarded merely as fellow-feeling, result in altruistic action? To explain it, we have to supplement Hume's account by showing how reason guides and

corrects sympathy. Reason does so by postulating general rules which, if followed, save us from superstition, enthusiasm, and the *partiality* of our moral judgment. The justification for wanting to overcome these defects is that otherwise we undermine our society which provides one of the conditions required by a good life for ourselves and those we love. This is why people are disposed to civility.[6]

On this view reason directs our limited sympathy "through the conventions that a particular society has established."[7]

But can civility, which requires conformity to convention, conflict with the genuine demands of morality? What if social mores demand racism, sexism, or dishonesty? Can a moral virtue really consist in following norms independent of their content? Cheshire Calhoun distinguishes the *holding* of moral attitudes from their *display:* "The function of civility . . . is to *communicate* basic moral attitudes of respect, tolerance, and considerateness. We can communicate these basic moral attitudes . . . only by following socially conventional rules for the expression of respect, tolerance, and considerateness."[8] This *expressivist* account makes the connection—and possible conflict—between social conventions and morality clear. Social conventions provide a common language for conveying moral attitudes in morally imperfect social environments. Thus, civility mediates between rational or ideal morality—that is, the moral positions justified by reasoned argument—and living in a shared social space. On this view civility is the virtue, and incivility the vice, for communicating moral attitudes. Sometimes the conflict between reason and convention is unavoidable, and difficult moral choices must be made.

Civility is thus (a) the expression of respect, tolerance, and considerateness through (b) established social conventions. Each constitutes a necessary condition; together they form a sufficient condition for civility. This definition contains a universal component, respect for persons, and a relativistic one, reliance on actual social norms. The potential for conflict is evident in Kekes's account since he makes no allowance for which conventions one should follow if one is to act civilly. Calhoun's account does, since it stresses rational moral attitudes such as respect and tolerance as necessary for civility. She acknowledges the conflict; for example, in our society men opening the door for women is a civil convention, even though it reflects inegalitarian attitudes.[9] Men are placed in a genuine quandary when trying to decide whether to comply with such norms. In sum, Kekes has shown why civility is important and what accounts for it, but his definition has not ruled out a duty to follow morally questionable practices, whereas Calhoun grounds civility in defensible moral attitudes.

I can now state my overall position: the game of golf, through its conventions of official rules combined with informal etiquette, promotes civility, probably empirically and certainly normatively. The rules require honesty in play and reporting of scores. To adhere to golf etiquette, players must exercise self-restraint and allow each other the mental and physical space to execute their shots; they must even care for the course, minimizing their effect on it for the sake of others.

Adherence to golf's conventions makes possible the distinctively civil tone that golf has. As such, the game helps work against the presence of *skloka*, Kekes's candidate for the vice that opposes civility: an ugly, pervasive, dark tone of partiality, selfishness, and lack of fellow feeling. The term was apparently given this connotation in the correspondence between Boris Pasternak and Olga Freidenberg to describe the social malaise that existed in the Soviet Union at that time. The critic John Leonard, in his review of *The Correspondence of Boris Pasternak and Olga Freidenberg, 1910–1954*, writes: "Olga, perhaps, was closer to the heart of the matter in her peculiar definition of skloka (which, in Russian, involves money and trouble): 'Skloka stands for base, trivial hostility, unconscionable spite breeding petty intrigues, the vicious pitting of one clique against another.'"[10] *Skloka* is found in abundance in many sports in which athletes stop at little to win. In this it reflects and perhaps helps sustain that attitude at large in our society.

Golf Etiquette Compared to Etiquette in Other Sports

Is golf the sole bastion of civility in sports? Imagine headlines announcing Fred Funk's arrest on dog-fighting or rape charges, Mike Weir taunting his opponent, or a player engaging in chatter during another's address. Instances of vulgarity, crime, and dishonesty are difficult to find in golf. Golfers call penalties on themselves, but in sports that rely only on "negative restrictions" to safeguard conduct, players cheat.[11] They strive to avoid detection of rampant rule breaking and claim credit for false gains; examples include receivers displaying the ball after trapping it, dishonestly indicating a catch, and soccer players "flopping," thus falsely accusing others of fouls. This tendency erodes the values that make sport a morally attractive enterprise.[12]

Tennis, once widely considered on an ethical par (sorry!) with golf, surrendered its civility to the antics of bad boys Ilie Nastase, Jimmy Connors, and John McEnroe. Grunts and other selfish behavior are now common on tour. A commentator once remarked that the innovation Connors and Company had contributed was to make the rules of tennis *part of the game.* The incident that prompted this remark was Connors's crossing the net at Roland Garros during the French Open in 1991 to rub out his ball mark to prevent review of a call. This unsportsmanlike act, a literal failure to respect boundaries, presents a fine example of incivility since it disallowed the operation of impartial rules. Though we can admire the skill of uncivil players, it is reasonable to think that our overall appreciation for them and, more important, the game itself is dimmed: the physical contest has become divorced from desirable ends.

But why *should* golf have its peculiar etiquette? Is civility in sports a relic? Is there any good reason for golf's etiquette apart from tradition? Why enforce quiet during a player's address? One reply might be that the golf swing, which is entirely self-initiated, requires great concentration. But what about making a free throw amid tremendous crowd noise? Any sport requires focus. One could add that if their attention were complete, athletes would remain unaffected by noise. Jack Nicklaus once replied, when asked how he handled crowd noise at the U.S. Open, "What noise?" Assume that crowd noise bothers players only because of the *expectation* of quiet. If noise were a constant, as it is in stadium sports, players might adjust to it. But this is beside the point. The answer is that golf should keep its etiquette, which is a morally good thing, intact. An atmosphere of quiet allows for diversity in sports: one sport, at least, that places a premium on contemplation. Players and spectators alike are alone with their thoughts. It makes the world of sports, and the larger human world, a better place: in golf, reason agrees with custom.

This gives rise to an objection: golf is classist and inegalitarian, and its much touted civility comes from this tradition. A critic might include civility among the quaint or tainted virtues such as gentility, gentlemanliness, or ladylikeness, outmoded notions that reflect class bias and exclusionary practices. The objection, however, commits the genetic fallacy by confusing the origin or cause of an idea with its justification. The fact that this is how the code of conduct arose is irrelevant to reasons that might be adduced in its favor. Golf etiquette remains justifiable in our more egalitarian times because it inculcates character. Golf is not elitist, at least not in the way that is usually meant: golf *extends* its nobility to whoever takes up the game in the right spirit, making anyone potentially a member of the elite. There are many people of limited means who play the game seriously; they are elite inasmuch as they personify the game. Affordable courses can be found; the golf swing can be practiced without hitting balls; used clubs are inexpensive. Golf can be much less costly than many other activities. It is the *way* golf is played, according to its conventions, that sets the game apart.

Competitiveness and Civility

A Titleist commercial asserts: "Every player wants to shoot lower scores." Why else play? If you want to shoot lower scores, and playing competitively is the only way to shoot lower scores, then you should play competitively. TaylorMade's ad contends: "This is the game we play today. . . . We use the latest technology to win. . . . We show no mercy." Gary Player says, "Get mean, get uptight, get serious on the golf course."[13] This doesn't sound very civil, does it? Since an obvious goal of golf is victory, how can golf promote civility?

The resolution of this problem is that golf has multiple goals. In Europe golf was regarded as a noble pastime, a ritual activity that established social class. Who one *is* was a more important consideration than winning. In the United States golf was likewise conceived mainly for amateur play. Professional golfers, although admired for their ability, were held in mild contempt as "ex-caddie class."[14] We can discern another contender for the goal of golf beyond winning, namely self-mastery. The argument for self-mastery appeals to the fact that one can play the game alone and not compete against anyone. Singles are allowed to count these scores toward establishing their handicaps. Each time a player goes out, the aim is to execute the golf swing as perfectly as possible in every situation. The objection is that even the single plays against phantom opponents in the form of the course, par, or his or her best score. Ultimately, one is competing against oneself. But playing *by* oneself, the objection continues, is but glorified practice: real golf must be played with others who witness one's play and provide pressure situations. But if Plato and Aristotle are correct, self-interest and morality are compatible: the well-developed personality requires concern for others. Golf's conventions temper competition with civility and foster a code of conduct even more important than "victory itself." Let us now turn to some developments that threaten golf's civil code of conduct.

Threats to Civility in Golf

TEAM PLAY AND THE RYDER CUP

The Ryder Cup was once an occasion more for camaraderie than for national team rivalry. Now jingoism and partisanship are not only present but also in some years rampant. Here golf surrenders its character as the individual sport par excellence. Players compete not for money, but for national pride. Winning a Ryder Cup event counts for no more than the Dream Team winning the Olympic basketball championship. Shouts of "USA, USA!" have abounded in recent years. Some players find the energy the Cup has generated admirable, as it adds to the excitement of the game and encourages a stronger fan base.[15]

But golf in the Cup takes on the uncivil character that team sports have come to exhibit. We have seen that partiality is one of the distortions of sympathy. My own view is that the Cup should be suspended until it can be played in accordance with the ideal of sportsmanship in which it was conceived. Though some would have none of this, Lee Trevino differs: "I wouldn't play in the Ryder Cup today. I remember when the Ryder Cup was friendly. We ate dinner with the players from the opposite team. The wives went shopping together. The fans gave me just as much applause when I lost as when I won. I don't like what I see now. It's almost like a contest of who can treat the other side the worst."[16] One writer, complaining of the Americans' infamous celebration on the seventeenth green during the 1999 Cup, alleges that golf has lost out to sumo wrestling as the remaining purveyor of civility in sport.[17]

But doesn't the behavior of Ryder Cup players constitute a counterexample to my thesis? If golf really promoted civility, we would not expect to see the pros behaving abominably with a change of venue. My reply is twofold. First, golf "changes guises" in the Ryder Cup. In the current ethos of team sports, the Cup calls up different and, for golf, I think, inappropriate norms of aggressive partisanship. Second, the example is relevant only to the empirical version of my thesis; the normative interpretation remains untouched. Golf promotes civility even though civil behavior among players occasionally takes a holiday.

A FISTFUL OF VICTORY: TIGER WOODS

Complaints about incivility in golf arise over individual players' behavior, including that of Tiger Woods. In this essay I am concerned exclusively with Woods's on-course behavior. Civility has to do with behavior in public; therefore, Woods's extramarital affairs, however immoral they may have been, do not raise questions about civility. Imagine a thief who robs a train's vault but is extremely courteous to passengers. Though his thievery mars his character, his civil manner remains intact.

Woods has been accused of acting uncivilly on the course. The golf critic Brandon Tucker criticized Woods's behavior during a recent tour event: "For being the world's most recognizable athlete and top endorser, Woods' on-course demeanor isn't exactly laudable—and when you can make a case for his younger Nike brother, LeBron James, as being the more civil under pressure between the two, it should raise eyebrows."[18] What had Tiger done? He had "unleashed a profanity-laced tirade at a photographer."[19] Tucker is making a misplaced appeal to civility here. For it was uncivil conduct *on the part of the photographer* that provoked Woods: he clicked the camera shutter during Woods's swing. Golf etiquette requires that others remain quiet throughout a player's address and swing. Thus, it is the photographer who was in the wrong and should have apologized. His behavior did not warrant a civil response.[20] Woods's reaction was one of justified anger. Aristotle did not include anger among behaviors that are bad by their very nature. Anger, he thought, was sometimes appropriate. If course officials fail to enforce golf etiquette, players should not have to tolerate such inappropriate conduct of spectators or photographers. Tucker continues:

> For many families, the main reason they introduce golf to their children, at programs like First Tee or their local golf club, is because the game teaches civility and etiquette in a manner you can't learn on the playground. Many kids learn how to grow up on the golf course. If golf's greatest icon consistently disregards that civility, it sends a dangerous message, and golf loses a piece of its nobility. Woods should be worried less about Jack's 18 majors, Sam Snead's 82 wins or Byron Nelson's streak of 11 victories, and strive harder to match them in integrity.[21]

This is a good statement of the empirical connection between golf and civility, but it misses the mark with Woods: his behavior does not represent disregard for golf etiquette. Demanding civility is not being uncivil.

Still, it is reasonable to regard profanity in public as always uncivil. We can distinguish between justified anger and its expression. Only the latter is at issue. This raises an interesting issue: Can a distinction always be drawn between the content and the manner of expression? The California Supreme Court argued in *Cohen v. California* that the distinction is problematic.[22] The defendant, Cohen, was arrested for wearing a jacket emblazoned with the words "Fuck the draft" during the Vietnam War. The Court argued that had Cohen used more polite language (imagine, instead, "The Selective Service is an abomination and ought to be abolished") he could not have expressed *the same thought*. The profanity, and its emotive force, was necessary to convey Cohen's vehement opposition to the war. Consider another example. Suppose that someone belches loudly and intentionally in a restaurant. Another patron says to him, "Shut up." Ordinarily, saying "Shut up" is rude and uncivil. But in this case no less firm and commanding a response could convey the individual's revulsion over and unwillingness to tolerate this boorish behavior. But suppose profanity were added to the retort: now it appears that the affronted party has also acted in an uncivil fashion.

Now, the issue with respect to Woods's behavior, unlike that of Cohen's, is not whether Woods's conduct should be prohibited. Rather, we are interested in determining whether Woods's use of profanity was uncivil. Could he have expressed the same objection to the photographer's action—which constituted a flagrant disregard for golf etiquette—without using profanity and issuing threats? Perhaps. But the photographer's action did not warrant a civil response. I think that in this case we should excuse Woods's outburst, provided it is not indicative of a pattern of behavior. We should not lose sight of the main infraction against civility: it is the photographer's violation of golf etiquette that is mainly at issue, and Woods's behavior was a *response* to it. Players are under a *general* obligation to exercise restraint when in the presence of others.

Whether or not his behavior constituted a breach of civility, the argument could be made that Woods's outburst constituted a loss of self-control, of equanimity and self-mastery, which are ideals that golf promotes. Woods would appear, then, to resemble Aristotle's portrait of the less than perfectly good, though not vicious, man: Tiger as *enkratēs* in the making rather than *sōphrōn*. Martin Oswald defines Aristotle's notions: "A *sōphrōn* is well-balanced through and through. . . . The *enkratēs*, on the other hand, has an intense and passionate nature which he is, indeed, strong enough to control, but not without a struggle."[23] Woods did not control himself on this occasion, and so failed even as a *enkratēs*. Since Woods has an intense, fiercely competitive temperament, the Aristotelian would recommend that he tend more toward restraint than those with milder dispositions. The profanity is hard to justify as staying within the bounds set by civility. If golf is to maintain its fragile position as an ethically model sport that promotes civility, players should restrain themselves most of the time and look for creative ways to express anger over insolent infractions of golf etiquette.

AMATEUR PLAYERS

The main threat to civility in golf comes from amateurs who fail to observe golf etiquette. You find these people on many a golf course, causing an agonizingly slow pace of play by hitting mulligans, making noise during others' addresses, failing to position themselves to hit, and remaining oblivious to the injunction to allow faster players to play through. Players who breach golf etiquette cause others to endure a slow, miserable round that can take upwards of five hours. It is almost enough to make one quit the game.

SPECTATOR BEHAVIOR

The ubiquitous, clichéd yells of "You da man!" and "In the hole!" erupting simultaneously with impact mar the civil quality of golf. Golf's conventions require restraint. Some will object to the polite smattering of golf applause as out of step with the times. To this I say, so much the worse for the times if they support a climate of rowdiness and boorishness. Spectators should rise to the standards of conduct of the events they attend, not the reverse.

THE NEWS MEDIA

When photographers click their shutters during someone's swing and blimps hover noisily above tournament leaders, the quiet, reflective character of golf is damaged. Further, commentators stoke the fires of controversy, focusing on players' rivalries and shortcomings. Jack Nicklaus writes: "The media was very different in my time, much more moderate in its approach, less eager to stir controversy, more sensitive to the people they were covering as people, as fellow human beings. Indeed, what I will never understand about today's media is the emphasis on the negative rather than the positive, how they look for bad rather than good."[24] Negative media coverage undermines the polite tone that characterizes golf. It signals the presence of *skloka*.

Golf appeals to our virtuous side, not our grabby, selfish side. The game has established conventions that further civil, respectful behavior. Golf is a thoughtful game that induces reflection and self-development on and off the course. As the most contemplative of sports, golf contributes to Aristotle's perfectionist ideal of contemplation and the well-ordered life. Oddly enough, in the early twentieth century the United States Golf Association (USGA) took a rather anti-intellectual stance against clubs that questioned its policies, stating that a questioning attitude was uncivil and barring the clubs from membership.[25] The notion of civility was stretched in this case beyond its proper meaning to bolster the USGA's heavy-handed and overly conservative style of institutional oversight, with the result that convention diverged too sharply from rational morality. Here is an instance in which it was wrongly thought that civility required conformity to social norms. There is no neat formula for adjudicating such conflicts; we must decide cases on the basis of moral reflection: what might be gained, or lost, by adhering to certain conventions?

Golf contributes to happiness and self-perfection, which can take place, as Aristotle argued, only within a good community that supports these virtues. Golf supplies the conventions that foster civility and integrity. As such, the game presents an image of a good community, one that harmonizes the desire to excel with civility. Golf elicits the aspiration to become a better person. Thus, the game of golf, in promoting self-mastery and civility, contributes magnificently to the examined life.

Notes

This paper is dedicated to Glennon Bazzle, founder and CEO of Global Golf Institute, who enhanced my appreciation for and understanding of golf. See his excellent book, *Anatomy of the Perfect Golf Swing: The Surest Way to Better Golf* (Birmingham, Ala.: Lobdell and Potter, 2006).

1. For example, see David C. Lewis, "How Golf Transformed a Blighted Neighborhood," April 22, 2008, www.msnbc.com/id/24185797/from/ET/print/1/displaymode/1098 (accessed April 29, 2008):

> The remade neighborhood of East Lake is wrapped around a spectacular new public golf course, which became the setting for another one of [Tom] Cousins' dreams: a free mentoring program that teaches golf lessons and life lessons. "One of the better things is that (that golf) teaches integrity," he said. "In other sports, basketball, football, you break the rules and there's a penalty. But there's no moral issue there. But in golf, it's all on your personal integrity. You don't improve the ball in the rough. You don't change the position." Cousins hopes kids can learn the cherished values of the game he loves. Phys-ed classes at the Drew charter school are taught on the golf course, and the school may be the only inner-city school in America with a golf section in its library.

2. *Golf Digest,* October 2008, 56.

3. P. M. Forni, *Choosing Civility: The Twenty-five Rules of Considerate Conduct* (New York: St. Martin's Press, 2002). See Forni's Web site at http://web.jhu.edu/civility for the full range of his projects. Judy Nadler and Miriam Schulman also have a good discussion of civility and its relation to virtue ethics; see their article "Civility" at the Markkula Center for Applied Ethics Web site: www.scu.edu/ethics/practicing/focusareas/government_ethics/introdcution/civility.html (accessed May 21, 2008).

4. J. J. Hermes, "Civil Engineering," *Chronicle of Higher Education* online, March 28, 2008 http://chromicle.com/weekly/v54/i29a00601.htm?utm_source=at&utm_medium=en (accessed March 28, 2008).

5. Forni, *Choosing Civility,* 177.

6. John Kekes, "Civility and Society," *History of Philosophy Quarterly* 1, no. 4 (October 1984): 439; emphasis added.

7. Ibid., 441.

8. Cheshire Calhoun, "The Virtue of Civility," *Philosophy and Public Affairs* 29, no. 3 (Summer 2000): 255.

9. One could point to the convention of women's tees in golf as a possible example. At least here, however, some relevant physical differences exist—namely, statistical differences in upper body strength between men and women. Removing the label "women's tees" might solve the problem: there would then be only a range of color-coded tees from shortest to longest, and no stigma or gender bias would be attached.

10. John Leonard, "Books of the Times," *New York Times,* June 23, 1982.

11. The distinction between positive and negative restrictions comes from Monica K. Varner and J. David Knottnerus, "Civility, Rituals, and Exclusion: The Emergence of American Golf during the Late 19th and Early 20th Centuries," *Sociological Inquiry* 72, no. 3 (Summer 2002): 426–41.

12. For a full discussion of the constitutive skills of a sport, intentional rule breaking, and the values that make sport a morally attractive enterprise, see Robert L. Simon, "The Ethics of Strategic Fouling: A Reply to Fraleigh," *Journal of the Philosophy of Sport* 32 (2005): 87–95.

13. The ads aired on the Golf Channel as well as Gary Player's comments in an instructional segment.

14. For a full discussion of the origin of American golf and the importance of its emphasis on civility, see Varner and Knottnerus, "Civility, Rituals, and Exclusion."

15. For example, Curtis Strange has said: "I don't think it's animosity toward the other team. You have to learn from your mistakes, and we're doing that. But I don't think the Ryder Cup was better back then. It's better now. You could arguably say it's the biggest event in sports." And Jesper Parnevik has noted: "I like the chaos, the energy that comes with the Ryder Cup. But there's a very small line between doing that and stepping over the line. It should be right on top of that line." The same article that quotes Strange and Parnevik documents incidents of jingoistic incivility that occurred in

Ryder Cups in the 1940s and 1950s. Mike Stachura, "Civility vs. Hostility," *Golf Digest,* September 2001, http:findarticles.com/p/articles/mi_m0HFI/is_9_52/ai_77453562/ (accessed May 5, 2008).

16. Cited ibid.

17. David B. Goldenson, "Golf Losing Out to Sumo Civility," editorial, *New York Times,* October 3, 1999, http://query.nytimes.com/gst/fullpage.html?res=9B02E4DA1 E3Ef930a35753C1A96F9582 (accessed May 5, 2008).

18. Brandon Tucker, "Game of Honor? Tiger Woods' Behavior Reveals Golf Has Lost Its Gentlemanly Ways," April 1, 2008, http://www.worldgolf.com/magazine/archive-2008/apr01.htm (accessed March 17, 2010).

19. Brandon Tucker, "Tiger Woods Feels No Need to Apologize for Profanity-Laced Threat at Doral Photographer," March 26, 2008, www.worldgolf.com/blogs/brandon .tucker/2008/03/26/hey_tiger_lay_off_the_photographers (accessed May 19, 2008).

20. On the "bounds of civility," that is, behavior that does not deserve a civil response, see Calhoun, "The Virtue of Civility," 267–72.

21. Tucker, "Game of Honor?"

22. *Cohen v. California,* 403 U.S. 15 (1971).

23. Aristotle, *Nicomachean Ethics,* trans. Martin Ostwald (Indianapolis: Bobbs-Merrill, 1962), 314.

24. Jack Nicklaus, with Ben Bowden, *Golf My Way* (New York: Simon & Schuster, 2005), 292.

25. Varner and Knottnerus, "Civility, Rituals, and Exclusion," 437.

HOW GOLF BUILDS AND SHAPES MORAL CHARACTER

Jennifer M. Beller and Sharon Kay Stoll

Historically, coaches, teachers, and advocates for sport argue that sport builds character. Many sport enthusiasts put great stock in the notion that sport builds positive character values such as honesty, responsibility, fairness, and respect, and they believe them to be one of the ultimate goals of sports participation. These individuals argue that athletic participation and the institutions of sport reflect American attitudes, values, and beliefs and that these values come through physical participation.[1] Jeffrey Stout argues that our moral vision and character are shaped by sport, a complicated and complex moral practice.[2] Moreover, Bernard Mullin, Stephen Hardy, and William Sutton argue that athletics teach lessons of teamwork, self-sacrifice, and discipline and that these are transferable from the playing field to the business world or factory.[3] More recently, Maureen Weiss argued before a congressional hearing that "educators and parents have long attested that participation in sport can teach children values such as honesty, respect, empathy, responsibility and fair play."[4]

"But," Weiss also noted, "there are critics who will argue that instead of building character, sports develops characters who learn, among other things, how to skirt the rules in order to win at all costs or who believe rules do not apply to them."[5] Bruce Ogilvie and Thomas Tutko state that "if you want to build character, try something else."[6] In support of the anecdotal evidence is strong empirical research that has found that sport participation in and of itself does not build moral character and that the longer one participates in sport the less able one is to reason morally about the weighty issues in and outside sport.[7] And though researchers have found that sport in general does not build character, team sport athletes appear more negatively affected by the competitive experience compared to individual sport athletes; within the individual sports, golfers appear the least negatively affected.[8]

Yet for over forty years this debate about sport as a character-building experience has intensified and not been quelled. Thus, with a major portion of American youths' after-school activity time engaged in the practice of sport and with estimates of between 30 and 40 million participants aged five to eighteen involved in community-, youth-, school-, and agency-sponsored sport, what is the truth about sport as a character-building experience? And, with approximately 30 million golfers (approximately 17 percent aged five to seventeen and 19 percent aged eighteen to twenty-nine) in the United States alone, responsible for about 500 million rounds of golf on more than 16,000 golf courses, what is it about the golf competitive experience that sets it apart from all other sports as having a greater influence on character development?[9] And what is the empirical evidence that participation in golf enhances one's moral character development?

To answer these questions we must examine the nature of character, how character is developed, the effect of competition on character development, and how the history, culture, and traditions of golf (as a game in which each player keeps her own score, calls penalties on herself, and follows its tradition and history of honorable behavior) set it apart from all other sporting activities as having the potential of being a character-building experience. What then is meant by moral character?

The Nature of Character

To the Greeks morality involved how individuals treated one another; they recognized that this treatment affected one's own well-being. Aristotle said that the notion of morality was decency to others, respectful behavior, fair play, and justice.[10] He called this character the life of right conduct, which entails knowing the right and doing the right, even when no one else is watching—so much so that it becomes habitual.[11] For Aristotle knowing what is right underlies one's ability to conduct right moral action in a habitual pattern. Thus, moral feeling is imperative to habitual moral behavior. Thomas Lickona, a psychologist, educator, and student of Lawrence Kohlberg, used the same Aristotelian notion of right conduct and expanded it to more fully develop the interconnectedness of moral feeling, moral knowing, and moral action to one's moral development. As a psychologist he noted that moral knowing includes moral awareness, perspective taking, moral reasoning, decision making, self-knowledge, and knowing moral values; moral feeling has to do with conscience, self-esteem, empathy, loving the good, self-control, empathy, and humility; moral action is competency, will, and habit.[12] The foundation of this character (knowing the right, valuing the right, and doing the right) is morality, "one's actions, intentions, and motives as they affect and impinge on others."[13] Moral character, then, involves how individuals relate to other human beings and the relative worth placed on such attributes as honesty, responsibility, civility, and decency: core universal values. Toward others the individual is responsible, the individual is civil, the individual plays fair, and so forth. A good example in golf is the tradition of golfers calling their own penalties. It is the only sport in which the participant is expected to value and follow both the rules and the spirit of the rules in all levels of play.

In contrast to the moral values that underlie character are social character traits. These are different from moral character traits in that social traits relate to the values that Western society places on hard work, dedication, sacrifice, intensity, and teamwork. These social values are greatly prized by Americans and considered integral to the sport experience. They focus on the individual's accomplishments: the athlete is a hard worker, the athlete is highly dedicated, the athlete is intense, and the athlete is a good team member. Much empirical evidence exists that sport builds or at least fosters the development of these social traits.[14] Although the social character traits are inherent to the character-building nature of sport, these values should not be the only part of a person's character. Strong social character requires a solid foundation of moral character to temper the individual's selfish wants, needs, and desires in relation to others. That is, one could be a very hardworking and dedicated rapist. Morality serves as a guide for promoting individual reasoning and personalized decisions.[15] As such, moral character is the sum of one's mental and emotional dispositions, and it has a distinct personal element.

Character Development

The concept of character development for most individuals is tricky, since everyone we have ever met believes that she, personally, is ethical, knows what it means, and could teach it to the world. At a recent major meeting on character education, a panelist stated, "We all know what it means, so all we have to do is teach it."[16] Taking that sort of perception into consideration, broaching the topic of developing character demands some quick sidestepping, especially given the empirical research over the past thirty years related to the competitive experience. It is not enough merely to think you know what is ethical; it requires study, thought, reflection, cognitive dissonance, and challenge of personal values relative to the professional and sporting practice.

The principal parts of moral character education revolve around different forms of learning, mainly: (1) role models, (2) the social environment, and (3) formal learning about ethics and character education.

LEARNING FROM ROLE MODELS

Significant people in our lives serve as roles models for us. We learn not only by hearing what these important people say but also through their nonverbal instruction—their gestures, facial expressions, and body language. These models can be parents, peers, teachers, coaches, coworkers, bosses, or even entertainers. Any person can serve as a role model and can teach others through actions, words, and behaviors. Parents bear a great responsibility in this regard; children learn from their parents, their first role models, what is morally right and wrong. To illustrate the importance of role modeling, there is an old story about parental role models and character education.

A father was home-schooling his twelve-year-old son about honesty. On Monday he taught the story of George Washington and the cherry tree. On Tuesday he used the example of Abraham Lincoln. On Wednesday he told his son about Mother Teresa. On Thursday he talked about Jesus Christ. On Friday they went to a movie. A sign stated that all children under the age of eleven get in free. The father said, "Today, you are ten."

The father taught his son more about character with his act than he did with his four stories. The point is that the first line of character education is through parents: if we are serious about character education, then parents must assume the duty of "walking the walk and talking the talk." Of course, we learn from many, many experiences, environments, and role models such as teachers, bosses, entertainers, athletes, and others. Golf has many such role models. In the 1925 U.S. Open Bobby Jones barely budged his ball while addressing it in the rough; no one saw the ball move except for Jones himself.[17] The tournament title hung in the balance, and as the scorecards were signed and turned in it became evident to everyone that Jones had assessed himself a one-stroke penalty. The movement of the ball did not benefit him and was not a great game violation, but he chose to take the penalty that the rules clearly stated he had to. He was tied with Willie Macfarlane at the end of regulation play because of that penalty, and he eventually lost the Open in a thirty-six-hole playoff. When asked why he chose to take the penalty, he simply stated that it was a part of the rules and the game. He also asked that reporters not write about it because "You might as well praise me for not breaking into banks." Similarly, Meg Mallon (four times an LPGA major tour champion) said that though many sports have as their motto "If you ain't cheating, you ain't trying," golf is different. Golf "started as a gentleman's game, and it has kept going. You learn that it is a badge of honor to play the rules and call penalties on yourself. It is a game of integrity." She assessed herself a 1-shot penalty when she dropped her golf ball on her coin. "You can't live with yourself if you don't call it. I just couldn't play feeling that way." In the 2007 Honda Classic, Mark Wilson assessed himself a 2-shot penalty when he realized that his caddie had inadvertently called out the loft of his high-bred club, thus potentially aiding another player. He won the tournament in a sudden-death playoff; the playoff probably would not have occurred had he not taken the penalty. Moreover, in the 1996 Bayhill Invitational, Jeff Sluman, who was two strokes from the lead, disqualified himself because he thought he had taken an improper drop, even though he wasn't entirely sure. Thus, following both the letter and spirit of the rules in golf is so internalized by players that, unlike participants in any other sport, they not only take personal responsibility for their actions, but they see doing so as essential to the nature of the game and to who they are as they play it.

LEARNING FROM THE SOCIAL ENVIRONMENT

Our lives are also influenced by our environment. Our first environmental influence comes from our immediate families. We are indirectly educated through our family traditions, family values, religious training, and family history. Our next environmental experience comes at school, at work, or at play. We learn from what our peer group practices, from the values of the group, and from watching what the group does. The environment also instructs us through the greater societal norms, values, and actions. Today our societal influences are highly affected by media presentation—for example, by television, sports, movies, the Internet, and print journalism. For this to work toward character development, parents have to take an active role in monitoring what children and teens are exposed to. Television and Hollywood productions generally have no interest in teaching children what it is to have good character. Rather, the majority of entertainment is focused on just the opposite of what we would define as good character: deceit, dishonesty, infidelity, irresponsibility, and so forth. Hence, parents must play an active role in all forms of education, especially that which comes from "the box" (computer and television) and the big screen.

FORMAL LEARNING ABOUT ETHICS AND CHARACTER EDUCATION

A specific type of thinking must occur if ethical reasoning is to improve. The process is called cognitive dissonance, which is an intellectual challenge through moral reasoning—a systematic process of evaluating personal values, realizing that they may be in conflict with one another, dealing with the anxiety that conflict causes, and developing a consistent and impartial set of moral principles to live by.[18] Moral reasoning, we believe, is imperative if we are to subdue the personal, internal turmoil of cognitive dissonance. Moral reasoning is a process based on philosophical reasoning. It is highly beneficial to anyone who undertakes it. Research for the last forty years has shown significant positive cognitive moral growth for all ages enrolled in specifically designed programs or classes. Moral reasoning is not ideology or theology or some mystical practice of making people good. Rather, it is based on the assumption that as reasoning individuals, each of us, through self-examination of personal values and those values in relation to a higher standard, can cognitively develop our moral decision-making process. Moral reasoning does not guarantee behavioral change, but it does promise individual soul-searching and reflection on personal beliefs, values, and principles. Without this process, dealing with dissonance is impossible and neither cognitive moral growth nor behavioral change will occur.

In support of the philosophical process of moral reasoning is current research concerning the neuroplasticity of the brain. Researchers note that frontal-lobe development is affected by a specific kind of moral education, types of experiences, and the practice of moral reasoning.[19] Frontal-lobe development is not complete until the early to mid-twenties. What we know about this development is that young people need an educational program that is built on higher-order reasoning. First-order reasoning, for example, would involve a question like "Is it wrong to cheat?" and second-order, "Why is it wrong to cheat?" It is more important for brain development to ask third-order questions, such as "Let us consider why you say it is okay to cheat in class, but it is not okay for your girlfriend to cheat on you?" The latest research in neuroscience is quite clear that the human brain is actually hardwired for morality.[20] That is, because the brain has continual plasticity, which is the ability to grow, training and education in morality are an important undertaking. This plasticity is affected by challenging norms and critical reasoning, so higher-order reasoning is essential to changes in the brain. The frontal lobes of psychopaths are small, whereas those of highly moral individuals are large and well-developed—the result of neuroplasticity. According to Laurence Tancredi, "Neuroplasticity is what we can use to build moral strength through positive experiences and training. Unless we are one of those with a serious biological defect—genetic or acquired— our brains are able to reshape themselves at virtually any age to improve our physical and psychological conditions. Neuroplasticity can be our best friend if we've gone wrong and want to reform."[21] These challenges cause discussion, thought, and reflection about the importance of being a "good human being," which develops the frontal lobe and, we hope, develops a good human being in action, word, and deed. Thus, the higher-order question forces the individual to examine value structures, inconsistencies in thought, and differences in the value of experience, as well as the ramifications of those differences. Applying this perspective in a discussion within a teaching format is a wholly different method of instruction; it requires the teacher to ask the tougher questions and to know the students well enough to challenge them to reflection and deep thinking.

Knowing, Valuing, and Doing the Right

Development of character therefore can be both systematic and nonsystematic; in other words, it is taught formally and informally. In the best scenario, the three elements (role modeling, environment, and cognitive dissonance) come together to give the individual a strong base of values and a way to think about them. These elements affect moral knowing, moral valuing, and consequent moral action, which are an overall reflection of moral character. Lickona calls these valuing and knowing the right—when the pieces are together, the individual has the keys to doing the moral right.[22]

Knowing and doing the right, though, are predicated on several interrelated factors that have a symbiotic relationship to the reasoner and his or her place and being in the world: moral knowing, moral valuing, and moral acting. Moral knowing is a specific type of knowing that encompasses a variety of skills, of which moral reasoning is one integral piece.[23] One must first recognize whether a moral question even exists. One must know and understand the underlying moral values that drive one's actions as well as be able to take another person's perspective. To have any potential effect on one's behavior, one must also have moral feeling: conscience, self-esteem, empathy, love for the good, self-control, and humility. We know from the research on neuroplasticity of the brain that there are individuals (such as psychopaths and sociopaths) who never truly develop a sense of moral valuing.[24] Yet for individuals to develop a strong sense of what is right requires that they be immersed in a moral community that supports, models, and teaches the good.

The Characteristics of a Moral Community

There are several components of a moral community. The first is warm and nurturing surroundings. Children typically learn to be by what they admire. Thus, if they live in an environment that is warm and nurturing with admirable adults, they are encouraged to learn. Second, clear limits and expectations must be set, communicated, and understood. Children must have clear rules, standards, expectations, and a vision of the goals they are to achieve and the people they are to become. Third is the multigenerational nature of the community: children learn from being around loving, caring individuals in all life's stages.[25] And fourth, a moral community reflects and transmits a shared understanding of what it means to be a good person.[26] In sum, for children to learn what it is to be a part of a moral community, and thus what it is to be good, to value the good, and to do the good, they must live, be loved, and be nurtured in an environment filled with individuals of all ages who help to set and model clear expectations and standards and who reflect and thereby transmit a shared understanding of what it is to be good.

Aristotle said that character is the composite of good moral qualities, whereby one shows firmness of belief, resolution, and practice about moral virtues such as honesty, justice, and respect. He also said that character is right conduct in relation to other persons and to self. Aristotle further argued that our humanness resides in our ability and capacity to reason and value results when we use our reasoning ability to control and moderate ourselves.[27] For example, courage is a mean between being cowardly and foolhardy. Reason helps us find that mean. Lickona builds on Aristotle's theme to broaden the definition: "Good character consists of knowing the good, desiring the good, and doing the good—habits of the mind, habits of the heart, and habits of action."[28] Lickona argues that reasoning is inadequate by itself; one must have a strong value system that resides in the psyche, which one understands and can articulate. Just to say "Cheating is wrong" is inadequate. One must know why it is wrong and what values are violated. For example, when Tiger Woods was asked why he did not stop his extramarital affairs before they became public, he said, "Well I didn't know I was that bad . . . stripping away denial, rationalization. You strip that away and you find the truth."[29] The true and final test is putting into action what one values, knows, and reasons is right, hence the concept of "doing." It is easy to say that one does not cheat; it is entirely another thing not to cheat when others around you are cheating. Lickona also stresses that such "doing" must become habitual and one must have courage to practice the art of character. Shields and Bredemeier follow this same sort of theme in their definition of "character . . . [as] the possession of those personal qualities or virtues that facilitate the consistent display of moral action."[30] That is, character is the attribute of an individual who values others and so attempts to practice certain principles toward others. These principles show a valuing of certain beliefs, for example that it is important to be honest, trustworthy, just, respectful, and civil. Character, then, in an ethical sense, is the sum of the principles, the valuing of the principles, and the behavioral action of the individual while following those principles.[31] From our past twenty-five years of study in the field of athletics and character we have derived our own definition: character is the ability to be honest, fair, and civil, even when no one is watching and even when no one else is practicing ethics. Character is having the courage to stand for the right even in an environment where gaining advantage rather than doing what is right carries the day.[32]

In most competitive activities we teach and socialize practices that violate the rules and nature of those games as well as individuals within them. For example, in such team sports as football, hockey, lacrosse, and basketball, individuals have historically been taught and socialized to believe that gamesmanship (pushing the rules to the limit by dubious means without getting caught) is acceptable. Individuals are realists rather than idealists and do whatever they need to do both inside and outside the game's rules to help ensure a win, whether that means taking an opponent out of the game to play the second or third string or outright breaking of rules. How we play the game is not as important as the win. The ultimate goal is to gain an advantage, no matter who is or is not watching, to ensure victory.

A number of the character-building elements of sport come from what many consider the immediacy of results associated with the social character traits of dedication to task, teamwork, sacrifice for the common good, self-lessness, self-reliance, overcoming obstacles, and so forth. These traits are highly prized and deemed the "character-building qualities" of sport. But individuals can display these traits in a moral vacuum. One can be highly competitive and successful and at the same time be immoral in motive, intention, and action. Whether one scores or does not score, wins or loses, plays or does not play can also affect one's character development, but that character could be only social rather than moral.

The demands and complexities of the competitive experience appear to affect the athlete's sporting experience negatively. Researchers have found over the past twenty-five years that athletes reason morally from a perspective very different from that of their nonathlete peers; athletes reason at a significantly lower level.[33] Lacrosse, football, ice hockey, and basketball players score the lowest. Their reasoning tends to be based on being told what is right and wrong, following only the letter of the rules and personal interests. Moreover, male athletes appear more negatively affected by the competitive environment than female athletes, although the moral reasoning of female participants in team sports more closely mirrors that of male team sports athletes. Interestingly, no difference exists between male and female golfers, who score significantly higher and reason from a perspective in which they take into account others, societal rules, and the intentions behind the rules.[34] These findings fly in the face of the age-old argument that women would score significantly lower on moral development instruments. Carol Gilligan and others claim that because women are more caregiving and altruistic and are more driven by these values, they would not score as high as males on these instruments.[35] To measure women with these instruments is misleading and incorrect. Gilligan's point, however, appears to be moot because, in our twenty-five years of collecting data from both competitive and noncompetitive populations, women have always scored higher.[36] Males have lower reasoning scores than females, but both are dropping at a constant rate. Men have always scored lower than females, perhaps not only because of the competitive environment of athletics but also because men are earlier and more often rewarded by their peers, fans, and parents for their athletic successes. Yet when we examine golfers' scores, they are generally the highest on these instruments, regardless of gender. Thus, it appears that the nature of how a game is taught and modeled has had an influence on how players view moral issues—cheating, gaining an advantage, retaliation, and so forth.

Essentially, athletes, especially team sport athletes, follow a code of gamesmanship as the standard of practice. Within this environment many athletes are taught and coached by role models who believe that rules exist to bend and manipulate for the sake of victory. As a result, new rules must be written to cover the latest infraction, and rule books become lengthier and more complex. Rules have evolved and changed, making it even more difficult for athletes to take personal responsibility. For instance, in the past, regardless of whether an official called an infraction, volleyball players were required to yell "Touch" if they touched a ball when it went out of bounds, and basketball players were required to raise their arms to show responsibility when they fouled. To do so now merits a player's removal from the game either by the officials or by her coaches and being ostracized by teammates who make such comments as "If my teammate ever told someone they touched the ball, I'd kick them in the head."[37] Moreover, even if coaches encourage their players to call "Touch" and raise arms, they are often told by officials to have their players refrain from such action; this occurred in a volleyball game between the U.S. Military Academy at West Point and a conference foe.[38] A major goal of the academy is to "develop leaders of character for the common defense." Character development is taken seriously, and thus all that cadets do, including mandatory sport participation, has it as its goal. When the rules were changed so that athletes were not to yell "Touch," the leaders at the academy felt that the rule change diffused athlete responsibility and was thus an attack on character development; their response was to coach their athletes to yell "Touch." Partway through the game an official stepped up to the coach and asked him to have his athletes refrain from calling "Touch." When the coach explained why he had his athletes call "Touch," the official explained the rule. After the game concluded, NCAA officials stated that if the academy continued disregarding the rule change, they would be asked to leave the conference, as they were not "following the official rules."[39]

In this view, it becomes the official's responsibility to see all infractions and make all calls; the athlete takes little personal responsibility for either the letter or the intention of the rule. This diffusion of responsibility encourages athletes to believe that cheating occurs only if one gets caught. And why the initial change in the rules? Athletes were flagrantly drawing attention to themselves, which disturbed the flow and purpose of the game. Thus, rules were rewritten probably with good intentions but with negative results in terms of athletes' taking personal responsibility. Consequently, if honoring, valuing, and playing by the rules lessens the chance of victory, doing so becomes very difficult for athletes.

Why do golfers appear different in terms of moral reasoning and character development from team sport athletes? Why do golfers take a penalty for movement of a ball, knowing they may lose a championship, even when no one else knows the ball moved?

Building and Supporting a Moral Community

Some similarities and differences exist between golf and other organized sports, all of which affect character development. All organized sports are games of physical skill, athleticism, tactics, strategy, and competition. The philosopher Robert Simon argues that "sports contests can be regarded as tests of the competitor's abilities to meet the challenge created by the rules. More broadly, sports are arenas in which we test ourselves against others, where we attempt to learn and grow through our performances, and where we attempt to develop and exhibit excellence at overcoming the sport specific obstacles created by the rules."[40] All organized sports are rule-bound, in that there are clearly defined constitutive rules. Simon also specifies that sport "can be defined primarily by reference to the idea of constitutive rules and goals, or obstacles designated by the rules themselves, which are unintelligible apart from them"[41] Actions and moves within the game as well as what constitutes winning are determined by the constitutive rules. These are the rules that are typically manipulated to help ensure victory.

Sport is also governed by a set of rules relating to sportsmanship or morality. These rules are about respect for teammates and competitors, commitment to fair play, and honorable actions; in golf, for example, it is wrong when on the green to walk with spikes in an opponent's line. The intent behind the rules is that athletes should not interfere with their opponents' capacity to compete within the constitutive and sportsmanship rules of the game. Both types of rules are essential to the nature of the game. The constitutive rules are the rules that govern the play itself, whereas sportsmanship rules are rules developed by an organization about player, coach, and fan conduct on the field and sometimes off. As Carwyn Jones and Michael McNamee have noted, "The rules of sport are premised on the principle of fairness. Breaking the rules, therefore, changes the balance of the game illegitimately, violating the principle of fairness; all competitors are afforded fair and equal treatment in the pursuit of victory. The decision to play is seen as a kind of tacit promise to the sporting community as a whole to abide by the rules. To break the rules, therefore, is to renege on this promise."[42]

Thus, certain acts that are not regulated by constitutive rules should be performed because they enhance and further competition. For example, individuals may not intentionally lie about the time and place of competition or bribe officials in an attempt to ensure a win. There is a tacit understanding that competitors should help create conditions in which opponents can do their best. Interestingly, in response to a rise in violations of constitutive rules, the number of sportsmanship rules has significantly increased in most sports—except golf.

What Sets Golf Apart?

Though all sports are governed by both constitutive and sportsmanship rules, golf has several elements that set it apart from other sports. First, golf has a rich history, tradition, and culture that support a strong sense of what is considered right action in both a constitutive and a moral sense. Golf may be the only sport that at all levels has a self-policing component that lends a critical dimension to the competition. Many argue that the same can be said of tennis, but at its professional and elite levels officials are present and make line, net, and other foul calls. Golf appears to be the only sport in which even professionals are required to be responsible for their own calls and scores. Golf relies on the simple premise that only the golfer truly knows how many swings were made during the play. Golf is simply nothing if not a game of honor, which leads to the traditions and expectations of the game.

Role models, themselves educated and socialized in an environment of honor and integrity, set high expectations for behavior. One need only examine the membership requirements of most country clubs and golf clubs to find the statement that an applicant must be of "good moral character." Few if any other sport activities make that requirement. Here is an example from one such club: "At Hillandale Golf Course, we recognize not only the value our junior golfers bring to the great game of golf, but also the importance of a well instructed program that includes character development. Our PGA and LPGA staff is trained to not only teach our 'juniors' the important fundamentals of a great golf swing but also the importance of enjoying their 'journey' in golf."[43]

And though good moral character is seldom explicitly defined, the expectation is that one must have a moral character in order to apply and that club members will encourage that morality. If we return to our discussion of how individuals learn moral character, we can see from these statements that golf has a rich tradition and culture that expect players not only to know but to follow the letter and spirit of the rules. The integrity of the game and the win require it. Obviously, what is expected may not be played out consistently, but the point is that there is a tradition and expectation of it, even though some clubs have exclusionary rules that violate the basic premises of honesty, respect, and responsibility.

Therefore, the culture of golf does not appear to support the concept of gamesmanship in the way that most other sports do. In the game of golf one can learn much about a person's moral and social character. The golf course challenges athletes' decision-making processes, reasoning, and problem-solving abilities through their club choices, shot selections, and course management. Within these contexts golfers are challenged continually by both the constitutive and sportsmanship rules. Much can be observed about their moral (integrity, honesty, responsibility, fairness) and their social (patience, modesty, logic, wisdom, dedication) character. And, though most sports are driven by the social values of competition, golf appears defined by its moral nature. Golfers who lie and cheat will not make it in the competitive game, for few if any would want to play against them. In other team sports, though, the underlying theme is often "Do unto others before they do unto you."[44]

Golfers are thus steeped in the honor and integrity of the game. These values are so deeply ingrained in participants that by the time golfers reach the elite and professional levels they would rather lose than improve a lie to ensure victory, as victory won through gamesmanship or cheating has little to no value. For example, several years ago a highly talented high school golfer was competing in his state high school championship when he accidently improved his lie with his foot on one of the last holes. He was in the final round and in contention to win. Much was on the line. If he won, he would be offered a full-ride golf scholarship at a very prestigious university. No one was watching. He could have continued as though nothing had happened or taken the stroke. He chose to take the stroke and lost. Had he not taken the stroke, he would have won. Later he said that he never even considered cheating to gain the scholarship. He would have violated the ethos of the game, and he would have known that he had not truly won the match. In contrast, most team sport athletes would think the golfer crazy: no one was looking; who would know?

Similarly, the professional golfer David Duval discussed how golfers should view their opponents: "One of the great things about golf is that you don't have to have any ill-will in this game. If I come head-to-head against him [Tiger Woods] at say, the U.S. Open, I want him to be playing as good as he can play because I want to beat him when he's playing his best. It would be a heck of a lot better, if you know he gave you all he's got, and you beat him."[45]

The spirit behind the rules guides and promotes honor and integrity in golf competition. And competition that raises the overall level of competition is the main goal. Some may argue that golf requires less physical conditioning or absolute athleticism compared to most other sports, but to excel in golf requires all the same social character traits as other sports: dedication to task, sacrifice, selflessness, self-reliance, overcoming obstacles, and so on. Golf's traditions, history, and culture create an environment with set standards, expectations, and consequences that positively affect the neuroplasticity of the brain. All of these are very important because of how we grow and think and mature morally. The community works if it has a defined set of expectations, behaviors, and parameters—and consequences for not meeting them. If the community is very strong in its moral beliefs, individuals will typically grow and mature in a moral fashion. But does that mean all individuals in a specific environment will grow and mature in the same fashion, and that those without a moral compass will be unalterably different? Not necessarily. There are glaring examples of golfers acting immorally both on and off the course. Nonetheless, if they come into a loving environment, with strong moral standards, moral role models, and consequences for violations, they can also grow and mature in that situation. It just takes longer.

Golf has all the qualities to encourage moral growth, whether the golfer is six or sixty. And, interestingly enough, empirical research supports this very notion. Moral reasoning scores of golfers are the highest of individual sport participants, and significantly higher than team sport participants. Some argue that education and income affect one's moral reasoning. In other words, the more highly educated and affluent people are (as many who play the game of golf are), the better they are at making good moral judgments. Education and affluence, however, neither predict nor directly affect moral reasoning. For example, lawyers score low on moral reasoning inventories; theologians score high. Is there a correlation to income? James Rest reported that socioeconomic status does not correlate with moral reasoning. For example, some of the smartest, best-paid people in business were the leaders of Enron.[46]

Yet why are golfers different from all other athletes? The answer lies in the traditions of the game, from calling one's own errors to the expectations of honesty, and in role models like Greg Norman, who disqualified himself from the 1996 Canon Greater Hartford Open when he found he had used an illegal ball. Nowhere else in sport do we find this heightened sense of responsibility to the game, to self, and to one's opponent. This sense of integrity might best be summed up through Rannulph Junuh's comments in the movie *Bagger Vance*. When he moved a twig in a game against two of the best who ever played, Bobby Jones and Walter Hagen, his ball moved. "I have to call a stroke on myself." His young caddie, Hardy Greaves, said, "No, don't do it! Please don't do it. Only you and me seen it, and I won't tell a soul." Junuh says, "I promised. I will, Hardy. So will you." And that's it in a nutshell: golfers score higher in moral reasoning because, unlike players of other sports, they see their endeavors as more about others and the game than about themselves. They have a sense of duty to self and to others. This duty leads to a strong sense of honor and responsibility to the integrity of the game. They hold themselves and others to this standard—they model, mentor, and teach honor and integrity as an essential ingredient to the nature and play of the game.

Notes

1. Angela Lumpkin, *Physical Education and Sport: A Contemporary Introduction*, 3rd ed. (St. Louis: Mosby, 1994), 2–50. Jesse F. Williams and William L. Hughes, *Athletics in Education* (Philadelphia: W. B. Saunders, 1930). M. Vannier and H. Fait, *Teaching Physical Education in Secondary Schools* (Philadelphia: W. B. Saunders, 1957), 1–15. Thomas D. Wood and Rosalind F. Cassidy, *The New Physical Education* (New York: Macmillan, 1927). Clark W. Hetherington, "The Demonstration Play School of 1913," *American Physical Education Review* 20 (1915): 285. Thomas Shea, "Win-at-Any-Cost Attitude Disturbs a PE Veteran. Southern Illinois University News Release," *Journal of Athletic Training* 25, no. 2 (1990): 185. Daryl Siedentop, *Introduction to Physical Education, Fitness, and Sport* (Mountain View, Calif.: Mayfield, 1990), 2–65. Daryl Siedentop, Charles Mand, and Andrew Taggart, *Physical Education: Teaching and Curriculum Strategies for Grades 5–12* (Palo Alto: Mayfield, 1986), 5–8. Dorothy Zakrajsek and Qyingyi Mao, "A Ranking of Goals and Objectives for Secondary Physical Education," *Northwest Journal of American Alliance for Health, Physical Education, Recreation, and Dance* 1, no. 1 (Spring 1988): 17–19. Dorothy Zakrajsek and Qyingyi Mao, "Ranked Indicators of a Good Lesson in Secondary Physical Education," *Northwest Journal of American Alliance for Health, Physical Education, Recreation, and Dance* 1, no. 3 (Spring 1990): 18–19.

2. Jeffrey Stout, *Ethics after Babel: The Languages of Morals and Their Discontents* (1988; rept., Princeton: Princeton University Press, 2001).

3. Bernard J. Mullin, Stephen Hardy, and William A. Sutton, *Sport Marketing,* 3rd ed. (Champaign, Ill.: Human Kinetics, 2007), 3–30.

4. Maureen Weiss, "Character and Sport," June 28, 2006, www.virginia.edu/uvatoday/newsRelease.php?id=108 (accessed June 9, 2008).

5. Ibid.

6. Bruce Ogilvie and Thomas Tutko, "If You Want to Build Character, Try Something Else," *Psychology Today,* October 1971, 60.

7. Brenda J. L. Bredemeier and David L. L. Shields, "Moral Growth among Athletes and Non-Athletes: A Comparative Analysis," *Journal of Genetic Psychology* 147, no. 1 (1986): 718. Brenda Bredemeier, "Sport, Gender, and Moral Growth," in *Psychological Foundations of Sport,* ed. John Silva and Robert Weinberg (Champaign, Ill.: Human Kinetics, 1984), 400–413. Patricia Davenport, Jennifer M. Beller, and Sharon Kay Stoll, "Moral Reasoning and Doping in Division I Sport," *Research Quarterly for Exercise & Sport* 79 [abstract], no. 1 (March 2008): A 65. William Penny and Robert Priest, "Deontological Sport Value Choices of United States Military Academy Cadets and Selected Other College-aged Populations," unpublished manuscript, U.S. Military Academy at West Point. Robert Priest and Jerry Krause, "Four Year Changes in College Athletes' Ethical Values Choices in Sports Situations," *Research Quarterly for Exercise & Sport* 70, no. 2 (1999): 170–79. Thomas Wandzilak, T. Carroll, and C. J. Ansorge, "Values Development through Physical Activity: Promoting Sportsmanlike Behaviors, Perceptions, and Moral Reasoning," *Journal of Teaching in Physical Education* 8, no. 1 (1988): 13–22. Chung Hae Hahm, "Moral Reasoning and Development among General Students, Physical Education Majors, and Student Athletes" (Ph.D. diss., University of Idaho, 1989). Jennifer M. Beller, "A Moral Reasoning Intervention Program for Division I Athletes: Can Athletes Learn Not to Cheat?" (Ph.D. diss., University of Idaho, 1990). Elizabeth Ray Hall, "Moral Development Levels of Athletes in Sport Specific and General Social Situations" (Ph.D. diss., Texas Women's University, 1981). Jennifer M. Beller and Sharon Kay Stoll, "A Moral Reasoning Intervention Program for Student Athletes," *Academic Athletic Journal* (Spring 1992): 43–57. Jennifer M. Beller and Sharon Kay Stoll, "Moral Reasoning of High School Student Athletes and General Students: An Empirical Study versus Personal Testimony," *Pediatric Exercise Science* 7, no. 4 (1995): 352–63. Jennifer M. Beller, Sharon Kay Stoll, Barbara Burwell, and Jack Cole, "The Relationship of Competition and a Christian Liberal Arts Education on Moral Reasoning of College Student Athletes," *Research on Christian Higher Education* 3 (1996): 99–114. Jennifer M. Beller and Sharon Kay Stoll, "A 20 Year Empirical History of Moral Reasoning in Competition," manuscript in progress.

8. Penny and Priest, "Deontological Sport Value Choices." Beller and Stoll, "A 20 Year Empirical History."

9. National Golf Foundation, www.ngf.org/cgi/home.asp (accessed June 12, 2008).

10. Aristotle, *Nicomachean Ethics: Cambridge Texts in the History of Philosophy,* trans. Roger Crisp (Cambridge: Cambridge University Press, 2000).

11. Ibid.

12. Thomas Lickona, *Educating for Character* (New York: Bantam, 1991), 3–49.

13. Angela Lumpkin, Sharon Kay Stoll, and Jennifer M. Beller, *Sport Ethics: Applications for Fair Play*, 3rd ed. (Boston: McGraw-Hill, 2003).

14. Andy Rudd, "Moral and Social Reasoning of Student Athletes" (Ph.D. diss., University of Idaho, 1996). Andy Rudd and Michael Mondello, "How Do College Coaches Define Character? A Qualitative Study with Division IA Head Coaches," *Journal of College & Character* 7, no. 3 (April 2006), http://journals.naspa.org/jcc/vol7/iss3/4/ (accessed March 23, 2010).

15. William Frankena, *Ethics*, 2nd ed. (Englewood Cliffs: Prentice-Hall, 1973), 2–73. James Rest, "The Hierarchical Nature of Moral Judgment," *Journal of Personality* 41 (1973): 86–109.

16. Statement made by a panelist at the Clemson Symposium on Civility in Sport, sponsored by the Clemson University President's Office, Clemson, S.C., April 11–13, 2006.

17. Bob Harig, "Golf's Honor Code Limits 'Cheating' Incidents," August 9, 2007, http://sports.espn.go.com/espn/cheat/columns/story?columnist=harig_bob&id=2964423 (accessed February 18, 2009).

18. Lawrence Kohlberg, *The Philosophy of Moral Development: Moral Stages and the Idea of Justice* (San Francisco: Harper and Row, 1981). Richard Fox and Joseph DeMarco, *Moral Reasoning: A Philosophic Approach to Applied Ethics* (Englewood Cliffs: Prentice-Hall, 1990).

19. Steven R. Quartz and Terrence J. Sejnowski, *Liars, Lovers, and Heroes: What the New Brain Science Reveals about How We Become Who We Are* (New York: William Morrow, 2002), 9. Jeffrey M. Schwartz and Sharon Begley, *The Mind and the Brain: Neuroplasticity and the Power of Mental Force* (New York: HarperCollins, 2002), 68–69. Giacomo Rizzolatti, "The Mirror Neuron System and Imitation," in *Perspectives on Imitation: From Neuroscience to Social Science,* ed. S. L. Hurley and N. Chater (Cambridge: MIT Press, 2005), 55–76. John M. Edeline, "Learning-Induced Physiological Plasticity in the Thalamo-cortical Sensory Systems: A Critical Evaluation of Receptive Field Plasticity, Map Changes and Their Potential Mechanisms," *Progress in Neurobiology* 57, no. 2 (1999): 165–224.

20. Laurence Tancredi, *Hardwired Behavior: What Neuroscience Reveals about Morality* (New York: Cambridge University Press, 2005).

21. Ibid., 45.

22. Lickona, *Educating for Character.*

23. Ibid., 53.

24. Tancredi, *Hardwired Behavior.*

25. Arthur Kornhaber and Kenneth L. Woodward, *Grandparents, Grandchildren: The Vital Connection* (Garden City, N.Y.: Anchor Press, 1981).

26. Jerome Kagan, *The Nature of the Child* (New York: Basic Books, 1984), 11.

27. Aristotle, *Nicomachean Ethics*, book 4.

28. Lickona, *Educating for Character*, 50.

29. Jay Busbee, "Golf Channel, ESPN Conduct Five-Minute Tiger Interviews," March 21, 2010, http://sports.yahoo.com/golf/blog/devil_ball_golf/post/Golf-Channel-ESPN-conduct-five-minute-Tiger-int?urn=golf,229238 (accessed March 21, 2010).

30. David Shields and Brenda Bredemeier, *Character Development and Physical Activity* (Champaign, Ill.: Human Kinetics, 1995), 192.

31. Frankena, *Ethics*, 14–22.

32. Lumpkin, Stoll, and Beller, *Sport Ethics*, 6.

33. Davenport et al., "Moral Reasoning and Doping in Division I Sport," A 65. Penny and Priest, "Deontological Sport Value Choices." Priest and Krause, "Four Year Changes in College Athletes' Ethical Values Choices in Sports Situations," 170–79. Wandzilak et al., "Values Development through Physical Activity," 13–22. Beller, "A Moral Reasoning Intervention Program." Beller and Stoll, "A Moral Reasoning Intervention Program for Student Athletes." Beller and Stoll, "Moral Reasoning of High School Student Athletes and General Students." Beller et al., "The Relationship of Competition and a Christian Liberal Arts Education." Jennifer M. Beller, "Sport as a Positive Builder of Character," *ERIC Digest* (2002). Beller and Stoll, "A 20 Year Empirical History." Sharon Kay Stoll, Jennifer M. Beller, and Amukela Gwebu, *Anti-Doping Education in the United States* (Colorado Springs: United States Anti-Doping Agency, 2006). Sharon Kay Stoll, Jennifer M. Beller, Jack Cole, and Barbara Burwell, "A Comparison of Moral Reasoning Scores of General Students and Student Athletes in Division I and Division III NCAA Member Institutions," *Research Quarterly for Exercise and Sport* (Suppl.) 66 (March 1995): A-81. Sharon Kay Stoll and Jennifer M. Beller, "Do Sports Build Character?" in *Sports in School: The Future of an Institution*, ed. John R. Gerdy (New York: Teachers College Press, 2000), 18–30. Sharon Kay Stoll and Jennifer M. Beller, "Ethical Dilemmas in College Sport," in *New Game Plan for College Sport*, ed. Richard Lapchick (Westport, Conn.: Praeger, 2006), 75–90.

34. Priest and Krause, "Four Year Changes in College Athletes' Ethical Values Choices in Sports Situations." Penny and Priest, "Deontological Sport Value Choices." Beller and Stoll, "A Moral Reasoning Intervention Program for Student Athletes." Stoll and Beller, "Do Sports Build Character?" Stoll and Beller, "Ethical Dilemmas in College Sport," 88–90.

35. Carol Gilligan, *In a Different Voice* (Cambridge: Harvard University Press, 1982).

36. Davenport et al., "Moral Reasoning and Doping in Division I Sport," A 65. Penny and Priest, "Deontological Sport Value Choices." Priest and Krause, "Four Year Changes in College Athletes' Ethical Values Choices in Sports Situations." Beller, "A Moral Reasoning Intervention Program." Beller and Stoll, "A Moral Reasoning Intervention Program for Student Athletes." Beller and Stoll, "Moral Reasoning of High School Student Athletes and General Students." Beller et al., "The Relationship of Competition and a Christian Liberal Arts Education." Beller, "Sport as a Positive Builder of Character."

Beller and Stoll, "A 20 Year Empirical History." Stoll et al., "A Comparison of Moral Reasoning Scores." Stoll and Beller, "Do Sports Build Character?" Stoll and Beller, "Ethical Dilemmas in College Sport."

37. Beller and Stoll, "A Moral Reasoning Intervention Program for Student Athletes."

38. Colonel James Anderson, U.S. Military Academy at West Point, personal communication, 1996.

39. Ibid.

40. Robert Simon, *Fair Play: Sports, Values, and Society* (Boulder, Colo.: Westview Press, 1991), 5.

41. Robert Simon, "Internalism and Internal Values in Sport," *Journal of the Philosophy of Sport* 27 (1999): 3.

42. Carwyn Jones and Michael McNamee, "Moral Development and Sport: Character and Cognitive Developmentalism Contrasted," in *Sports Ethics,* ed. Jan Boxill (Oxford: Blackwell, 2003), 42.

43. Hillandale Golf Course, "Junior Clinics," www.hillandalegolf.com/junior.asp (accessed June 8, 2008).

44. Lumpkin, Stoll, and Beller, *Sport Ethics,* 12.

45. David Duval, interview, *New York Times,* February 3, 1999, D4.

46. James R. Rest, *Moral Development: Advances in Research and Theory* (New York: Praeger, 1986).

SIXTH HOLE

VIRTUE ETHICS

From *Caddyshack* to Better Golf

F. Scott McElreath

Justin Leonard knew that if he made his forty-five-foot birdie putt against José María Olazábal, then the U.S. team would win the 1999 Ryder Cup in Brookline, Massachusetts. He probably knew that it would be the largest come-from-behind victory in Ryder Cup history. But he could not have expected what happened after he nailed the putt: U.S. players, their family members, and their fans rushed onto the green and wildly celebrated for an abnormally long time while Olazábal waited for a chance to hit a potentially match-tying putt. Once the green was cleared, Olazábal missed the putt and a second celebration ensued. Many people still debate the morality of the first celebration. On the one hand, European players and media found it "disgusting" and disrespectful. Even U.S. players, such as the Ryder Cup captain, Ben Crenshaw, apologized for the behavior of their fellow citizens. On the other hand, some Americans responded that a European celebration in 1997 at Valderama was at least as raucous.[1]

How do we settle this controversy? One approach is to figure out which side offers good reasons. A plausible ethical theory is beneficial because it helps us determine if we have good reasons for our moral beliefs. After all, it is easy to have a belief about what is morally right or wrong. But what we really want is to be able to justify our moral beliefs. We would like to be able to explain why a person should add penalty strokes to her score when she violates a rule of fair play. "Just because" is not good enough. Similarly, in the movie *Caddyshack*, Judge Smails's simply yelling "Spalding!" at his grandson is an inadequate explanation for why he should behave better. We want to find a good ethical theory since it can provide a general justification of our moral beliefs.[2]

Consequentialism and Kantian ethics are two of the most popular ethical theories among philosophers. Defenders of consequentialism hold that consequences, or what happens after an act is done, are the only things that bear on whether an action is morally right. If an act causes better results than its alternatives, then the act is right. If an act produces worse consequences than the other options available, then the act is wrong. Defenders of Kantian ethics state that consequences do not matter at all. What counts instead are one's intentions. Kantian ethics considers whether the agent's maxim, or the general rule in her mind when acting, is rational.[3]

It is hard to deny that consequences are morally important. Whether a golfer makes the right choice to play on a given day depends on whether and to what extent playing increases her happiness and the happiness of others. For example, it is wrong to play golf on a workday when working will produce much more good. But consequences are not everything. When Judge Smails in *Caddyshack* kicks the ball with his foot while his competitors are not looking in order to get an unfair advantage, he acts wrongly even if no bad consequences result for him or for others. His maxim or general rule seems to be "Whenever I am in a situation in which I want to benefit myself, I will deceive others." His act is immoral because his maxim condones deception. Consequentialism correctly evaluates the choosing-to-play example, but incorrectly evaluates the moving-the-ball case. As we will see, the opposite is true for Kantian ethics. So neither theory adequately accounts for our commonsense moral beliefs.

What we need is an ethical theory that holds that consequences matter but are not the only things that matter. Virtue ethics holds that our actions should be modeled on what an ideally virtuous person would characteristically do in our circumstances. In this chapter I will argue that virtue ethics is plausible because it does a better job than consequentialism and Kantian ethics at accounting for our moral intuitions about golf. Moreover, the game of golf would improve if golfers and golf policy makers were to use virtue ethics, because they would more explicitly embrace acting on such virtues as benevolence, justice, and tolerance.

Consequentialism

According to the form of consequentialism I will discuss, an action is morally right if and only if there is no other available action that produces better consequences overall. One consequence is better overall than another if it produces a greater balance of pleasure over pain for all individuals affected.[4]

Let us suppose a recreational golfer is considering taking the afternoon off from work in order to play a round of golf on her own. To figure out if this act is morally right according to consequentialism, we must first identify all the options available to the golfer. She can golf, work, spend time with friends, go to a bar, write letters to her congressperson; the possibilities are endless. To keep our example simple, let us imagine that golfing and working both produce better consequences overall than any of the other choices available. Additionally, suppose our golfer is a single postal carrier. If she works, then she will be glad to be paid, her customers will receive their mail on time, and her coworkers will be happy to have her doing her share. If she plays golf, then she will enjoy the time off, though not as much as the money she would have been paid, her customers will still receive their mail, but after an annoying delay, and her coworkers will resent her absence. No one is affected by her choices other than her customers, her coworkers, and herself. There is a greater balance of pleasure over pain if she chooses to work. So consequentialism implies that it is right for her to work: there is no other available action that produces better consequences overall. Golfing, therefore, is wrong because working produces better consequences overall.

Consequentialism correctly assesses this example. In these circumstances, the recreational golfer should not golf. Of course, this is not to say that golfing is always wrong. Perhaps in another situation golfing would provide relaxation and enjoyment for her that no other activity would provide, her customers would get the same service, and her coworkers would want her to be happy. If so, then she would be obligated to hit the links because the balance of pleasure over pain from golfing would be greater.

We have now identified a particularly desirable implication of consequentialism. Pleasure and pain matter morally, and whether an action is right depends on the circumstances, to the extent that different circumstances provide different amounts of pleasure and pain.

But pleasure and pain are not the only morally relevant factors to consider. In golf, for example, the rules of fairness are far more serious than the rules of etiquette. At some clubs wearing a T-shirt violates a rule of etiquette, but doing so nonetheless seems morally acceptable. There is nothing unjust about wearing a T-shirt. Golf's rules of fairness, on the other hand, are typically morally important. It is morally wrong for someone to carry and use an extra club because doing so gives her an unfair advantage over her competition. Intentionally moving one's ball with one's foot to get a better placement is wrong for similar reasons.

Let us pursue what consequentialism would say about moving one's ball by focusing on Judge Smails. He has two options: to move the ball or not to move the ball. If he moves the ball, then he will get the pleasure of a better placement and no guilt because he is unconcerned about the rules of golf. Nobody else will get any pleasure or pain because only his caddy, Danny Noonan, will find out, and Noonan will not mind. Noonan will be too preoccupied with earning Smails's favor for a golf scholarship. Also, Smails's opponents will not notice any difference in Smails's scorecard because he will play particularly poorly that day anyway owing to the distracting antics and gamesmanship of Al Czervik. If Smails does not move the ball, then he will be frustrated that he did not move the ball when he had the opportunity, and no one will think any differently about him.

Given that no one else is affected in the situation, we need only focus on Smails's pleasure and pain. Because of his selfishness, moving the ball produces better consequences overall than any other available action. Consequentialism mistakenly implies that his action is morally right.

Kantian Ethics

Kantian ethics avoids this problem. According to this ethical approach, an action is morally right if and only if the maxim (intentional rule) of the action is universalizable. Kant holds that every agent acts with a maxim. A maxim is universalizable if and only if the maxim can be rationally conceived and rationally willed. This language is cumbersome and abstract mainly because of Kant's difficult prose. Not only did he write in German, in the eighteenth century, and with abstract terms, but he made up German words too. Let us focus on understanding his terminology.

The maxim of an act can be rationally conceived if the act can be done in a world in which everyone follows the maxim. Let us consider the maxim of Smails's act of moving the ball with his foot. The following statement describes the way the world must function if everyone obeys his maxim: "Whenever anyone is in a situation in which she wants to benefit herself, she will deceive others." Everyone wants to benefit herself. So in this world everyone deceives others. Before too long, everyone will notice that everyone is deceiving others, since many people will be saying that they will do one thing but then do another. The expectation of honesty will disappear. But for someone to deceive another, the latter person must have an expectation that there is no deception. Thus, deception is impossible in this fictional world. If so, then Smails's rule cannot be obeyed by everyone. Or, using Kantian language, the maxim of his act cannot be rationally conceived. Smails's act is wrong because the maxim of his action is not universalizable.[5]

Kantian ethics does a better job than consequentialism of explaining our intuitions about Smails's act of moving the ball. What makes the act wrong is that it is deceptive. Kantian ethics arrives at this conclusion without even considering the consequences of Smails's act. Instead, we identified Smails's maxim and asked a number of hypothetical questions in order to arrive at the rationality of acting with his maxim. Wrong acts, then, are irrational, and right acts are rational. Many philosophers agree with Kantian ethics that we determine the morality of an act by focusing not on the act's consequences but on its rationality.

As the choosing-to-play case instructed us, however, sometimes consequences are morally important. Yelling your opponent's name when she tries to putt is wrong since it has the bad result of distracting her. Moreover, a person's maxim can be morally irrelevant. If the recreational golfer plays golf, then she will act with the following maxim: "Whenever I am in a situation in which I can help others without harming them, I will help without harming." Maybe she believes that playing golf helps her colleagues because they do not like her anyway and that golfing does no harm since her customers will still get their mail on time. Neither of these beliefs is true, but for psychological reasons let us suppose the recreational golfer has them. The recreational golfer's maxim is universalizable because it passes both of Kant's tests. First, the maxim of her act can be rationally conceived. The act of helping without harming can be done in a situation in which everyone obeys her rule.

And her maxim passes the second test since it can be rationally willed. That is, rational agents can want to be in a world in which everyone follows this maxim. For example, if free choices are available in such a world, then there is reason to believe that rational agents can desire to live in that world. In a world in which everyone helps without harming when she can, free choices are available. In some cases, a lot of options help without harming, and when none of those options is available because there is no way to avoid harming, people can still help while causing the least harm.[6]

So the maxim of the act of golfing is universalizable, since the maxim can be rationally conceived and rationally willed. Thus, golfing for the recreational golfer in this case is right, according to Kantian ethics. This is not a good result for Kantian ethics. We said earlier that golfing here is wrong because of the bad consequences of playing.

Virtue Ethics

These examples make no trouble for virtue ethics. This theory says that an action is morally right if and only if it is an available action that an ideally virtuous person might characteristically do in the agent's circumstances. Virtue ethics is more than two thousand years old and originated in ancient Greece during the time of Socrates, Plato, and Aristotle. Many present-day philosophers are trying to revive it, and religious manifestations can be found now in popular culture with the slogan WWJD? (What would Jesus do?)[7]

The form of virtue ethics that we will focus on leaves open the possibility that there are multiple ideally virtuous people. Jesus may be one, but so may be Gandhi, Martin Luther King Jr., and others. That a person is ideally virtuous simply means that she has each of the virtues. A virtue is a stable character trait that tends to benefit the trait possessor or others. Benevolence, justice, and tolerance, for example, are virtues, since a person with those traits tends to benefit herself or others.

Can virtue ethics hold that knowledge of the rightness of actions is easy to possess? No. To know what some person might characteristically do, we need to know what her character traits are and what someone with those traits is disposed to do. Since an ideally virtuous person has each of the virtuous character traits, there are many traits to consider. And it can be hard to figure out what someone with those virtuous character traits is disposed to do. For a soldier in battle, for instance, messy circumstances may leave us unaware of whether bravery requires jumping on a grenade to save a comrade or instead running toward the enemy to prevent further attacks. So knowledge of which available act an ideally virtuous person might characteristically do is difficult to possess, and thus, knowledge of rightness is sometimes hard to possess. But this criticism applies equally well to consequentialism and Kantian ethics: sometimes it is hard to predict future consequences and to articulate someone else's maxim or intention.

Reasonable belief about rightness, on the other hand, is in fact easily accessible. To have reasonable beliefs about what available act an ideally virtuous person might characteristically do in specific circumstances, we must attempt to identify all the virtues possessed by an ideally virtuous person that appear to be relevant. Let us call these the *relevant virtues*. What are all the relevant virtues in the example of Smails's moving the ball? Prudence does not seem to be relevant. There is no reason to think that one action is prudent while the other is not. Moving the ball is prudent because it helps him win, but not moving the ball is also prudent since he gets the pleasure of taking a big swing at the ball and dirt. Of the virtues possessed by an ideally virtuous person, it is possible that only justice and honesty are relevant when determining any difference in the virtue status of Smails's options. Not moving the ball is just because he is not taking an opportunity that he does not deserve, and it is honest since his scorecard is accurate and he is not attempting to deceive. Moving the ball is neither just nor honest. A person with justice and honesty alone, then, is disposed not to move the ball. If an available action seems to be such that a person with the relevant virtues alone appears disposed to perform it, then there is reason to believe that an ideally virtuous person would characteristically perform that action in those circumstances. So there is reason to believe that an ideally virtuous person would characteristically not move the ball. Virtue ethics correctly implies, therefore, that Smails is required not to move the ball.

Similar claims are true about the choosing-to-play example. Working is benevolent because it helps her colleagues, and it is an indication of loyalty since it keeps a work promise. Playing golf in her circumstances is neither benevolent nor a sign of loyalty. A person with benevolence and loyalty alone is disposed to work in this case. So an ideally virtuous person would characteristically work in these circumstances. Virtue ethics agrees with our moral intuition that our recreational golfer should work, given her situation.

Virtue ethics correctly evaluates the examples we have seen, and consequentialism and Kantian ethics have trouble doing so. It follows that virtue ethics is plausible and worthy of our consideration when deciding what is morally right to do. But, as often occurs with advancement of a theory, there are some potential problems that need to be examined.

Let us consider some initial concerns someone might have about the plausibility of virtue ethics. According to one objection, virtues can conflict, and consequently, virtue ethics can provide contradictory advice. Benevolence (benefiting others) may require that a doctor withhold the truth about a patient's terminal illness, but honesty necessitates the opposite. In my view, however, an ideally virtuous person has a virtue that disposes her to do either of the acts when the virtues conflict. So either action is permissible according to virtue ethics. Fortunately, careful consideration of the virtues reveals that they rarely conflict. For instance, upon further reflection, we may find that for the doctor, telling the truth really is benevolent because it helps the patient accept and prepare for death.

Someone else might object that because an ideally virtuous person, like any other human being, need not be acting in character at all times, there may be some cases in which it is wrong to do what she does. For example, an ideally virtuous person might uncharacteristically falsify an opponent's scorecard out of revenge in the heat of the moment. If so, virtue ethics incorrectly implies that it is morally right to alter an opponent's scorecard out of revenge in the heat of the moment. But this objection rests on a misunderstanding. "Doing what an ideally virtuous person would characteristically do in our circumstances" means "doing what an ideally virtuous person would do in our circumstances if she were acting because of her virtuous character traits." None of an ideally virtuous person's virtues necessitates falsifying an opponent's scorecard out of revenge.

From another perspective, virtue ethics leaves room for more conflicting advice. One ideally virtuous person might do one thing and another might do something else, even when both are acting in character in identical circumstances. There may be latitude in a virtue. Benevolence may allow for congratulating an opponent for her great shot immediately or for waiting until later. So one ideally virtuous person might characteristically congratulate the opponent immediately and another may wait until later. Virtue ethics appears to require that we congratulate the opponent immediately *and* later, which seems incoherent. But this objection fails to notice that virtue ethics says it is right to do an available act that an ideally virtuous person might characteristically do. Either action is right in this situation because either action is one that an ideally virtuous person might characteristically perform.

Because people may have different conceptions of what an ideally virtuous person might characteristically do, someone might worry that virtue ethics reduces to the untenable, relativistic view that a person can rightly do whatever she thinks an ideally virtuous person might characteristically do in her circumstances. While foolishly thinking that an ideally virtuous person might characteristically do this in her circumstances, a crazed fan may yell, "You da man!" at Tiger Woods during his swing on the eighteenth hole at the U.S. Open. Virtue ethics would be mistaken to imply that this act is right. This is a misinterpretation of virtue ethics. Virtue ethics does not say that an action is morally right if and only if it is an available action that, *according to the agent,* an ideally virtuous person might characteristically do in her circumstances. The agent's thoughts are excluded because agents can be mistaken. Virtue ethics assumes that there is a fact of the matter about what an ideally virtuous person might characteristically do. The virtues are good independently of one's thoughts. For reasons mentioned earlier, it may be hard to know that fact, but it is something about which we can have reasonable beliefs.

None of these initial objections to virtue ethics appear to succeed. So, unless we are missing a good objection, this theory remains valuable as a way to provide a general justification of our moral beliefs.

Better Golf through Virtue Ethics

What if golfers and golf policy makers were to embrace virtue ethics? The game of golf would get better. It would not be perfect because people might not identify all the relevant virtues in their situation and so might not apply virtue ethics correctly. Also, some people perform actions that they know are wrong. But the increased emphasis on acting virtuously would help tremendously. For example, recreational cheating and gamesmanship, as described by Angela Lumpkin in the next chapter, may still exist, mainly because the culprits feel compelled to perform these wrong acts. But we would still find fewer of these infractions if conscientious golfers focused more on acting virtuously. Cheating, as we said when discussing Smails's moving the ball, is unjust and dishonest. Gamesmanship may cause an opponent to improve, but it manifests vice by belittling, insulting, or deceiving another competitor.

Moreover, golf policy makers can do much more for women, minorities, people with disabilities, and homosexuals. Women professional golfers are certainly thriving, but they still do not receive equal marketing. Tennis policy makers, by contrast, have successfully promoted women's tennis. Ticket sales, TV ratings, and advertiser interest have consequently increased. As a result, women professional tennis players receive equal pay at major tournaments. Golf policy makers can follow tennis's lead. To deny women professional golfers equal marketing is unjust because they deserve equal opportunities if such options are readily available.

Additionally, golf club policy makers can abolish rules that bar women or minorities from joining a club. For instance, the Augusta National Golf Club, home of the Masters, still excludes women from membership. Even if the rules are legal because of the private status of the club, the policy makers' acts are maleficent, insulting, and unjust since women do not deserve the negative message they receive.[8]

Much has been said about Casey Martin's desire to use a golf cart on the PGA Tour owing to a debilitating circulatory disease that makes it painful for him to walk and stand for long periods. The main argument against his request seems to be that a cart provides him an unfair advantage. But a fair policy maker is disposed to provide the same opportunities to everyone affected by a policy. A game policy maker with integrity is disposed to create, adjust, or delete the game's policies in ways that retain the essential components of the game. Striking the ball, not walking the course, is a necessary part of golf. So a fair-minded golf policy maker with integrity would recognize that the core of the game would be maintained if golf carts were available to all professional golfers or if golf courses were reconfigured to be more accessible to people with disabilities.[9]

Homosexuals also are not treated well by people in the golf community. Homophobia runs rampant in all sports, but that does not make it excusable. I suspect that homosexual professional players justifiably fear that coming out of the closet would cause them to lose endorsements and appearance invitations and to suffer from alienation from peers. Some golf clubs do not allow partners of homosexual members the same privileges as spouses of heterosexual members. The people in golf who support a climate of fear of homosexual professional players or who endorse homophobic club membership policies express intolerance. An intolerant person fails to acknowledge the beneficial differences in someone or treats her poorly merely because she is different.[10]

Golfers and golf policy makers will not become more virtuous overnight. The challenges are to find virtuous role models, to identify their virtues, and to develop the habit of performing acts of those virtues. Fortunately, golf already promotes virtue. By requiring both consideration for an opponent during play and the self-imposition of penalty strokes, the game of golf encourages respect and integrity. Moreover, some steps have already been taken to emphasize greater virtue in golf. The PGA Tour and the USGA praise honesty and courage in public advertisements. The First Tee, created by the World Golf Foundation, provides opportunities and resources for young people to develop their characters while learning about and playing golf. For example, in life skills training, participants learn to appreciate diversity, manage emotions, resolve conflicts, plan for the future, and create step-by-step goals. In these character-building experiences and in golf clinics, the First Tee incorporates the following nine virtues: honesty, integrity, sportsmanship, respect, confidence, responsibility, perseverance, courtesy, and good judgment.[11]

These efforts should help golfers and fans avoid immoral actions like the unjust and disrespectful celebration that occurred at the 1999 Ryder Cup. The Europeans may have had similarly distracting celebrations in the past, but virtuous persons, unlike the characters from *Caddyshack*, know that two wrongs do not make a right. Being completely virtuous is impossible; nonetheless, the more virtuous we become, the more the game we all love will improve.

Notes

1. "Unbridled Celebration," September 26, 1999, http://sportsillustrated.cnn.com/golf/1999/ryder_cup/news/1999/09/26/celebration_sidebar_ap/; and "A Mob Demonstration," September 28, 1999, http://sportsillustrated.cnn.com/golf/1999/ryder_cup/news/1999/09/28/ryder_abuse_ap/.

2. A moral belief is a belief that holds something as moral. In the moral belief "Telling the truth is morally right," that something is telling the truth and the moral is morally right. Unfortunately, "morally right" is ambiguous between "morally permissible" and, more strongly, "morally obligatory." For the sake of simplicity, in this chapter "morally right" means "morally permissible."

3. Immanuel Kant, *Grounding for the Metaphysics of Morals*, in *Kant's Ethical Philosophy*, trans. James Ellington (Indianapolis: Hackett, 1983); and John Stuart Mill, *Utilitarianism*, ed. George Sher (Indianapolis: Hackett, 1979).

4. I am focusing on the most popular type of consequentialism, which is also known as "traditional act utilitarianism." Other kinds of consequentialism, such as motive utilitarianism, rule utilitarianism, or egoism, are beyond the scope of this chapter.

5. For this interpretation of what it means for a maxim to be able to be rationally conceived, see Allen Wood, "Kant on False Promises," in *Proceedings of the Third International Kant Congress*, ed. Lewis White Beck (Dordrecht: D. Reidel, 1972), 614–19; and Wood, *Kant's Ethical Thought* (Cambridge: Cambridge University Press, 1999), chap. 3.

6. For this interpretation of what it means for a maxim to be able to be rationally willed, see Christine Korsgaard, *Creating the Kingdom of Ends* (Cambridge: Cambridge University Press, 1996), chap. 3.

7. Current historians of philosophy disagree over which famous philosopher or philosophers actually endorsed this theory. I will sidestep this debate and just say that virtue ethics came from the ancient Greeks.

8. "Augusta Defends Male Only Members Policy," www.golftoday.co.uk/news/yeartodate/news02/augusta5.html.

9. "Disabled Golfer May Use a Cart on the PGA Tour," May 30, 2001, www.nytimes .com/2001/05/30/sports/golf-disabled-golfer-may-use-a-cart-on-the-pga-tour-justices-affirm.html.

10. Marcia Chambers, "At Country Clubs, Gay Members Want All Privileges for Partners," September 21, 2004, www.nytimes.com/2004/09/21/sports/golf/21clubs.html.

11. "The First Tee Homepage," www.thefirsttee.org.

III. Ethical Issues within Golf

SEVENTH HOLE

CHEATING AND GAMESMANSHIP AMONG AMATEUR AND PROFESSIONAL GOLFERS

Angela Lumpkin

To understand golf it is essential to realize its initial connection with class and amateurism. Organized golf began for upper-class males with the foundation in 1754 of the Society of St. Andrews Golfers, which became the Royal and Ancient Golf Club in St. Andrews, Scotland. The United States followed by emphasizing elitism and amateurism and in 1894 established the Amateur Golf Association of the United States, which became the United States Golf Association (USGA). The Royal and Ancient Golf Club and USGA collaboratively write, interpret, and govern the rules of golf with a lasting heritage that makes golf unique among sports. For example, only in golf does the first section of the rules describe etiquette and behaviors that demonstrate courtesy toward others. In playing by the spirit of the game, players are expected to demonstrate integrity and sportsmanship at all times.[1]

The rich heritage among upper-class males in Scotland, Europe, and the United States, along with the influence of the British amateur sport ideal of playing the game for the game's sake, shaped the rules of social and serious golf, and these rules apply equally to amateur and professional golfers. In contrast, media and anecdotal reports indicate that professionals in baseball, basketball, and football are more likely to engage in gamesmanship and cheating than are golfers. The cultures in these team sports, in comparison with that of golf, include greater acceptance of unethical behaviors.

This chapter will explore whether, and to what extent, amateur or professional golfers cheat and engage in gamesmanship. A part of this examination will be to investigate whether individuals who choose to play golf for fun and recreation differ in their demonstrated values from professional golfers. I will argue that amateur golfers tend to use a series of illogical rationalizations for cheating that, fortunately, professional golfers do not use.

Amateur Golfers

The appeal of trying to successfully strike a ball (or small item) with a stick, pole, or long object toward a target goes back centuries. It is the difficulty of meeting this challenge that may have propelled golf to its status as one of the fastest-growing participatory sports in the United States. Golf has become a game for anyone and everyone; golf courses, golf schools, and golf leagues are designed to appeal to males and females of all skill levels and ages. And aspiring golfers have learned that the game can be played recreationally with only a cursory understanding of the rules. Since anyone can try to hit the ball with a club as many times as it takes to get the ball into the hole, let the play begin.

Unlike aspiring professional athletes in the team sports of baseball, basketball, and football, amateur golfers rarely learn rules from watching live or televised golf events because interpretations or even applications of rules seldom occur. Those who watch professional golf typically see outstanding players consistently hitting balls on the fairways and greens. If errant shots are hit, professional golfers know what to do, and there is rarely any involvement by officials. Since amateur golfers seldom have read the rules of golf or observed their enforcement, they have quite limited knowledge of the rules. Through simply playing, though, amateurs learn something about the unique etiquette of golf. For example, they may learn that in the absence of officials, golfers are expected to penalize themselves for mistakes and behave in specific ways, but most do not fully understand when, how, and why.

The overarching protocol in golf, as stated in the rules, is to be courteous to every other golfer and to display sportsmanship at all times. This includes avoiding distracting another golfer, for example by moving out of the line of vision during an attempted stroke, by not talking while another player is hitting, by not walking in the line for a putt, and by quieting electronic devices. Many golfers, though, ignore the rules associated with distractions. Golfing buddies, for example, often attempt to distract their friends and thus interfere with their concentration or ability to hit successful shots (possibly having learned these psychological ploys from watching sports such as professional football and basketball). The goal is intentionally and adversely to affect the strokes of others by talking and moving around. Of course, this is a type of gamesmanship, or trying to gain a competitive advantage by causing another player to hit more shots and lose the round or hole.

Golf rules and etiquette require maintaining a steady pace of play and allowing faster, smaller groups or more skilled golfers to play through. Inferior players frequently hit errant shots. Since looking for badly hit balls slows down the pace of play, golfers are allowed a maximum of five minutes (USGA Rule 27-1c) to look for a potentially lost ball before declaring it lost, taking a penalty stroke, and resuming play. Whenever golfers do not want to incur the cost of replacing lost balls, however, they tend to spend excessive amounts of time looking for and hoping to find their balls. If an abandoned ball is found instead, often the golfer uses this ball without penalty, even though the rules clearly require replaying the ball from the original spot and taking a penalty stroke.

The number of shots adds up quickly when balls are whiffed, hit out-of-bounds, and lost. Often these poorly skilled players choose not to assess the penalties associated with these actions, even though the number of shots taken to hit the ball into the hole should be counted exactly, as stated in USGA Rule 3-2. This rule does not set a maximum score for any hole. Yet amateurs do have the option of using the USGA Handicap System to adjust scores per hole, per the specific course being played, on the basis of Equitable Stroke Control, which suggests that even the USGA does not expect amateurs to score faithfully by the rules.

The golfers who know and choose to violate the rules or etiquette of golf often claim that they are only playing a game and nothing is riding on the outcome. Trophies, prize money, and media acclaim are not given for the lowest score in their foursome. Bragging rights are the only reward, so no one else should care how many shots have been made or recorded. Such golfers often then use several additional rationalizations for their unethical behaviors that we will examine next.

One rationalization is a logical fallacy called an appeal to ignorance, which claims something is right just because it is not believed to be wrong or has not been shown to be wrong. For example, the golfers in the playing group who claim they do not know the USGA rules of golf and local course policies may, out of ignorance, move an object that is impeding a shot. They do not know it is an infraction, so it is not an infraction. Ignorance is not just bliss; it results in lower scores.

A second rationalization for cheating is the fallacy of appeal to popularity. The act is right since everyone else does it. Many golfers claim that all players at one time or another fail to add a required penalty stroke or play their balls from more desirable lies. Many who play social golf say that not correctly counting the number of shots taken is accepted by all as the way a social game is played. This seems to justify everyone's counting strokes any way he or she prefers. In fact, if one golfer wants to cheat, she or he simply encourages others to cheat as well, as if to justify this behavior.

Some golfers who gamble on their games claim that everyone cheats sometimes to increase the chances of winning. These players may move another golfer's ball, intentionally not count shots, or use someone else's ball when they cannot find their own because money is involved. Sometimes these golfers simply want to be able to brag about winning money from those with whom they have been playing or to avoid buying beverages in the clubhouse.

A third rationalization for cheating is the similar appeal to tradition, because cheating is thought to be the current standard or norm. David Callahan argues persuasively that Americans are cheating more and feeling less guilty about it.[2] For example, the accountant who falsifies financial documents may claim that such actions are not as bad as when lawyers bill excessive hours, stock analysts engage in insider trading, and corporate executives artificially inflate stock prices in order to cash out their stocks before bankrupting the company. Callahan alleges that it should not be surprising that golfers cheat because many also lie on their tax returns and to their insurance companies, since they perceive their taxes and premiums as excessive.

Some golfers have convinced themselves, as they have in other aspects of their lives, that cheating is an inherent part of golf and has become normalized within golf culture. They use irrational reasoning as they seek to balance or level the playing field through cheating because others are doing the same. These golfers have convinced themselves not to be the chump who counts every shot or follows every rule. They play golf under the assumption that if you are not cheating, then you are not trying hard enough to win.

The fourth and maybe ultimate rationalization for cheating may be that no one will ever know. So when a golfer moves his ball while addressing it, he believes that no one else will ever know and thus assesses himself no penalty. When a golfer, after an errant shot, finds a different ball, since no one will ever know, she or he plays this ball and assesses no penalty. After all, a similar approach appears to be quite successful in the world around these golfers: those who cheat on tests in school, steal from their employers, and falsify their credentials to secure jobs are seldom discovered and almost never punished. The conclusion is that if the act is unpunished then it is morally permissible, which confuses the question "Why be moral?" with "What is moral?"

When faced with these ethical dilemmas, many golfers choose to violate the rules, cheat their opponents, and deceive themselves into believing that they are playing by the rules. These justifications place individual self-interest ahead of the integrity of society and the game. Golfers who engage in these behaviors choose to ignore the rules because they believe more benefits and fewer penalties come to those who cheat.

These accusations do not implicate all amateur golfers. There are many moral amateur golfers. But the extent of cheating and gamesmanship seems to indicate that such behaviors have come to be accepted within the culture of amateur golf. Golfers who act in these ways, though, are unlikely to categorize themselves as morally bereft. Rather, they are more likely to describe how they play golf as consistent with how they seek to advance themselves in their careers. They emphasize winning, even in a friendly competition, and rationalize taking whatever actions are needed, regardless of the rules, as long as these behaviors can be personally justified.

Professional Golfers

All professional golfers began their careers as amateurs. Early in life they began to learn the etiquette and spirit of the rules. But they also were exposed to how amateurs actually play. So why do professional golfers end up acting differently? One reason is that professional golfers are closely observed and governed by the rules of golf. In fact, when young golfers join high school and college teams, they often have to unlearn behaviors they previously had assumed were acceptable, such as touching their balls while in play. When golfers become skillful enough to play in leagues, tournaments, and championships, they quickly find that the culture of the game changes from tolerance of cheating and gamesmanship to a standard of sportsmanship and an expectation that they consistently follow the rules and etiquette of the game.

By way of comparison, amateur and professional baseball, basketball, and football players are taught and coached how to cheat and engage in gamesmanship in order to gain competitive advantages. Baseball players are rewarded for stealing signs from opponents and taught how to slide forcefully into a shortstop or second baseman to break up an attempted double play. Basketball players are taught how to grab an opponent's jersey on a rebound attempt and are rewarded for trash-talking to distract opponents. Football players are praised for making violent and hurtful hits on opponents and coached how to hold on the line of scrimmage to gain advantages. The cultures of these sports are more likely to characterize actions such as these as good strategy or tactics rather than as cheating or gamesmanship.

Though professional golfers are expected to acknowledge inadvertently moving a ball when addressing it, baseball, basketball, and football players are rarely taught or coached to call mistakes on themselves. The cultures of these team sports, rather than encouraging players to admit failing to catch a ball that hit the ground first, or to acknowledge violating a rule, advocate taking advantage of officials' errors and intentionally deceiving officials. By contrast, professional golfers consult with officials in order to comply fully with the rules.

Although an occasional instance of a professional golfer's violating a rule for personal advantage, such as having a fifteenth club in the bag, may occur, it is more likely that professional golfers will admit their mistakes. A professional golfer's character is displayed whenever this person chooses to do the right thing. For example, J. P. Hayes knew he did the right thing when he admitted to using a ball not on the USGA's approved list. Although he had made an inadvertent mistake, he informed an official and was disqualified from a PGA Tour qualifying tournament in 2008.

Professional golf maintains a high standard of conduct for players. Every professional golfer is expected to play fairly and show sportsmanship at all times. Doing the right thing and adhering to an imperative of integrity is reinforced on a daily basis by other professional golfers. These individuals appear to have internalized the values of respect, responsibility, honesty, and justice and seek to act on these bases. Professional golfers may be the best examples of class acts in sport.

Rewards and Punishments in Golf

One reason that amateur golfers and professional golfers behave differently is because the rewards and punishments for cheating and gamesmanship vary dramatically. Amateur golfers are almost never punished for violating the rules. There are no rewards for playing according to the rules, which makes sense given the relative insignificance of most rounds of golf. It should not be surprising that many amateur golfers, as rational human beings, find the temptation to cheat irresistible: cheating can be personally rewarding. Similar behaviors served them well when they played baseball, basketball, football, or other sports, so there seems no reason they could not be applicable to golf.

The rewards from such behaviors also may extend beyond the golf course. Amateur golfers interact professionally and socially with many of the same individuals with whom they play golf. Social relationships may be strengthened at the nineteenth hole over beverages bought by the person who lost the day's wager. Willingness to do whatever it takes to win or record the lowest score can boost one's status at the office or within a group of friends. And as Callahan claims, most amateur golfers live, work, and socialize in a society that has increasingly accepted the cheating culture as a way of life.[3] So amateur golfers may cheat because it is in their self-interest to do so.

Just the opposite is true of professional golfers' situation. Adherence to the letter and spirit of the rules is the accepted norm for professional golfers, and anything less than this will lead to on-course disqualification and off-course exclusion from social interactions or commercial endorsements. Certainly, some professional golfers may comply with this expectation because of self-interest. But when admitting to violation of a rule of golf results in disqualification, as it did for J. P. Hayes, a higher moral standard has been followed. The social contract within professional golf demands no cheating and gamesmanship, and peer influence and official rule enforcement reinforce this prohibition. For example, the professional golfer who immediately admits a mistake, even if doing so results in a penalty stroke or the loss of an event, is praised as the consummate example of good sportsmanship. It is this person who is said to exemplify the integrity of the game.

Moral Development and Reasoning

The reason for the higher standards of professional golfers is that they tend to be more morally developed and show a higher level of moral reasoning than do amateur golfers. Kohlberg suggests six stages of moral development, as well as three essential components of the moral reasoning process that provide some helpful insights into examining this assumption.[4] At the lowest levels of moral development, individuals behave obediently to avoid punishments, out of self-interest, and to meet the expectations of others to gain their approval. In applying these moral development levels to amateur golfers, it seems that golfers comply with the rules and etiquette of golf only for these same reasons.

Many amateur golfers will choose not to assess penalty strokes for playing balls hit out-of-bounds or fail to repair divots or marks on the putting green. If cheating and lack of golf etiquette are personally beneficial, many amateur golfers may engage in these behaviors. Peers on the golf course, and especially in a foursome or playing group, help shape the actions of amateur golfers. For example, regardless of course rules, some golfers will drive golf carts wherever they choose if their buddies expect this or do likewise. It would appear that many amateur golfers, like most individuals, live their lives at these lower levels of moral development.

At higher levels of development, Kohlberg, like proponents of the non-consequential moral theory, states that certain rules and rights have universal application. For example, telling a lie and killing are wrong because they infringe on the rights of others. Professional golfers seem to have accepted the social order within professional golf and have agreed to fulfill the social contract, inherent in their sport, of showing genuine interest in the welfare of others. That is, almost all professional golfers have adopted the universal ethical principles of right and wrong that make golf the unique sport it is. Nearly every professional golfer consistently adheres to the letter and spirit of the rules, even when the outcome of a major championship is on the line. Therefore, in the way they play in tournaments, professional golfers demonstrate Kohlberg's higher levels of moral development more often than do amateur golfers.

This development is achieved through the moral reasoning process, in which individuals evaluate their personal values and develop consistent and impartial sets of moral principles by which they live their lives.[5] The first step in this systematic process is moral knowing, or the cognitive phase of learning about moral issues and how to resolve them. The second step is moral valuing, or the normative basis of what each individual believes about himself, society, and others. The third step is moral acting, or how people act on the basis of what they know and value.

Bredemeier as well as Rudd and Stoll report that the longer athletes participate in sport, the lower their moral reasoning.[6] This may be true for athletes in team sports like baseball, basketball, and football, but actions of professional golfers seem to indicate just the opposite. Amateur and professional baseball, basketball, and football players are often coached to act in unethical ways to gain competitive advantages, and many teammates expect each other to do whatever it takes to win. Professional golfers, unlike amateur golfers, play a game without on-course coaches and teammates who encourage cheating and gamesmanship and in which playing by the letter and spirit of the rules is revered.

Many amateur golfers who are playing for fun often choose not to play according to the rules of golf. This may be because amateur golfers believe that it is acceptable to lie about their scores and openly violate the letter and spirit of the rules. In contrast, almost all professional golfers comply fully with the social contract of their sport. Maybe they do so because other professional golfers do the same and officials enforce the rules. In summary, the moral reasoning process and actions that are based on the values of professional golfers have been shaped by the culture of golf that rewards and recognizes principled behaviors, not cheating and gamesmanship.

Golf has benefited from its historical roots as a pastime for the upper class, in association with amateurism, and playing the game for its inherent benefits. From its earliest years, including the time when golfers began to compete for prize money, the traditional rules and etiquette of golf remained strong. This game has retained its timeless connection with playing by the letter and spirit of the rules. Golf's emphasis on sportsmanship has shaped the values displayed by generations of amateur and professional golfers.

As this game has become more egalitarian, however, erosion in the moral fabric of golf has begun to occur. As all comers have been welcomed to public and private courses, the playing of golf has reflected changing values in American society; self-interest has taken priority over other people and principled behaviors. The use of rationalizations—pleading ignorance, claiming everyone does it, appealing to tradition, and believing that no one will ever know—has replaced a strict adherence to the rules and etiquette of golf. Cheating to win has become the way the game is played by many, as they rationalize their actions to make them acceptable.

Since the outcome of a casual round of golf among amateurs is truly inconsequential, players would be better off not keeping score rather than keeping a mythical score. Golf can be played for fun and enjoyment as well as for the challenge, without the need to fabricate a score. In fact, the rules and etiquette of golf are more likely to be learned in the absence of the perceived pressure of a scorecard. Once players have developed sufficient skill, they can be free to learn to play by the rules. That is, rather than having to unlearn unethical behaviors, golfers should earn the right to keep score when they know and agree to follow the rules.

Professional golf provides a model for a different way to play the game. Professional golfers demonstrate sportsmanship, integrity, and respect for others and the game. Amateur golfers would be well served to learn from professional golfers that cheating and using gamesmanship in golf are unprincipled and immoral. Professional golfers illustrate how to play for fun while displaying integrity and sportsmanship.

Notes

1. United States Golf Association, *The Rules of Golf* (Far Hills, N.J.: United States Golf Association, 2007).

2. David Callahan, *The Cheating Culture: Why More Americans Are Doing Wrong to Get Ahead* (Orlando: Harcourt, 2004).

3. Ibid.

4. Lawrence Kohlberg, *The Philosophy of Moral Development: Moral Stages and the Idea of Justice* (New York: Harper and Row, 1981).

5. Angela Lumpkin, Sharon Kay Stoll, and Jennifer M. Beller, *Sport Ethics: Applications for Fair Play*, 3rd ed. (Boston: McGraw-Hill, 2003).

6. Brenda J. L. Bredemeier, "Divergence in Children's Moral Reasoning about Issues in Daily Life and Sport Specific Contexts," *International Journal of Sport Psychology* 26, no. 4 (1995): 453–63; Andy Rudd and Sharon Stoll, "What Type of Character Do Athletes Possess? An Empirical Examination of College Athletes versus College Non Athletes with the RSBH Value Judgment Inventory," *Sport Journal* 7, no. 2 (2004): 1–10.

EIGHTH HOLE

Playing Through?

Racism and Sexism in Golf

John Scott Gray

> I know just the place to build housing for the homeless: golf courses . . .
> land that is currently being squandered on a mindless activity engaged in
> by white, well-to-do business criminals who use the game to get together
> so they can make deals to carve this country up a little finer among
> themselves. . . . Golf is an arrogant, elitist game that takes up entirely too
> much space in this country . . . [and] another thing: race. The only blacks
> you'll find in country clubs are carrying trays. And don't give me that
> Tiger Woods bullshit.
>
> —George Carlin, *Napalm and Silly Putty* (2001)

In the feature article of the December 23, 1996, issue of *Sports Illustrated*,
"The Chosen One," dedicated to its Sportsman of the Year, Tiger Woods,
his father, Earl, remarked that his son would "do more than any other
man in history to change the course of humanity." The reference here is
not merely to sports history, which would put Woods in competition with
figures like Jackie Robinson and Muhammad Ali, but the whole of history,
ranking him among figures like Gandhi, Jefferson, and Buddha. When
questioned on this point during the *SI* interview, Earl Woods asserted: "He
has a larger forum than any of them. Because he's playing a sport that's
international. Because he's qualified through his ethnicity to accomplish
miracles. He's the bridge between the East and the West. There is no limit
because he has the guidance. I don't know yet exactly what form this will

take. But he is the Chosen One. He'll have the power to impact nations. Not people. Nations."[1]

Though these expectations might seem a burden to most mortal individuals, Woods has sufficiently handled the golf courses of the PGA Tour, continuing to carry a confidence that has distinguished him as one of the most accomplished golfers to play the game. He has achieved these goals while largely transcending issues of race, as he continues to be seen less and less as a racial minority and more and more as simply the greatest player in the game. Regarding the transcendence of race, however, Woods has been criticized by some, including the Basketball Hall of Famer Charles Barkley and the Hall of Fame football player Jim Brown, for not being responsible in addressing issues of race and racism. In particular, Brown believes that Woods should have been less concerned about being politically correct in responding to the on-air comments by the Golf Channel's Kelly Tilghman, who said that other players could challenge him by getting together to "lynch him in a back alley," and he was also faulted for not adequately responding to a resulting January 19, 2008, *Golfweek* magazine cover story on race in golf that featured a noose on the cover.[2]

Though Woods's achievements may have changed the way he is viewed as an individual, it is unclear how those changes rank next to his late father's expectations. Recent events surrounding Woods's personal affairs may have done a great deal to remove some of the prestige from the Tiger Woods brand; this essay will not address these issues but will focus instead on the place some believe he holds as a symbol of racial inclusion and equality in golf. Regardless of whether Tiger Woods has thus far been successful at changing the world in the ways his father intended, at the very least one could hope that he has helped bring change to the world of golf. It is the golfing world that *SI*'s Gary Smith writes about, saying that it is a "white canvas . . . the moneyed, mature and almost minority-less world." This is the view echoed by the late George Carlin when he repeatedly bemoaned the game of golf as an elitist and arrogant waste of time and space. Are Smith and Carlin correct in their depiction of the game of golf, or is the game changing and becoming more inclusive, and if so, what do these changes tell us about our society as a whole?[3]

Is Golf a Model of Good Behavior?

Much has been made of the great strides that our society has seen in the awareness and exclusion of racism as well as sexism in the United States.

Advances in academic and business environments have often been antici-
pated or at the very least mirrored in sports, as there have been slow but
steady increases in the presence and numbers of minorities in senior positions and more opportunities for women to participate. The times have
changed since 1987, when Al Campanis, general manager for the Los Ange-
les Dodgers baseball team, discussed on national television the perceived
inadequacies of minorities, saying that blacks "may not have some of the
necessities to be, let's say, a field manager, or, perhaps, a general manager."
Changes have certainly not happened overnight, but today nearly every sport
includes numerous minorities at every level, from the field to the highest
levels of management.[4]

Along these lines, some might argue that we should hold golf as a model
for equality, because it is one of the few sports that has allowed women
and men to compete against each other at the highest level. Even among
recreational golfers, the handicap system as well as the use of multiple tees
to even out various skill levels is said to allow anyone to play anyone else,
regardless of age or sex. As for race, some might point out that the recognition of Tiger Woods, whose ethnic heritage is black, Chinese, American
Indian, Thai, and white, as the greatest player of his generation has led to a
changing of mind-sets regarding race and organized golf in general. Though
early numbers concerning minority participation in golf are unavailable,
the number of African Americans, as well as Asians, Hispanic Americans,
and other minorities, playing golf has increased significantly over the last
fifteen years; a recent study by the National Golf Federation estimates that
one in seven golfers in the United States is a minority. The study estimates
that minorities from the three largest groups make up 5.5 million of 36.7
million total golfers: 2.3 million African Americans, 1.5 million Asian
Americans, and 1.7 million Hispanic Americans. The survey also reveals
that interest in the game was much higher than actual participation for all
three groups. For example, the survey estimates that more than 10 million
African Americans are at least somewhat interested in playing the game. For
all three racial groups the average participation for men was nearly double
what it was for women, although in the United States as a whole the participation ratio is three to one. Furthermore, it is telling that the recent attempt
to discuss racism and golf in the controversial *Golfweek* cover story led to a
discussion of the selection of the cover art and the editorial choices that led
to it rather than the actual contents of the magazine itself.[5]

While much has changed, much more remains the same. Racism and sexism still exist in and around golf. Improvements in the post-Tiger era have been made, as the PGA has invested millions in programs, such as First Tee, to spread golf to communities that previously had not been exposed to golf. That said, there still is much more that needs to be done. Social exclusion remains; both women and minorities face what some call "interactional barriers" to their participation in golf. "I Just Want to Play," an essay by Lee McGinnis, Julia McQuillan, and Constance Chapple that appeared in the August 2005 issue of the *Journal of Sport and Social Issues,* discusses these barriers as well as the strategies employed by women as they attempt to overcome them. The barriers of social closure are "established when a social group, seeking to monopolize its own life chances, organizes itself against competitors who share some positive or negative characteristics."[6] The concept asserts that white males have established barriers against women and minorities in golf, and that these obstacles are extensions from other arenas of human conduct, in particular the business world. In *The Unplayable Lie,* Marcia Chambers refers to these barriers as the "Grass Ceiling." Though one might not agree with the assertion that many of the inroads made in the golf community in terms of race and sex qualify as mere tokenism, this chapter argues that the social closure discussed by McGinnis and others is still a problem faced by many Americans in the clubhouses and on the greens of America's best golf courses.

Masters of the Universe

In recent history much of our discussion of race and sex in golf has centered on the famed Augusta National Golf Club, home of the Masters Golf Tournament. For starters, it was Woods's amazing twelve-stroke victory over the 1997 Masters field that announced his presence with authority to the world. The victory itself is jaw-dropping, but the importance of his winning at Augusta National, which had been without a single African American member until a mere six years earlier, cannot be understated. There had been other African Americans who played in this tournament in the past, starting with Lee Elder's qualification for the 1975 edition. Yet the view of much of the membership at the private club mirrored that of Clifford Roberts, cofounder and longtime chairman of the club and tournament, who remarked that "as long as I'm alive, golfers will be white, and caddies will be black."[7] This attitude was certainly not unique to Augusta, however; the PGA of America added a provision to its constitution in 1943 mandating that only "professional golfers of the Caucasian Race ... shall be eligible for membership." This clause remained part of the PGA constitution until 1961.[8]

Though these aspects of golf's history may not be part of the public consciousness today, the protest of the 2003 Masters Tournament by Martha Burk, chairwoman of the National Council of Women's Organizations (NCWO), is certainly fresh. According to a *Washington Times* article, Burk and her protest were "mentioned in 4,424 stories in major U.S. newspapers and magazines" during the seven months leading up to the 2003 tournament, a massive amount of coverage and pressure that led Augusta National to choose to protect its sponsors by broadcasting both the 2003 and 2004 tournaments commercial-free. Burk and the NCWO maintained in their letter to the club that they were "concerned that the nation's premier golf event, the Masters, is hosted by a club that discriminates against women by excluding them from membership. . . . We urge you to review your policies and practices in this regard, and open your membership to women now, so that this is not an issue." Hootie Johnson, then chairman of Augusta National, responded in a three-page press release that the club was a separate entity from the Masters Tournament, a private club with a private membership process; he characterized Burk's request as one that "strongly urged [us] to radically change our membership." Johnson added that though the club might one day allow women members, "that timetable will be ours and not at the point of a bayonet."[9]

One reason offered by Alan Shipnuck, author of *The Battle for Augusta National,* for the forcefulness of Johnson's response was the controversy that had surrounded another private club in 1990—Shoal Creek Golf Club in Alabama. That course, home to the PGA Championship, was put on the spot for its lack of minorities. Hall Thompson, founder of Shoal Creek and a member of Augusta National, responded to these inquirers by saying that those in the club had the freedom to associate with whomever they desired, adding that "I think we've said we don't discriminate in every other area except the blacks." Shipnuck points out that the idea of inviting an African American to join a country club in Birmingham, Alabama, was an amazing rarity. Among seven clubs containing a total of more than 6,000 members in Birmingham, there were only 2 African American members. Nine days before the PGA Championship the club buckled under the pressure of protest and admitted its first minority member, a move that was followed at other clubs around the country as the PGA instituted a policy requiring that clubs hosting PGA Tour tournaments do not discriminate. (The next two courses to host the PGA Championship had been all-white before this declaration was made.) The specific language of the new policy stated that potential tournament hosts had to guarantee "that the membership practices and policies do not discriminate on the basis of race, sex, religion or national origin." Augusta National and the Masters are exempt from this requirement because the PGA considers this tournament, as well as the other three majors (the PGA Championship, the British Open, and the U.S. Open) as non–PGA Tour cosponsored events, so this nondiscrimination policy does not strictly apply.[10]

Ironically, it is the transcendent Tiger Woods who has received a touch of criticism in relation to the Augusta controversy, including an article by the *USA Today* columnist Christine Brennan that predated the Burk protest by three years, "slamming [him] for his lack of an overt social conscience." It was Brennan's series of articles discussing the exclusionary practices of Augusta National that sparked Burk to focus on the issue. Though the actual protest did not attract large numbers of participants during the tournament itself, concerns regarding how these private clubs are viewed and the degree to which that perception reflects on the game of golf are still worthy of serious consideration, especially given that as many as one-third of all golf courses are private.[11]

Some might read the preceding pages and simply respond that these events, however sordid and embarrassing, are all simply part of golf's colorful (pun certainly not intended) history and in no way represent the true and current state of the game. Unfortunately, though the PGA may have implemented a policy against discrimination, there is no oversight in terms of verification, as all a hosting club needs to do is assert in writing that it has nondiscriminatory practices. An April 2003 *USA Today* article by Jill Lieber made public the results of a survey of 129 golf courses (ranging from wholly private to public) hosting PGA, Champions (Senior PGA), and LPGA events regarding their membership. Though 86 percent of the private clubs and all the semiprivate clubs freely shared the size of their membership as a whole, "only 26% of the private clubs and 40% of the semi-private clubs revealed their gender breakdowns. Only 5% of the private clubs divulged their racial breakdowns." Harry Edwards, a renowned sociology professor emeritus at the University of California, believes that the reason these clubs are so reluctant to open up about their gender and racial breakdowns is that, simply put, the facts of the matter do not match their nondiscriminatory rhetoric. Edwards states that "when it comes time to ante up, to show their policies are working, that they've opened up, they don't have the numbers." Some, including Barbara Douglas, president of the National Minority Golf Foundation, believe that most minorities would simply not be interested in a private club membership; Douglas feels that "it's not reasonable to expect multiple numbers."[12]

This view leads me to wonder, however, exactly why expecting minority membership at private clubs is unreasonable. It is certainly true that social and cultural backgrounds influence one's recreation possibilities, as Washington and Karen point out in their essay "Sport and Society." They remark that "social class is a key component of our understanding of sports. It is important to understand what connects particular groups of people to particular sports activities and what role these play in the reproduction of inequality in a given society."[13] They argue that sociologists should make the study of sports a central aspect of their larger analysis of society at large, a position I wholeheartedly agree with. Still, though it may be true that not everyone is willing or able to spend the $25,000–50,000 in membership fees necessary to join Augusta National, certainly there is a wide range of possibilities in terms of cost. Even though the greens fees and equipment can make golf an expensive game to play, there are numerous opportunities to lower the hit to the wallet, including affordable used equipment and reduced greens fees at off-peak hours. It may certainly be granted that golf is expensive compared to other sports, but to what degree that economic difference translates into the ratio of Caucasian males to minorities or women remains to be clarified. Furthermore, work is being done to open the game of golf to nontraditional populations, as programs such as the First Tee, a World Golf Foundation project started in 1997 to expose children to golf and its nine core values, have expanded access to the game to many who might not ordinarily be introduced to it.[14]

Having Sex on the Golf Course

If one looks past the cost involved in playing golf as a dominant factor in determining who does and does not play, then other factors need to be considered. If we focus on issues of sexism, one of the key ways in which women are made to feel unwelcome on the golf course, according to McGinnis, McQuillan, and Chapple, is through the ways in which golf courses are defined "as men's spaces." Their research centered on a series of interviews with female recreational golfers who had various levels of experience, skills, and seriousness about the game. Many of these women felt that they were singled out and stereotyped as being poor or slow players. This response expressed itself in one of two ways: either feeling pressured to play like men to deserve to be on the course (driving distance being a major concern), or a sense of "role entrapment," which "translated into emphasizing the femininity of golf and exaggerating differences between men and women on the golf course"; this led to suggestions that women, to be accepted as golfers in their own right, should attempt not to appear masculine, aggressive, or too intense. It is this concern that led the LPGA commissioner, Ty Votaw, to emphasize the "five points of celebrity" (performance, appearance, passion, relevance, and approachability) during a mandatory Player Summit meeting. The degree to which sex appeal, long a controversial element in the marketing of women's golf, plays in this conception of celebrity is not clear, but what is clear is that Votaw wants the LPGA players to be more than just great golfers.[15]

The issue being raised here does not concern whether there should be a women's professional golf tour and a men's golf tour (although there are critics whom I will discuss below who might make this argument). Instead, the issue is one that arises on golf courses across this country and around the world: the degree to which social expectations that dictate how a "lady" is supposed to play—which is fundamentally different from how a man is supposed to play—are placed on women. The false dualism that suggests that there are two ways of playing golf, one being a superior, male style of play and the other an inferior, female style, is what must be examined more carefully.

This form of role entrapment is amplified by the classification of the red tees as the women's tees. McGinnis, McQuillan, and Chapple cite R. W. Connell's work in this area, particularly the concept of "hegemonic masculinity." According to Connell, the hegemonic masculinity concept (in the current case, the big-hitting driver) "is always constructed in relation to various subordinated masculinities as well as in relation to women." The blue tees (the manly tees) are in contrast to the white tees (for seniors and lesser-skilled men), and are entirely separate from the red (women's) tees. They add that, "according to the rules at many courses, people should select tees according to ability; however, . . . the unwritten, gendered rules regarding 'men's tees' and 'women's tees' usually prevail." Instead of letting skill decide where one should play from, there is a stigma to playing from the forward tees. In fact, many male players have heard the threat of having to play their next shot with their pants around their ankles or endure other punishments if their drive does not go past "the women's tees." To take one more example of how the tee confusion makes certain gender roles manifest, male members of the Golf Association of Michigan are allowed to enter scores only from the back and middle tees and are not even given the option of registering a score from the forward tees. Furthermore, when I use the free internet golf handicap service offered by Yahoo to keep my own ratings, the forward tee boxes on my local courses are automatically referred to as a ladies' tee box, whereas the middle tees are automatically referred to as the men's tees.[16]

A recent book by the political scientist Eileen McDonagh and the journalist Laura Pappano attempts to analyze the ways in which social closure relating to sex in sports is created and institutionalized in the first place. In *Playing with the Boys,* McDonagh and Pappano focus on the problem of coercive sex-segregation in sports, an accepted traditional practice that is based on what they see as three false assumptions: the inferiority of female athletes to males, the need to protect females from being injured by males, and the possible immorality of females competing directly with males. These false assumptions have allowed the institutionalization of sex-segregation in sports in six different ways; examples include the idea that there should be different versions of a sport for males and females (baseball versus softball) or that the same sports, if played by both sexes, involve sex-segregated teams (basketball). Furthermore, the concept of the same sport being played with two sets of sex-based rules or styles is a way of institutionalizing the sex-segregation found in golf, as evidenced by the differences in tee box practice. This work is important because knowing the genesis of social closure helps enable us to prevent its continued existence in the future.[17]

Another of the key elements mentioned in discussions of the social closure in golfing communities resistant to the acceptance of women and minorities is the makeup of the role models within that community—the membership of the PGA of America. Professional golfers, the teachers and stewards of the game, are underwhelmingly female (3 percent), and very few are African Americans (by some accounts, there are only 44 black Class-A certified professionals among the nearly 20,000 total in the United States). With the explosion of the LPGA in recent years, one would think that there would be qualified women, but they are either not seeking jobs as PGA instructors or not being hired. Regarding the lack of female PGA instructors and women in upper management positions, McGinnis, McQuillan, and Chapple argue that "it takes extreme courage for women to enter golf professionally when there is little gender-specific social support." This lack of female role models for other women is similar to the lack of minority role models, especially when Tiger Woods is taken out of the equation.[18]

The National Golf Federation survey mentioned earlier, which covered the participation of minorities and women in golf, contains a summary of recommendations for the game's economic growth. These include pursuing "the strength of the female market . . . lower barriers to entry . . . welcome minorities at the golf course, the retail shop, etc." The last two were the most telling, given the ground that we have covered, calling for golf courses to "reduce intimidations and increase comfort level . . . [and] provide a social network." It seems that these are the very things that McGinnis, McQuillan, and Chapple are calling for in their work.[19]

Putting Out

In conclusion, though the times may be changing for the better in our society, old feelings of exclusion die hard. Even if there is less overt discrimination on the golf course, there is still a widespread impression that the game and its clubs are places for wealthy white men first and others second. This sentiment is perhaps the strongest element leading to social closure, regardless of the degree to which it is true from one course to the next. As McGinnis, McQuillan, and Chapple point out, women who take up the game are not as likely to stay involved and continue playing as men are. If golf truly wants to turn over a new leaf and escape its racist and sexist past, clubs and golf professionals will need to do more in order to have a real effect on altering the impressions, felt by many women and minorities, of not being wanted. This process can begin by an increased level of transparency on the part of golf's leading institutions, including openly disclosing how many women and minorities are in their clubs and discussing why the numbers are what they are.

These considerations are important for both the health of the USGA and the game of golf as a whole. A February 21, 2008, *New York Times* article, bearing the title "More Americans Are Giving Up Golf," raised the issue of how many golf courses were struggling to stay economically viable in today's society.[20] According to the author, Paul Vitello, golf is in its own recession both in terms of the number of people who play a round a year and in terms of the hard-core players who play more than twenty-five rounds a year (down from 6.9 million in 2000 to 4.6 million in 2005). Many believe that the main problem is the time factor, as fewer people are willing to invest four to five hours in a round of golf, but some owners admit that there is a need to market more to women and younger players. "When the ship is sinking, it's time to get creative," said Walter Hurney, principal owner of the Great Rock Golf Club in Wading River, New York. This creative thinking must include a reevaluation of past golf course business methods, including their interactions with women and minority groups. Golf, after all, is one sport that through the handicap system offers an opportunity for an equal playing field, and an equal playing field is needed to ensure the moral and participatory health of the sport.

Notes

1. Gary Smith, "The Chosen One," *Sports Illustrated,* December 23, 1996, 28–53.

2. ESPN News Services, "NFL Hall of Famer Says Tiger Should Have Decried Remark," http://sports.espn.go.com/golf/news/story?id=3212224 (accessed September 12, 2008).

3. Smith, "The Chosen One."

4. *Nightline,* ABC, April 6, 1987.

5. C. L. Cole, "The Place of Golf in U.S. Imperialism," *Journal of Sport and Social Issues* 26, no. 4 (2002): 331–36. Data regarding minority participation in golf can be found in the National Golf Foundation's 2003 study "Minority Golf Participation in the U.S.: African-American, Asian-American, Hispanic-American," www.golf2020 .com/Reports/Minority_Golf_Participation_in_the_US.pdf (accessed June 20, 2008).

6. Lee McGinnis, Julia McQuillan, and Constance L. Chapple, "I Just Want to Play," *Journal of Sport and Social Issues* 29, no. 3 (2005): 317.

7. Rick Reilly, "Strokes of Genius," *Sports Illustrated,* April 21, 1997, 30–49.

8. Alan Shipnuck, *The Battle for Augusta National: Hootie, Martha, and the Masters of the Universe* (New York: Simon and Schuster, 2004), 25. Also see John H. Kennedy, *A Course of Their Own: A History of African American Golfers* (Lincoln: University of Nebraska Press, 2005).

9. "Burk Fails to Make Cut at Masters," *Washington Times,* March 21, 2004; Shipnuck, *Battle for Augusta,* 6, 9–10.

10. Shipnuck, *Battle for Augusta,* 26; Jill Lieber, "Golf's Host Clubs Have Open-and-Shut Policies on Discrimination," *USA Today,* April 9, 2003, www.usatoday.com/sports/golf/2003-04-09-club-policies_x.htm (accessed June 11, 2008).

11. Brennan's articles, in turn, were inspired by the ongoing work of Marcia Chambers, including the previously mentioned *Unplayable Lie: The Untold Story of Women and Discrimination in American Golf* (New York: Pocket Books, 1996) and her essay "Ladies Need Not Apply," *Golf for Women,* May/June 2002, 108–13.

12. Lieber, "Golf's Host Clubs."

13. Robert E. Washington and David Karen, "Sport and Society," *Annual Review of Sociology* 27 (2001): 190.

14. The nine core values are honesty, integrity, sportsmanship, respect, confidence, responsibility, perseverance, courtesy, and judgment (www.thefirsttee.org, accessed May 6, 2008).

15. McGinnis et al., "I Just Want to Play," 324.

16. R. W. Connell, *Gender and Power: Society, the Person, and Sexual Politics* (Stanford: Stanford University Press, 1987), 183. McGinnis et al., "I Just Want to Play," 325. The Golf Association of Michigan can be found at www.gam.org. Also, the Yahoo handicap service is at http://golf.sports.yahoo.com/tracker.

17. Eileen McDonagh and Laura Pappano, *Playing with the Boys: Why Separate Is Not Equal in Sports* (New York: Oxford University Press, 2008), 10–15.

18. McGinnis et al., "I Just Want to Play," 327.

19. National Golf Foundation, "Minority Golf Participation in the U.S.," 4, 6–7.

20. Paul Vitello, "More Americans Are Giving Up Golf," *New York Times,* February 21, 2008, www.nytimes.com/2008/02/21/nyregion/21golf.html?pagewanted=1&hp.

IV. Golf and Rationality

Is Golf Inherently Irrational?

David Shier

Woodrow Wilson famously described golf as "a game in which one endeavors to control a ball with implements ill adapted for the purpose." Yet President Wilson was an avid golfer—so much so that he even used black golf balls so he could play in the snow. This learned and seemingly rational person spent his *leisure* time doggedly pursuing an activity that he himself characterized as inherently frustrating. Was he insane?

In general, if people deliberately place obstacles in the way of achieving their own goals, we have reason to question their rationality. ("Hi, Sue. Are you on the way to the meeting?" "Yeah, I'm trying to get there, but I might be a little late because first I need to build a pit full of razor wire and flaming kerosene in my driveway and then jump over it.") Yet this is precisely what golf requires of its participants—that they play by rules and on courses designed to make it much more difficult to achieve the goal of holing the ball in the fewest possible strokes. The rules place regulatory restrictions on the golfer (governing how a player may cause the ball to move, the equipment he or she may use, etc.), and the features of the courses place environmental restrictions on the golfer (such as hole length, grass conditions, bunkers, water hazards, etc.).

Characterizing golf as the "pursuit of a tiny and fantastically expensive ball, in a fanatical attempt to direct it into a hole the size of a beer glass half a mile away," Mike Seabrook comments, "If anything could be better calculated to convince one of the essential lunacy of the human race, I haven't found it." One might seriously wonder why anyone ever plays the game, since golf certainly can look irrational, or at least paradoxical, in this light.[1]

The intuitive explanation, of course, is that golf wouldn't be worth playing if it were easy. It simply wouldn't be fun. Well, maybe much of the time it's not exactly fun anyway, but it surely wouldn't be interesting, and it wouldn't ever be gratifying. Golfers place obstacles in the way of achieving their own goals in order to make the sport more challenging and, consequently, more interesting and enjoyable.

There is nothing wrong with this intuitive answer—in fact, I think it's the right one. But one of the great values of philosophy is the way it encourages all of us to challenge the intuitive answers to questions (which are, after all, quite often found upon reflection to be incorrect) and to explore the concepts involved in order to discover whether and, perhaps more important, *why* the intuitive answers are correct. Philosophical reflection aims at unpacking a network of ideas to get a fuller, clearer, more satisfying explanation, and much of the following will be concerned with doing just that on the issue of rationality. The robustness of the conceptual framework developed in this explanation (i.e., its applicability to other phenomena) will then be illustrated by applying it briefly to a few other issues, including ad hoc course changes, handicapping, and new technologies in golf.

Internal and External Goals of Golf

The apparent insanity of golf derives from the tension between engaging in an activity with a definite goal (such as holing the ball in the fewest strokes possible) and at the same time placing various limitations and obstacles deliberately in the way of one's own achievement of that goal—or at any rate tacitly agreeing to play with these limitations and obstacles.

So one of the key concepts that we need to unpack is that of the goal or goals of the sport. What are the goals of golf? If you ask a golfer, you may get an answer in terms of low scores, fewest strokes, winning, and so on. But many golfers will also say their goal is something like the excitement or challenge of competition (against others or for personal best), exercise, recreation, fresh air, social interaction, or even income. All these may reasonably be described as goals or aims of golf, since they can all be answers to the question, "What are you trying to accomplish in playing golf?" But on reflection they fall into two categories, dividing neatly along an important line.

The first category comprises all those goals that are inherent to the sport. These are the goals that any golfer has *in* playing the game, as opposed to reasons *for* playing the game—or better, the goals golfers have in playing a particular form of the game, since these goals will vary with the form of competition (stroke vs. match play, handicapped vs. raw score, individual vs. team, etc.). These goals will include such objectives as completing the course in the fewest total strokes, winning the most holes, and the like. The goal for the individual golfer on any individual hole, though, will still be some variation on holing the ball in as few strokes as possible.

We might call the members of this first category the *internal goals* of the sport, for they are a part of the game in the sense that they are, or can at least always be presumed to be, goals of anyone playing that sport. Someone who hits golf balls with golf clubs in pursuit of other goals simply isn't playing golf. Someone driving balls at a range is using golf equipment and practicing some golf skills but is not playing golf, because the activity doesn't have the right goals. Or we can imagine "giveaway golf"—analogous to give- away checkers—the goal of which is the *highest* number of strokes, but such a ridiculous activity is not really golf at all.

The second category of goals comprises what we may call its *external goals,* since these goals are not inherent to the sport. One may play without these aims yet still be playing golf. Essentially, these are reasons *for* engaging in the activity at all—reasons to play. Notice that the question, "Why are you playing golf in the first place?" can sensibly be answered by items from this category—for example, "Because I desire the challenge of the competition." But it can't sensibly be answered with an *internal* goal—for instance, "Because I desire low scores." You don't golf because you desire low golf scores; you desire low scores *because you are a golfer.*

Typical external goals are competition, exercise, recreation, fresh air, social interaction, and money. Many of these are quite naturally associated with golf, but not everyone plays with all (or even any) of these goals. For many the outdoor activity is among their main reasons for playing, but for many others it is at most a minor benefit. For some the camaraderie is a high point, and others may regard the social interaction as a necessary evil. For many professionals income is a primary goal (though they surely love the competition, the excitement, etc., as well), but for most players it's at best a fantasy they keep to themselves. Furthermore, although most people have some of those standard goals of challenge, competition, and the like, the category of external goals is necessarily open-ended and extremely varied, since there are as many potential external goals as there are conceivable reasons to play. You might play golf in order to impress your golf-loving boss, to spy on someone who plays, to conduct psychological research on obsessive-compulsive disorder (for which golf courses are abundant sources of experimental subjects), to wear some stylish golf clothes, or for countless other reasons.

The Rationality of Golf (First Shot)

With the distinction between internal and external goals in mind, we can begin to resolve the apparent tension between wanting to achieve certain goals and yet at the same time *deliberately* making it extremely difficult to achieve them. What appeared to be tension begins to look like harmony when we consider internal versus external goals. In an important sense, the external goals are the more important, fundamental goals of the two, for if we had no external goal for the activity, then by definition we would have no reason to play in the first place, and hence no reason to seek internal goals such as low scores. Achieving (or even attempting to achieve) our internal goals is of value to us only because of the external goals we can achieve by doing so. There is no reason to seek low scores unless the quest brings us challenge, enjoyment, or the like. Even more to the point, by making it *difficult* to achieve the internal goals, we make it *possible* to achieve certain external goals. For example, if the course is too easy or the competitors unchallenging, the goals of compelling challenge and enjoyable competition cannot properly be satisfied.

Not all the common external goals, however, are connected so directly to the difficulty level of achieving internal goals. Whether the course is difficult or not, we're still going to get the fresh air. On the other hand, a goal such as getting fresh air probably isn't a golfer's *only* external goal in playing, since there are plenty of other ways to get fresh air. Why golf and not hiking, tennis, or whatever? So we may infer that golfers who have getting some fresh air as a goal typically have some additional goal or goals more specifically related to the activity of playing golf, and the same goes for other generic external goals (exercise, socializing, etc.).

Even goals such as competition and challenge, when they are described so generally, are not reason enough to play golf, as opposed to performing other activities that provide competition and challenge. Those who are drawn to golf's challenge and competition are drawn to it in large measure because of its *particular* blend and balance of certain physical and psychological skills, and because of its *particular* type of competition in the particular sort of environment created by a golf course. We might call these sorts of things the *primary* external goals of golf—for example, enjoyable or exciting competition of that particular type, with respect to that specific skill set, in that specific type of course environment.

Regulatory and Environmental Restrictions on Golfers

The difficulty level of achieving the internal goals is a function of several sorts of variables. A great many of these are governed by the rules of the sport, which, depending on the various forms of play, restrict the types of clubs and balls that may be used, the ways in which one may and may not cause the ball to move, the movement of other items on the course (flag-sticks, obstructions, impediments), the assessment of penalties, and many other aspects of the sport. We call these the *regulatory restrictions.*

There are, of course, many different sorts of rules. Some rules are argu-ably such that any activity that didn't include the regulated action just wouldn't be golf—for example, that you strike the ball with a golf club and not, say, with your foot. Such a rule could be called *intrinsic* to the sport. Most rules in a normal rulebook, however, are not intrinsic in this sense. Consider the USGA Rule 17-4: "When a player's ball rests against the flag-stick in the hole and the ball is not holed, the player or another person authorized by him may move or remove the flagstick, and if the ball falls into the hole, the player is deemed to have holed out with his last stroke; otherwise, the ball, if moved, must be placed on the lip of the hole, with-out penalty." If the rule instead allowed only the player to remove the flag-stick, or if it required the ball, if moved, to be played where it lies, surely this would still be *golf!*[2]

The other variables that go into determining the difficulty level of achiev-ing the internal goals are *environmental restrictions*—primarily, those hav-ing to do with the physical features of the golf course. Many popular sports are played in uniform spaces, such as football fields and basketball courts, with their identical regulation rectangles. Baseball parks, on the other hand, vary quite a bit in their overall dimensions and shape. But these variations, though they do affect the game in important ways, are still rather periph-eral. It's not as if home plate is 60.5 feet from the mound in Yankee Stadium and 70 feet in Fenway. Golf courses, however, do differ significantly from one another with respect to many basic features that directly affect central aspects of play. The variations in distance, shape, topography, hazards and bunkers, turf, and so on are central to how difficult it is to achieve the internal goals of the sport. This virtually unlimited variability of course design quite directly affects the prospects of achieving the internal goals of the sport.

We should note, too, how this is connected to another question: Don't all sports, and all recreational competitions, involve the placing of obstacles in the path to players' own objectives? Indeed, this is arguably the case. We design other sports and games so that there are obstacles to overcome along the way to internal goals, so that players may enjoy certain benefits in overcoming them; the process is not unique to golf. Indeed, Bernard Suits insightfully characterizes game playing in general as "the voluntary attempt to overcome unnecessary obstacles."[3] For example, soccer requires that hands not be used.

But in golf the question of why we make it so hard to achieve our goals has a special resonance. First, golf is harder to play well than most of these other activities; it really is insanely difficult. But more to the point, the placing of obstacles in the way of the golfer's internal goals is so much more obvious, so outwardly manifested in golf, since there are literally hazards and traps placed in the way of the player. We don't put a bunker between first and second base, or a pond on the twenty-yard line.

The Rationality of Golf (Second Shot)

We can now return to the question of why it's not insane to make golf insanely hard, and address it within the framework of goals (internal or external) and restrictions (regulatory or environmental). If the regulatory and environmental restrictions do not combine to make it difficult enough to achieve the *internal* goals, then the primary *external* goals cannot be achieved, so that golfers are deprived of their reasons for playing golf at all. Therefore, instead of standing in the way of achieving fundamental goals, the regulatory and environmental restrictions golfers place on themselves (in the pursuit of the internal goals) make it *possible* to achieve their (primary external) goals. That is to say, placing these obstacles in one's own path is not irrational, but rather a requirement of the activity's being rational at all, for without these restrictions, there is no reason to engage in the activity.

We should keep in mind, however, that it is also possible for the regulatory or environmental restrictions to make it so difficult to achieve the internal goals that the primary external goals cannot be achieved, which also deprives golfers of their primary reasons for playing. If the course is so difficult that no one can really play it, then there can be no real competition, no genuine (i.e., potentially surmountable) challenge, and so on. So really, the ideal is a balance between too difficult and too easy. Echoing Aristotle's phrase about virtue, we might say that excellent golf conditions lie at the mean between these extremes of excess and deficiency.

This suggests a general approach to the often hotly contested issues about the rules of the sport, the features of the courses, and the practices of golfers. One should identify the relevant external goal or goals and determine whether the rule, feature, or practice in question will, by altering the prospects of achieving the internal goals, enhance or impede the prospects of achieving the relevant external goal or goals. Of course, that's not the only criterion, as there are certainly other important goods that must be considered in evaluating rules and courses. For example, fairness of the rules and courses is a moral requirement—an aspect of our broader social and institutional commitments to fairness and justice. But preserving the possibility of achieving external goals is a necessary condition to justify a rule or course change.

HELPING BY HANDICAPPING

The goals and restrictions framework is useful in straightforwardly articulating the role and the value of handicapping, a practice almost unique to golf. The difference in abilities among amateur players can easily be so considerable that, because of the environmental restrictions of a particular course, the internal goal in competitive play of a lower score than a player's opponents is too difficult for some to achieve and too easy for others, making it impossible for the competitors to fully satisfy their primary external goals, such as the enjoyment of genuinely *competing* against others.

One method of bringing the goals and restrictions into balance would be the imposition of asymmetrical environmental restrictions on the players in different ability classes, such as different tee positions (in effect relaxing the environmental restrictions on less accomplished players). Handicapping, however, addresses the situation by changing the internal goals instead of the restrictions. The previous internal goal (lower raw score than your opponent's) is replaced by another internal goal (lower net score than your opponent's), which makes the possibilities of winning and losing much more realistic for all the competitors, and therefore greatly increases the likelihood of satisfying the external goal of a competitive golf experience.

AD HOC CHANGES TO THE GAME

Another issue that can profitably be addressed within the goals and restrictions framework—one that has arisen several times in the Tiger Woods era—concerns ad hoc changes to features of golf courses. Striking changes to some tournament courses (such as grass length, tree placement, tee location, etc.) seemed to many commentators to be implemented with the aim of diminishing Woods's advantage and making the tournaments more "competitive."

But the imposition of such ad hoc environmental restrictions undermines, rather than enhances, the true competitiveness of tournaments. One of the primary external goals of professional golfers is genuine, uninhibited competition in which they can fully test their skills and mettle against their peers'. Of course, they want to win, and to win prize money, but they want to achieve those goals in competition against opponents who have the opportunity to play their best. The ad hoc restrictions artificially make it more difficult for targeted players to achieve the internal goals than the other players, thus undermining the external goal of satisfying, *authentic* competition. It is important here to note the motivation for these changes in the restrictions—that is, holding back a particular player, or a small group of players: if it were, for example, to change the character of play for all (say, to a shorter game), they would not be ad hoc changes, and the issue would be quite different. Such changes are considered in the next section, which concerns newer technologies in golf equipment.

We should also note that there is substantial variety in golf courses, and therefore to some extent different skill sets are always going to be rewarded on different courses. What is problematic with the course changes in question is the fact that they are ad hoc—that they target only some players. Thus, the grounds for objecting to the changes can be seen as also rooted in fairness considerations. But the goals and restrictions framework brings into sharp relief the fact that there are independent grounds for objections rooted in the practical self-interest of the other competitors. Even the golfers who are not targeted, who we might think would have selfish reasons to tolerate restrictions on others, will have *self-interested* grounds to object, because their own external goals of genuine competition are undermined.

At first pass this may seem to be at odds with the previous point about the role of handicapping in ensuring competitiveness. But the apparent tension is just a reflection of the different situations of professional and amateur golfers. The amateur's external goals involving enjoyable competition require real possibilities of success and failure, and the differences in abilities among amateurs are so great that this goal sometimes cannot be achieved without handicapping. For touring professionals, among whom the differences are small enough that relative success and failure are real possibilities, satisfying the external competitive goals requires genuine, unfettered competition.

NEWER BUT NOT ALWAYS BETTER TECHNOLOGIES IN GOLF

The final issue to which the goals and restrictions framework will be applied here is one of the most controversial in golf—the extent to which there ought to be restrictions (if any) on the dramatic technological advances in equipment, especially those involving increased distance. Solid core balls, improved driver faces, and the like have radically increased average drive distances in professional golf. In 1995 John Daly led the PGA Tour with an average drive distance of 289 yards. In 2007 ninety-three players averaged better than 289, led by Bubba Watson's 315.2 yards; the forty-one-year-old Daly came in second, 23 yards better than when he was twenty-nine years old.[4]

As I suggested earlier, new technologies should be permitted only if their effect on the difficulty of achieving internal goals does not undermine the prospects of achieving the relevant external goals. Although there is some trade-off in accuracy, the primary effect of distance technologies is to position players much more frequently for eagles and birdies. Thus, unless the courses are altered accordingly, the player gains an advantage—not over other players, provided they have access to similar technologies, but over the course. And golf, even when it involves competition against others, is at root a struggle against the course. Distance technologies help the player in this struggle by making it easier to achieve the intermediate internal goal of reaching the green quickly and thereby making it easier to achieve internal goals such as lower scores.

The question is: Do the newer technologies make it too easy—so easy that external goals are undermined? If so, then introducing additional restrictions on these technologies is justified. What is clear is that they are changing the *character* of play (especially of the pro game, where the increases have been more pronounced) by encouraging an aggressive approach that emphasizes distance over accuracy and radically de-emphasizes the geometrical nuances of the middle game. As Hal Sutton commented, "If you were to ask everybody out here whether they wanted distance or accuracy, they'd all tell you distance. Forget accuracy. The fairways are soft, the greens

are hard, and there is no rough. Let's kill it. There's no such thing as thinking. It's just grab your driver and hit it as far as you can."[5]

This change in the character of play is analogous to the common complaint about American basketball: that it has focused on dunks and three-
pointers while almost entirely losing the midrange game—a game that
rewards a skill set different from the (admittedly awe-inspiring) athleticism
of dunks and the specialized skill of three-point shooting. Many lament
the way the game has changed, especially in the NBA. (Of course, we may
wonder whether they are simply nostalgic for the game as they knew it, or if
they are correctly noting that something of value has been lost in this shift.)

Golf has changed in a similar way, as raw power is rewarded at the
expense of other skills. But golfers have loved golf largely because of the *particular combination of skills* that it demands, and a prominent part of that skill
set has always been the cognitive game, the geometrical game that is being
crowded out by the distance technologies. That is, for golfers to achieve their
primary external goals involving entertainment, challenge, and competition,
they have had to compete against the course (and each other) with respect
to that particular skill set, with all its elements. (We should also note that
there is a similar consideration involving the fans of professional golf and
their external goals in following the sport. Whether fans find the changing
sport more, or less, entertaining surely must be a factor in the rule decisions
of organizations such as the USGA and PGA regarding equipment, etc.)[6]

Thus, distance technologies are radically de-emphasizing one of the
important skills and changing the character of play, undermining important external goals that most golfers have historically had. Viewing this issue
through the conceptual framework of goals and restrictions allows us to make
full sense of the suggestion that distance technologies should be limited or
even rolled back—and to understand it as a principled objection, instead of
merely some sort of reactionary, antitechnology nostalgia.

Of course, some may find the changed game *more* interesting and enjoyable. We may ask whether those who lament the changes are simply nostalgic for the game as they knew it, or whether there is something about that
particular type of golf game that is important, perhaps essential, to golf. The
conceptual apparatus of goals and restrictions frames this issue nicely but
cannot settle it, for it doesn't dictate what the goals of the sport *should* be,
which skills *should* be rewarded, or what the character of play *should* be.
Essentially, the dispute is over how golf is to be defined and by whom, and
those are different sorts of questions altogether.

Surely, though, there are limits to how much technological change of this sort the sport can absorb and still be interesting to anyone. Imagine the advent of the smart ball—a self-steering ball with an onboard GPS homing device, for example. You just hit the thing any way you like and it finds the cup all by itself. How fun would that be? No fun at all, actually. (Well, okay, maybe the first hundred times.) But a competition with smart balls wouldn't be a competition among players, but among engineers. And what would be the point? As we've seen, in golf, as in other sports, we place obstacles in the way of achieving our own internal goals in order to make it possible to achieve our external goals. The whole point of the obstacles is to challenge ourselves, our own skills—not the engineering skills of others. To the extent that golf becomes a contest of new technologies and not a contest of one's golf skills, it really will become irrational.

Notes

1. Quoted in Colin Jarman, comp., *The Hole Is More Than the Sum of the Putts: Ultimate Golf Quotations* (Lincolnwood, Ill.: Contemporary Books, 1999), 339.

2. United States Golf Association, "The Rules of Golf," www.usga.org/playing/rules/pdf/2008ROG.pdf (accessed July 10, 2008).

3. Bernard Suits, "The Elements of Sport," in *Philosophic Inquiry in Sport*, ed. William J. Morgan and Klaus V. Meier (Champaign, Ill: Human Kinetics, 1988), 11. This article first brought to my attention the tension inherent in sports in placing obstacles in the way of our own goals. His distinction between "pre-lusory" and "lusory" goals is similar (though not identical) to the distinction I advance here between internal and external goals, but he uses it to different ends, focusing his discussion on the roles of various types of rules and on developing a definition of sport in general.

4. "PGA Tour Statistics," www.pgatour.com/r/stats/ (accessed July 10, 2008).

5. Jaime Diaz, "The Growing Gap: Driving Distances Are Skyrocketing on the PGA Tour. So Why Is the Average Golfer Being Left Behind?" *Golf Digest,* May 2003, http://findarticles.com/p/articles/mi_m0HFI/is_5_54/ai_101967369/pg_1?tag=artBody;c011 (accessed July 10, 2008).

6. The important role of the external goals of the fans in following the sport was pointed out to me by the volume editor, Andy Wible. I am very grateful to Andy for this and for his many other helpful comments.

THE BACK NINE

V. Personal Reflections

Life Lessons

Tom Regan

Four. Three. Two. One. Seven-thirty, on the dot. We're talking rocket science here. You can't phone for a tee time before seven-thirty, the day before you want to play. And you don't want to be back in the queue (hundreds will be competing for a small handful of spots) when the call goes through. So timing is everything. And what timing means here is: seven-thirty, on the dot.

A menu answers. If you want a million dollars, tax free, press 1. If you want a villa on the Mediterranean, at no cost, complete with servants, press 2. If you want a tee time at Pebble Beach, press 3. I press 3.

"You want to play Pebble Beach?" a Valley Girl voice answers. "You mean, like, today even?"

"That would be great," I say, adding, perhaps a bit defensively, "Is there anything wrong with that?"

"No, there's nothing wrong with that. It's just that, you know, if you're staying at the Lodge, tee times usually have to be arranged six months in advance."

I am tempted to reply that I have decided not to stay at the Lodge this time because I found the $1,950-per-night, two-bedroom suite overlooking the eighteenth fairway a bit too confining. But common sense prevails, and I say, as cordially as I can, lust catching in my throat, "Thank you, but I'm not staying at the Lodge . . . this time. I was just wondering whether, well, maybe . . . I mean, perhaps . . . someone has had to cancel?"

"Let me check."

She's gone, lost in a shower of music. "Who's kidding whom?" I'm thinking to myself. "The chances of walking on at Pebble Beach? Today? Tomorrow? Any day? Get real."

"What about eight-thirty? We have a cancellation. A medical emergency or something."

"You mean eight-thirty today?"

"Yes. Eight-thirty. Today."

"Let me think a minute." I do some fast calculations. Here I am, in the middle of San Francisco. I have just gotten up, haven't dressed, haven't eaten, haven't wakened dear Nancy. And I don't know my way out of the city. But I figure if I forget about showering, forget about breakfast, don't forget about Nancy, don't get lost, and average, say, 260 miles an hour, I can make it. Dangerous, but doable.

"That's cutting it a little close," I say. "Do you maybe have anything later? Possibly?"

"What did you say?"

"I said, do you maybe have anything later? Possibly?"

That sweet voice speaketh not. Nor is there the need to. I know what she's thinking. What she's thinking is, "You've got to be an idgit. Someone gives you a tee time at Pebble Beach, on the very day you call, and you're flotsam enough to ask for another one?"

"Sometime tomorrow would be fine," I venture.

"Let me check."

This time the music goes on, and on, and on. I figure the young woman is putting my commitment to the test. How much do I really want to play Pebble Beach? Well, she'll see. There's no way I'm backing off this phone, even if I have to listen to most of the gazillion tunes recorded by the Beach Boys. Then she's back.

"What about one-thirty tomorrow?"

"One-thirty? Tomorrow? Are you kidding?"

"One-thirty. Tomorrow. I'm serious. A medical emergency or something."

"Oh, my God," I say. "I'll take it!"

The rest is about credit card numbers, proper dress, directions. I keep thinking, "This is too good to be true." Then, after a hearty breakfast and several wrong turns, I find Highway 1 heading south out of San Francisco, Nancy by my side, our children back home safe in their skins, a leisurely drive ahead. I see myself as the Lou Gehrig of golf: I am the luckiest man on the face of the earth.

Beginnings

Golf has been a fickle part of my life, dating back to the early 1950s. That was when I began caddying at Shannopin Country Club, about ten miles down the Ohio River from Pittsburgh. A trolley line passed directly in front of our house and made a stop at the foot of a long, steep hill that led to the golf course. The trolley run could take up to half an hour, depending on traffic; the trek up the hill, another twenty minutes. During the golfing season, if you wanted your name near the top of the caddy master's list, you had to leave my neighborhood no later than six o'clock in the morning. Many were the days of summer, and on weekends in spring and fall, when I left home sleepy-eyed but full of anticipation.

Part of the anticipation was the money. Back then you earned seventy-five cents a bag for eighteen holes. And almost everyone would throw in at least a quarter tip. Caddies who arrived early enough to carry doubles twice could pocket four dollars, even more by also shagging balls or, if you were big and strong enough, carrying three bags at a time. I remember once carrying triples twice, with good tips all around.

But it was not only the money that motivated my younger self to rise when most boys my age were still in bed. There was something about a golf course, something about the game itself, that claimed my sensibilities at that early age and that continues to do so to this very day. Probably all golfers have experienced the same things I have, more or less; but none of us, I think, has found the words to capture what we feel.

- The mystical tranquility of so large a space, especially at sunrise, after the crickets grow silent and the birds begin their morning song; the grasses, thick with dew, without a single human footprint breaking their pristine surfaces, shimmering in earliest light; and not a single human syllable shattering the earth's mysterious silences.
- The sight of a ball well-struck: a Platonic dot of evanescent whiteness, rising resolutely into the wind, holding its line, searching for the place where it belongs, soaring without human will or whim to guide it; and then, like a bright afterimage viewed against the darkness, the moment passes, the shot forever part of the past, to live only in memory, talked about in boasts and incredulity, the game moving inexorably forward, forever forward, the players crafting other shots, birthing newer memories.

- The jocular camaraderie of friends in fierce competition, none wishing ill to the other, but none any particular good either; their laughter and cursing; the words exchanged, in praise and denigration; grown men acting at being boys, and women being girls, bonded in an oasis of stolen time, away from home and job, finding space in life for play again.

Of such moments are golf courses and the game of golf made, such the riches given to those who would receive them; these were things that, from the first day I sauntered down the first fairway at Shannopin Country Club, a single bag working its wages on my bony shoulder, I took happily, greedily. And then, for the better part of thirty years, for reasons I can give but don't believe, I took almost nothing at all.

Gathering Dust

As is true of others who played the game in their youth, golf became something "I used to do" when (here come my reasons) I could no longer find the time to play it. It's not hard to say when this happened. Nancy gave birth to our son, Bryan, in 1966; I took my first real job in 1967; we built a house in 1969; and our daughter, Karen, was born in 1970.

After these developments, except for maybe three or four rounds a year early on, then none at all for most years thereafter, I threw myself into being a good husband, a good father, a good provider, a hardworking teacher, a productive scholar, and a former golfer.

True, I continued to follow the game; but the passion and dedication were gone. I had too much else I had to do, too much else I wanted to do. At least that's what I kept saying to myself even as, inside, I questioned my own veracity.

My first set of clubs had wooden shafts and bore names like Brassie, Spoon, and Niblick; they had been my father's, given to him over the years by wealthy golfers for whom he had caddied in his youth. When golf was no longer part of his life, he gave his clubs to me. Blessed with a slow, graceful swing, characterized by an intensity when playing that made Ben Hogan look like Bill Murray by comparison, I have no doubt that he could have been a scratch golfer if circumstances had not prevented him from working at his game. "You have to practice if you want to be good"; my father never tired of sharing his simple wisdom with me, especially when, my Tommy Bolt temper venting steam, I took to cursing and throwing clubs. "Don't expect to be good at this game," he would say, "if you don't take the time to practice."

I don't think he ever knew this, but I did take the time to practice. I all but wore the brass off that Brassie, snapped the head off that Spoon, callused my hands hitting that Niblick, all to no great purpose. Almost from the start, when caddies were permitted to play one morning a week at Shannopin, I had the skills to break 100; but try as I might, I could not get much better. I was, you might say, born to be a bogey golfer, that and nothing more.

Which was why I was never comfortable with the reasons I gave for letting golf drop out of my life. When I was honest with myself, I had to admit that the game had gotten the best of me. Here's what I mean.

For as long as I could remember, I had a golfing doppelgänger, another golfer-self who embodied all that I was capable of—or, more accurately, all that I believed I was capable of. This never-seen-by-anyone-else companion of mine didn't think in terms of failure. He always expected me to drive the ball straight and far, always expected me to hit fairway woods and irons long and true, always expected me to pitch and chip with accuracy and finesse, never expected me to leave a putt short or miss a two-foot comebacker.

Of course, all this was about *my* game. My doppelgänger didn't expect me to hit the ball as far as Bubba Watson or putt as well as Steve Stricker. No, my doppelgänger wasn't that unreasonable. He just always expected me to play at the top of my game, whatever shot I was hitting. By way of example: more than once in my life I'd hit a drive more than 250 yards. Well, since I'd done this a few times in the past, my doppelgänger expected me to do it every time I took the big stick in my hands. And more than once in my life I'd hit a sand wedge out of a deep bunker to within a few inches of the cup. Because I'd done this a few times in the past, my doppelgänger expected me to do it every time I was in a greenside trap.

Logically, it didn't make any sense. Ninety-nine percent of the time (at least) my drive did not go that far and my sand shot did not end up that close. When it came to my doppelgänger's expectations, however, logic made no difference. If I did thus-and-so in the past, then I should be able to do thus-and-so in the present. And if I should be able to do thus-and-so in the present, then, by gum, my doppelgänger didn't see any reason why I didn't just do it. Every time.

As Joe Thiesman might have said, you don't have to be Norman Einstein to see that my relationship with my doppelgänger was not a happy one. The expectations never yielded. The sense of failure never weakened. The harshness of the verdict ("No! Not good enough!") never softened. Why play a game, I asked myself, that all but guarantees disappointment and frustration, not just a little but a lot? Why not find some other athletic pursuit—long-distance running, for example, where you can spend an hour or two a day, with friends, everyone running at the same pace, no winners or losers except on race day. That is the path I took for most of the next thirty years of my life, my golf clubs gathering dust in the attic. The game, as I've said, had gotten the best of me. Not the children. Not the house. Not the job. It was the game.

Try, Try Again

My father died in 1995, at eighty-five. He hadn't touched a club in twenty years, maybe more. Near the end, he was hobbled by Parkinson's. He no longer walked, he shuffled; and he slobbered some, his speech slurring the more the muscles in his mouth weakened. Over time he withered away, leaving a shell behind, brittle as kindling. You could have crushed his chest if you weren't careful when you embraced him. Even so, even up to the moment he breathed his last inaudible breath, I never doubted that he could have thrashed me soundly, on any links of my choosing, still saying, "Don't expect to be good at this game if you don't take the time to practice."

A few years before he passed away, I had made a futile attempt to return to the game. There I was, pounding balls on the range—hundreds of them a day—with a rapacious appetite of a famished vegan turned loose in a tofu factory. Did my game improve? Had my doppelgänger exited, stage left? Don't bet on it. The only thing my irrational exuberance earned me was not one but two golfer's elbows—that and (to my enduring gratitude) a two-year medical leave from my home course.

Then, after my father's death, I decided to try again, one last time, but now with a more prudent sense of purpose and commitment. It goes without saying that I wanted to become a better player, and that I was willing to practice regularly and hard (but not to the point of physical destruction) if that was what it took. But I also wanted to immerse myself in the wonders and history of the game, to rediscover, with the fresh eyes of maturity, what it offers to all who play it, whatever their level of skill. For a good six months, as time permitted, I worked at every phase of my game until, in 1999, not long after my sixtieth birthday, judging myself to be as ready as I ever would be, I found myself driving south out of San Francisco, destination: Pebble Beach.

Pebble Beach

Islam has its Mecca. Christianity has its Bethlehem. And Judaism has its Jerusalem. Golf in America has its Pebble Beach. Granted, the country's cup runneth over with remarkable courses. Merion. Baltusrol. Oakmont. Augusta National. Olympic. Cyprus Point. There is no risk of being at a loss to name twenty-five great American courses. Or fifty. Or a hundred. But when the "Best Courses in America" dust settles, there is only one agreed-upon number one public golf course in this land of ours, and that is Pebble Beach. Merion, Baltusrol, Oakmont, Augusta, Olympic: private clubs, one and all. As for Cyprus Point: Cyprus is so private that Bob Hope once quipped, "It had a membership drive, and drove out forty members."

But Pebble Beach? From its inception the course has been open to those paying members of the golfing public who could afford to play it. Every American golfer, every golfer anywhere, is eligible to play the fabled links, to stand where Palmer and Nicklaus, Watson and Miller, Mickelson and Woods have stood. And—at more than $300 a round when I played and $500 today, not counting cart or caddie fee—Pebble is one place where you want to take your time standing.

The course, which opened for play in 1919, is not America's oldest. That honor goes to Oakhurst Golf Club, in White Sulphur Springs, West Virginia, founded in 1884. Even Oakmont, in Pennsylvania, is older by fifteen years, and Merion, also in Pennsylvania, by almost ten. But what it lacks in age, Pebble Beach more than makes up for in tactile, olfactory, auditory, and just plain staring-you-in-the-face beauty of the breathless variety, especially at holes six through eleven (collectively known as the Cliffs of Doom), which work their way in and out of Carmel Bay, heading south, and at seventeen and eighteen, played into and along the bay, eventually heading north to the Lodge.

Pebble's remaining holes, though more difficult than their slumbering reputation would have you believe, lack the breathtaking blend of sky and water, rugged cliffs and crashing surf that combine to create Pebble's aesthetic trademark. The novelist Robert Louis Stevenson, who walked these grounds, described the space now known as the Cliffs of Doom as "the most felicitous meeting of land and water in creation." And this was before there was a golf course.

For his part, Nicklaus has said that if he could play only one round of golf in his life, it would be at Pebble Beach, not, I think, merely because of the many challenges the course presents, but also because of the mesmerizing prospect in which it presents them.

Pebble's history, especially its U.S. Open history, remains vivid in the memory banks of scratch and high handicappers alike.

- 1972: The seventeenth hole, the final round. Nicklaus smashes a one iron into the teeth of a thirty-five-mile-an-hour wind, hitting the flagstick on the fly, the ball coming to rest inches from the hole, leaving a tap-in for birdie en route to his third Open victory.
- 1982: The seventeenth, again, and the final round, again. Tom Watson, facing certain bogey, chips in for birdie out of thick rough from behind the green on his way to defeating a stunned Nicklaus by a single stroke. There's Watson—who can forget the scene?—dancing around the green, wedge held aloft, that gap-toothed grin of his big enough to garage an RV.
- 1992: No heroics on seventeen for a change; this time, it's the seventh. Tom Kite, in the back bunker; it's a downhill lie, virtually no green to work with. Out comes the ball, heading nonstop to Tijuana. But wait: traveling full tilt, the ball hits the flagstick, hangs in midair for an instant, then drops straight down the pole, into the hole. Birdie two. That miraculous shot saves Kite's round, certainly. But that the bespectacled, owlish Kite had a round to save (he shot an even par 72 on a day when the average score was 77, in winds gusting to forty-five miles an hour) is the real story.

Pebble Beach having hosted the Open in 1972, 1982, and 1992, one would have expected to see the tournament back there in 2002. It says something about the hallowed status the course enjoys that the USGA would break the mathematical progression and have the Open's one hundredth playing, and the first one of the new millennium, hosted by America's course.[1]

A Better Idea

I arrive almost an hour before my tee time, feeling so pumped up I could sign autographs: "May your putter be hot—Yours, Hulk Regan." But here's the wonder: the most impressive thing about Pebble Beach, for someone visiting for the first time, is how overwhelmingly underwhelming it is. At least at the start.

The scale and style of the buildings (the Lodge, the Pro Shop, the smattering of high-end specialty stores), despite the Bill-Gatesian prices associated with the place, are—well, "early Best Western" seems apt. The main entrance? That's so laid-back California, it's hard to find. A putting green? It's a short walk from the first tee to a small practice area. How small is it? Let's just say that if you have four people putting at the same time, you have two too many. As for a practice range: a shuttle bus takes you to a bush-league, beaten-down facility where balls are dispensed by a coin-operated machine.

And about that first tee: it's a narrow, squat affair, hard by the front entrance to the Pro Shop, eternally surrounded by legions of vocal golf kibitzers, and elevated so that those striking their tee shot are directly in the sightlines of the good folks wolfing down hors d'oeuvres at the Lodge's restaurant. Talk about a public golf course.

Even the first hole is something of a yawner: 338 yards from the white tees, slight dogleg right, easily within the repertoire, I think, of the players in my foursome. Two are late-forties chaps, originally from Taiwan, who work at Pebble Beach and exult in the gift of beneficence they feel in being able to play the course, free, once a month. The fourth, who makes a point of flashing his custom-made driver, featuring a head the size of a Lincoln Town Car, is a bronzed, blond, muscular type from somewhere down the coast. He is accompanied by his diminutive, buoyant fiancée, about the size of his lob wedge, whose job today is to prove her fitness to the fullness of his manhood by lugging his pro-sized leather bag, loaded with more than its full complement of clubs, for the next five hours, more or less.

The Blond Bomber hits first, smashing a prodigious duck hook that registers 6.2 on the Richter scale. I allow myself the faintest of smiles. Nothing pleases me more than the public spectacle of too much Teutonic testosterone gone awry. Next, the two Taiwanese Americans flail away, each hitting the middle of the fairway about 170 yards out. I smile again. The stage is set. It's my turn.

I survey the milquetoast efforts of my playing companions. Most times I drive a ball 210 to 220 yards. And straight. Everyone who knows my game knows that. I know that. But my doppelgänger, he has a better idea. This is no time to leave the pedal off the metal. This is Pebble Beach. Visions of 250 dance in his head.

An anticipatory hush falls over the boisterous golf cognoscenti adjacent to the tee. Diners at the Lodge hold their canapés in midair. Left arm straight. Shift weight right. Full body turn. Swoosh! Crack! History! Ben Hogan hit from this very tee. Sam Snead threaded this very fairway. Now, fellow golfers, add to that illustrious list the name Tom Regan.

When the ball finally lands—and it takes a very long time for it to find the place where it belongs—it is maybe a hundred yards out, nestled in a tangle of trees thirty yards to the right of the fairway. We're talking classic pop-up here. I stare in amazement, limp as a Kleenex in a tsunami. The Blond Bomber looks me over, contemptuously. The two friends shake their heads, knowingly. Twiggy, the caddie, smiling beamishly, chirps, with a sincerity not to be denied, "Nice shot!" And my doppelgänger? He is throwing clubs and stomping all over the place inside my mind.

Without a doubt, I think, I am in for a very long afternoon.

"I Love This Game!"

Lee Trevino once remarked that if you're 5 over after Pebble's first five holes, "It's a good time to consider suicide." Remarkably, standing on the sixth tee, I am only 1 over, having bogeyed the first and fourth holes, parred the second and third, and birdied the par-3 fifth, sinking a coiling, side-hill putt from twenty feet. This is followed by another par on number six, hard into the wind off Carmel Bay, where I manage to get up and down from just off the green. Heading to number seven, the memory of the fiasco on the first tee all but forgotten, I am brimming with confidence. I love this course! I love this game! I even love the Blond Bomber, who, having declared that he is having "a bad day," and who must be at least 12 over by now, has decided not to keep score.

The seventh is one of Pebble's signature holes. It measures a mere 103 yards from the middle tee, 107 from the back. It requires a little dump shot from an elevated tee to a minimal green. A piece of cake. There's just this small problem: that aforementioned green is almost completely surrounded by deep traps and crashing waves. Also, there is a gusting wind that blows in any direction and at any speed it chooses; on this day it is straight into our faces, at about twenty-five miles an hour. You don't want to be short, which almost certainly puts you in one of the bunkers; and you don't want to be long, which risks the briny deep.

Does the wind make a one- or two-club difference? Maybe more? It can be more. Ken Venturi once hit a four iron here into gale-force winds and came up short. I choose an eight iron. The perfect club. There's just this other small problem: the ball lands in the kikuyu, a thick, clinging grass that has been compared to a nest of tarantulas, a good twenty yards left of the green, leaving a menacing bunker between moi and the hole.

No, I do not dump the ball in the bunker. Nothing that good. I chop my second shot short of the bunker, then hit my third shot forty feet past the pin before 2-putting for double bogey 5. Sleepy old Pebble Beach is beginning to bare her nasty teeth. As for Herr Doppelgänger, he is fuming. The names he called me you never hear in polite company.

"The Most Terrifying Second Shot in All of Golf"

No words can prepare you for the eighth hole. The tee is adjacent to the seventh green and requires that you hit a blind drive up and over a steep rise. Hit the drive too far right, you are out-of-bounds. Hit it as far left as you can, you are in bounds but face an impossible shot to the green. Dumb luck has me hit the ball just about as perfect as I can, leaving me with what Nicklaus calls "the most terrifying second shot in all of golf."

Try to picture this. You are standing over your ball, about 180 yards from a small, shallow green that slopes toward the water. Between you and the green there is a vast chasm that falls from the height of the fairway to a mix of craggy rocks and sand, a good eighty feet below, then rises maybe sixty feet to the level of the green. There is no room for error here. If you want your second shot to be on the green, you have to hit your second shot to the green. Anything shot at the green that is short of the green becomes part of the ever-churning ecology of Carmel Bay.

The eighth does offer a coward's way out. This is to forget about carrying the chasm, forget about the green, forget about par; just play it safe by laying up left, then hit a short iron on, take your two putts, and get out of there with a heart-pounding bogey. I take the coward's way, and follow this with another bogey at the ninth. A front nine of 6 over par, 42, on a true test of golf. Not bad. Not bad at all. All that practice is finally paying off.

Sand . . . and More Sand

My most vivid memories of the back nine are of sand, lots of it, having spent a good part of the rest of the afternoon in no fewer than eight traps. Sand, yes, but also wind and length, the second nine measuring almost

350 yards longer than the front. The result? Standing on the tee at seventeen, I am sixteen over. A bogey-bogey finish will put me at—well, you can do the math.

"If you finish bogey-bogey, you shoot ninety. If you par one of those holes, and bogey the other, you shoot eighty-nine. It's just one-shot difference," Nancy tells me on our next day's drive. "What's the big deal? It's just one shot. I just don't get it."

"Hmm," I think to myself, loving my wife dearly, calling her attention to the bilious clouds overhead, the blue waters of the Pacific below. Only golfers who have struggled with the game as I have would recognize the immense difference between two scores separated by a single stroke.

"Yeah, you're right about that," I remember saying.

The wind is howling directly in our face when we hit our tee shots at seventeen, the hourglass-shaped green some 180 yards away, guarded by traps galore, one of which I manage to find before getting out, then 2-putting for bogey 4. As for the two friends from Taiwan, first one and then the other sinks an impossible sixty-foot putt for par. Their only par of the day. They are both so happy, each doing a little dance reminiscent of the one Watson did on this same green in 1982. I cannot help thinking that they have never felt closer in their life, never more convinced that they belong in this game; both are so happy, the unbridled joy of one multiplying the unbridled joy of the other.

The Blond Bomber evidently has been saving his best for last, beginning with a prodigious drive off the eighteenth tee, followed by a no less prodigious three iron that stops some forty feet from the hole. "That's more like it," he declares, full of conviction.

"Nice shot," the little one chirps yet again as the rest of us applaud, each of us genuinely happy for her man (he would go on to 4-putt for bogey) because of the good that golf has given him this day.

My story on eighteen begins less spectacularly. I hit a good (for me) drive slightly right of center, then a solid three wood that leaves me about a hundred yards from the green. The pin is tucked behind a trap guarding the green on the right. You don't want to hit it short. Better to be long. Any idgit knows that. So it only stands to reason I would hit it short.

Here's what the day comes to, then. After a solid front nine, I have squandered away any hope of a decent round by giving my best imitation of Lawrence of Arabia on the back. What could have been a score in the low to mid-80s now is at risk of becoming 18 over, 90. All I have to do is not get up and down out of this godforsaken bunker, and that's what I go home with. Bogey golf. Been there. Done that. More times than I want to remember.

My doppelgänger (who has been berating me throughout the back nine) moves into command mode.

"Enough, already! You've done this before. You can do it again! You can do it now!"

I dig my feet into the sand, open my stance, and try to get a sense of how hard I need to swing to blast the ball over the lip of the trap and onto the green. The tempo on the backswing is good; the distance behind the ball at impact seems right; the follow-through feels complete. When I look up and see the ball drop gently onto the putting surface, then wend its way ever so slowly toward the hole, finally stopping only inches away, leaving a tap-in for an 89, I feel . . . I feel more than I can say.

"Nice shot," says the charming blond guy from down the beach as he and the others join in a friendly round of applause, this time for me.

"Just don't whiff the friggin' putt!" my doppelgänger hisses in my ear.

Being There

Pismo Beach is several hours' drive south of Pebble along the coast highway through Big Sur. Nancy and I have made the drive before but still marvel at the large vistas of black mountains falling into blue waters. We spend the night at a motel perched precariously atop craggy cliffs. Arriving early in the afternoon, I play a nine-hole course, Pismo State Beach Club, which measures less than 1,500 yards and plays to a par of 33. Greens fees are eight dollars for nine holes, twelve for eighteen. No Lodge. No onlookers loitering around the Pro Shop. Just the bare essentials: this is a tee; that is a green; there is a hole. Pebble Beach it is not.

I am paired with a husband and wife who run a hot-dog stand and a middle-aged plumber, Jason, who has taken the afternoon off. The concessionaires slice and dice their way around the course for nine holes, giddy with laughter, not giving their scores a moment's bother. The plumber, by contrast, is quiet, relaxed, at peace with himself; he's a good striker of the ball, focused, dutiful when it comes to course maintenance.

Jason and I play the nine holes a second time. Our conversation on our tenth tee goes like this:

"Play much?"

"As much as I can."

"Plumbing must be hard."

"Some days, yes; some days, no."

"Lived in Pismo long?"

"A while."

"Where'd you live before?"

"Folsom."

"Folsom?"

"Yeah, Folsom. Folsom State Prison."

Oh, my God, I think to myself, what do I say now? Nice place, that Folsom, eh?

Fortunately, Jason has the good grace to fill the awkward silence.

"I made a lot of mistakes when I was young. A lot of mistakes. But I've paid for them and learned from them."

"Yes," say I, still not knowing what else to say.

"And one thing I've learned, something that's really obvious but a lot of people, probably even a lot of philosophy professors, don't know. Know what that is?"

"No, what?"

"I've learned it doesn't really matter how good you are at golf as long as you're there when you play. Ever thought of that?"

"I'm not sure I know what you mean."

"Well, think about it." For the first time, he smiles. "I mean, just to be out here, in the sun, feeling the wind, the grass under our feet. It doesn't matter whether it's Pebble Beach or Pismo Beach. The shots we hit. The shots we miss. That doesn't matter. It's about being there, wherever we play, whatever our score. You know what I mean?"

I try to understand him. I know he is saying something he thinks is important.

"You know what I mean?" he asks again.

"You mean not to think about golfing and instead just golf?"

"Exactly."

"That's hard to do."

"If you let it be."

"Can you do it?"

"Sure. It's the easiest thing in the world. Just let it go. You know what I mean? Just let it go."

He smiles again.

"You still have the honor, by the way," he adds, stepping to one side. "Just let it go."

What happens next is hard to describe, and even harder to explain. All I remember is that, at the top of my backswing, I felt like a tumbler had been turned and a lock had been opened.

Heading Home

After we finish (we both shoot 77), Jason says he plans to play about the same time the next day and asks whether I'll be around. Sorry, but no, I say, my wife and I will be moving on in the morning.

"Well, that's okay then," he says.

"It's been special, Jason," I say. And mean it.

"For me, too. Never played golf with no philosophy professor before. Geez."

In the parking lot we shake hands and say good-bye, wishing each other the best of luck. On the drive back to the motel, I let my mind wander over the events of the last two days, still a jumble of impressions. One thing is clear, though, and clearer today than it was at the time. Some golfers I've met are good; fewer are wise. That teacher I met back at Pismo, that Jason, he was one of the few.

It's only after I lock the car and begin to climb the stairs that I embrace the full measure of what has happened.

I have just played nine holes of golf without thinking about playing golf. For nine holes, I was there.

Nine holes without so much as a word, without so much as a whimper, without so much as a snarl from my doppelgänger.[2]

I think about barging into our room and shouting what I had learned, but decide against it. There are some things even those closest to us will never understand.

Notes

1. Tiger Woods won the 2000 Open, finishing 12 under par, the first player in the 106-year history of the event to finish seventy-two holes at double digits under par.

2. My doppelgänger passed away at the Pismo State Beach Club in the fall of 1999.

VI. Golf, Mysticism, and
Self-Understanding (Amen Corner)

PHILOSOPHY IN THE KINGDOM

Golf, Mysticism, and Philosophy

Mark Huston

Michael Murphy's best-selling 1972 golf novel, *Golf in the Kingdom*, and the more recent movie *The Legend of Bagger Vance*, directed by Robert Redford, exemplify one of popular culture's main attitudes toward the sport of golf: mysticism.[1] The average, and even pro, golfer would in all likelihood probably never claim to have had a mystical experience while playing golf, but there is nevertheless a fairly pervasive and even influential view that there is a relationship between golf and mysticism. The most striking example of this is *Golf in the Kingdom*, which not only continues to remain in print and sell even though it is more than thirty-five years old, but also has spawned a society named after the main character of the book, the Shivas Irons Society, which started in 1992. I contend that one of the reasons for this surprising endurance is that the book struck a popular, mystic nerve, if you will.[2] In this chapter I will attempt a diagnosis of this attitude by examining these works in light of certain core philosophical discussions of mysticism. First, a brief description of *Golf in the Kingdom* and an even briefer description of *The Legend of Bagger Vance* are in order.

Golf in the Kingdom and *The Legend of Bagger Vance*

Golf in the Kingdom is broken into two parts, each containing several subsections. The first part is characterized by a traditional story line, and the second part presents pearls of golf wisdom that the author is supposed to have gleaned from events related in part 1. Though it is a novel, the book gives the impression of being a memoir because it is written in the first person by a character named Michael Murphy, the name of the author of the book.

Part 1 describes a 1956 trip Murphy makes to Scotland, where he plays golf at a course named Burningbush. There he plays a round of golf with the local golf pro, Shivas Irons, and one of Irons's students, Balie MacIver. As we'll see, the round is quite strange, as Murphy witnesses and receives instruction from Irons. Murphy describes various emotions—frustration, joy, and so on—that he experiences, as well as his increasing ability to get "the feel" of the game and finally seeing the "aura" of some of his shots. This "aura" is dubbed "true gravity," a mystical term if I have ever heard one, and is described in part 2.[3]

After the round of golf, Murphy goes to dinner at the home of some friends of Irons. During the dinner he has various strange conversations about life and golf, such as a discussion about how golf leads to an understanding of the "simultaneity of past and future."[4] After the party Murphy goes with Irons to the lair of Irons's teacher, Seamus MacDuff, whom we never meet, where they use MacDuff's old club to hit balls. Finally, they end up back at Irons's house, where Irons gives Murphy a collection of various writings and scraps that record his views, thoughts, and theories, most of which are quite mystical in tone and content. Murphy then uses these writings for the second half of the book.

The Legend of Bagger Vance takes place in Savannah, Georgia. Told from the perspective of Hardy Greaves in flashback, we get the story of Junuh. Junuh, we are told, was a great amateur golfer who joins the army during World War I. Upon his return, he is unable to assimilate back into society, and so he becomes almost a hermit. He is finally lured back to golf by his wife (whom he had abandoned) to play against Bobby Jones and Walter Hagen in order to reinvigorate the local economy, which is in peril because of the Depression.

As Junuh is hitting golf balls he is mysteriously approached by a stranger named Bagger Vance. Vance gives Junuh advice, bits of wisdom, and even condemnation when necessary, in much the same way Shivas Irons does to Murphy, until Junuh is able to find his "authentic swing." This signals that Junuh has regained his zest for life, including his relationship with his wife, and so Vance drifts away as mysteriously as he arrived.

As I proceed, I will periodically use examples from these two works as illustrations of various points that arise in relation to golf and mysticism.

Mysticism

Before attempting a specific examination of the relationship between golf and mysticism, it is important to try to get some sort of handle on the nature of mysticism; however, this is no easy task. Definitions and criteria of mysticism are almost as diverse as the number of scholars who have written on the topic. For example, one definition states that a mystical experience is a "(purportedly) super sense-perceptual or sub sense-perceptual experience" that relates us to "realities or states of affairs that are of a kind not accessible" by standard means of relating to the world, such as sense perception or introspection.[5] Using a somewhat different definition, Hal Bridges stipulates mysticism as a "selfless, direct, transcendent, unitive experience of God or ultimate reality, and the experient's interpretation of that experience."[6]

Forming a definition is not particularly problematic, and it is usually necessary for the sake of clarity. There is, though, another option: to extrapolate general marks, or criteria, from the writings and reports of recognized mystics.[7] This option leads into murky territory since different writers emphasize different criteria. William James and Bertrand Russell, two of the greatest philosophers of the nineteenth and twentieth centuries, provide a prime example of this option.

Russell, who in general is very critical of mysticism, denying any of mysticism's claim to revealing truths of reality that are not accessible to science, presents three criteria: mystics claim (1) that "all division and separateness is unreal," in other words that "the universe is a single indivisible unity"; (2) that "evil is illusory"; and (3) that "time is unreal."[8] Russell's criteria have something in common with both definitions offered earlier but are different as well. All these criteria are supposed to be insights into the nature of the world, and it is clear from the way Russell frames the debate that he agrees with the first definition, that mystical insights are taken to be inaccessible by standard means, or, as he would put it, they are accessible only through "religious revelation."[9] Criteria (1) and (3), on the other hand, correlate nicely with Bridges's second definition, especially the notion of the unity or oneness of everything. Criterion (2) provides the primary area of difference, since the other two definitions fail to address evil in any direct way at all.

In contrast with Russell, William James provides, in his classic work *The Varieties of Religious Experience,* one of the most philosophically sympathetic accounts of mysticism ever written. Focusing on the mystical state as one of consciousness, and through his reading and interpretation of a wide and varying range of reported mystical experiences, James proposes four marks of mystical experiences: noetic quality, ineffability, passivity, and transciency.[10] Elsewhere James writes that mystical states are "very sudden and *great extensions* of the ordinary 'field of consciousness.'"[11]

I will explicate these terms. *Noetic quality*, as James thinks of it, means that mystical states are taken to be states of knowledge or illumination. *Ineffability* describes a state that "defies expression." A state characterized by *passivity* is one that cannot be forced to occur, although there are preliminary steps, such as focusing attention or meditating, that may make mystical states more likely to come about. Finally, James thinks that mystical states "cannot be sustained for long," and are hence *transient*.[12] Jerome Gellman directly attacks this last mark by pointing out that writings of mystics do not support transiency, claiming that the reported mystical experience "might be an abiding consciousness, accompanying a person throughout the day."[13]

The differences between the criteria of James and Russell are quite striking. The major difference is that James focuses exclusively on the psychological state itself, whereas Russell is concerned only with what the purported state is supposed to reveal about reality or the nature of the world. The only slight overlap is their agreement that the state usually has a noetic quality. James initially leaves it at that, but Russell presents what he takes the state to supposedly reveal about the world to the individual. The earlier definitions combine elements from both sets of criteria.

General Criteria of a Mystical Experience

Given the plethora of potential criteria, I will sum up those that seem to appear most often. None of these criteria, however, should be taken to be either necessary or sufficient for a mystical experience; their overlap merely provides family resemblance criteria.[14] In other words, for an experience to count as *mystical* it must have some overlapping subset or other of these marks: ineffable, noetic, providing insight, direct (i.e., not mediated), involving a sense of the loss of the self or ego, unitive (i.e., the sense that everything is part of one united whole), passive, lacking a real sense of time; they are sometimes thought to be *pure conscious events*, blissful, paradoxical, revelatory, and transformative.[15]

Because I am focusing on pop cultural representations, a couple more points are in order. Though the historical research often relates mystical states to religious revelation, the religious element typically plays at most only a minor role in popular culture works about golf. When religion does play a role, it is usually through a blend of Western and Eastern ideas. This blend is used most dramatically in *Golf in the Kingdom,* to obviously popular effect.[16] I will make a particular connection between Zen Buddhism and the book later in the chapter. In addition to downplaying most traditionally religious components, popular culture heavily emphasizes the personally revelatory or transformative elements. To put it slightly differently, the mystical state in pop culture has much more to do with an individual having a *life-changing experience,* and then possibly sharing what is learned from that experience, than it does with coming to some specific religious state, such as a perceived union with God. There are plenty of other philosophical debates related to mysticism, but these remarks should suffice for our purposes.[17]

Golf and Mysticism

Breaking this into two separate, but integrated, parts, I will first briefly compare golf and baseball, since baseball also has significant mystical representations in popular culture, and then examine the question: What best explains the association between golf and mysticism?

I focus on baseball since it seems to be the rival to golf when it comes to more obviously mystical elements in its representation in pop culture. *The Natural* and *Field of Dreams* are prime examples.[18] There are revealing differences between the two sports that I take to reflect different explanations of the role mysticism plays in their pop culture representations. One obvious explanation of the differences is that baseball is a team sport and golf is individual, so it is more difficult to present the story of an individual having a mystical experience through baseball. *Field of Dreams,* though, accomplishes this, yet even here the mystical experience does not come *through* playing baseball but only as a result of other, mysterious, factors, such as the hearing of voices by the lead character.[19]

I believe there is a deeper explanation for the differences between the representations. The history of baseball is tied deeply to the history of the United States in the late nineteenth and twentieth centuries, hence monikers such as "national pastime" and "America's game." My hypothesis is that baseball gets the mystical treatment so often in part because of this connection. Many of the works related to baseball were written by people who grew up in the 1940s, 1950s, and 1960s, when baseball was at its zenith. Kids grew up dreaming of baseball and worshiping baseball players in ways that they apparently no longer do. So I suspect some of these works can be explained as a kind of nostalgia or attempt to capture the essence of baseball in America.[20] I believe that the explanations for the role of the mystical in representations of golf are substantially different. This leads to an attempt to explain more specifically the relationship between golf and mysticism, thus responding to, and integrating, both parts of this section.

First, there is the important historic component: golf's origin is usually traced back to Scotland in the 1400s. In addition, there are four key elements that, I will argue, when taken together at least begin to explain why golf often gets the mystical treatment. Those components are its extreme individuality; the length of time it takes to play and the consequent opportunity for contemplation; nature; and freedom.[21]

In addressing the first component, I would argue that if golf is not the most individual sport, it is certainly near the top. Unlike a sport such as tennis, another sport considered to be an "individual" sport, one does not even need an opponent to actually play golf.[22] I use the term *actually* because an individual might shoot baskets or hit a tennis ball against a wall, but these are not instances of actually playing those sports anymore than hitting a bucket of balls is an instance of playing golf. Sports such as bowling or auto racing *may* be as individual in some sense as golf, but they lack the other components and so are less amenable to potentially mystical representations.[23]

The second and third components combine with individuality. As anyone who has ever played a round of golf knows, it takes awhile—especially if you get behind a slow group. If one is playing alone, or even with a good friend, at a fairly secluded course, however, there is time for *contemplation* that is simply not found in most other sports. This is due not only to the length of time it takes to play, but also to the time between shots. Unlike sports in which one is forced to react to other players, thus usually leaving little time for contemplation, the golfer is normally reacting to himself, which results in plenty of time for reflection. Additionally, the contemplation occurs in *nature,* the third important element. Though in some very weak sense any sport played outdoors could be characterized as "in nature," golf courses are clearly part of nature, comprising trees, grass, rocks, and so on, in a way that most other sports are not. For example, Junuh's final revelatory experience occurs when he loses a ball in the woods. His isolation in the woods allows time for a flashback, a contemplative experience that would make very little sense on, say, a football field or basketball court.

Ralph Waldo Emerson had astute poetic discussions about how the "lover of nature is he whose inward and outward senses are still truly adjusted to each other." Even more poetically he wrote that "standing on the bare ground . . . all mean egotism vanishes. I become a transparent eye-ball. I am nothing. I see all."[24] These statements clearly echo many of the general criteria associated with mystical experiences: they evoke unity (in this case with nature), they are noetic ("see all"), and there is a sense of the loss of self or ego. James continues these ideas about nature when he says that "certain aspects of nature seem to have a peculiar power of awakening . . . mystical moods." He then adds that almost all the cases he discusses, especially the most "striking cases," "have occurred out of doors."[25] In fact, James even has a special name for those, such as Emerson, who describe a mystical union with nature: naturalistic pantheists.[26] I hope that it is now fairly obvious that nature plays a significant role in attempting to describe and understand purported mystical states, and I take it that this carries over into an explanation of popular golf mysticism. Furthermore, given the qualitatively different role that nature plays in golf compared to other sports, that role goes a long way toward explaining the relationship between golf and mysticism.

Freedom: Cheating, Paradox, and Zen

The fourth suggested component of mysticism, freedom, also needs clarification. Golf provides a kind of Sartrean existential freedom that few other sports can offer.[27] According to Sartre's existentialism, "existence precedes essence," meaning that we are thrust into this world and we are then completely free to shape ourselves according to our own will. But in order to live authentically, we must accept full responsibility for our actions, and it is only our actions that define us as individuals—not beliefs, not judgments, not emotions: only actions. In other words, each individual is the totality of her actions. In turn, with complete freedom comes fear because of the fullness of our responsibility. Yet we are also free to overcome fear and to live authentic and happy lives.[28] So where does golf come in?

Recall the earlier point that golf is one of the more individual sports. Along with that extreme individuality there is a special kind of freedom, particularly in relation to the rules of golf. Sartre points out that play (read: sport or game) is "an activity of which man is the first origin, for which man himself sets the rules."[29] Thus, games present a microcosmic example of macrocosmic existential freedom. Though there are rules that must be followed in any sport, rules that we follow because of either other players, as in the case of tennis, or referees, in nonprofessional golf there is a much greater degree of latitude as to how closely or loosely we follow those rules. Even when one is playing with other people, there are plenty of occasions to cheat, such as slightly moving the ball for a better lie.

Alan Shapiro, in his book *Golf's Mental Hazards,* asks the question: Do you cheat?[30] He emends this, however, to ask what kind of cheater you are and whether you are in denial about your cheating. For example, are you above-board with your playing companions, or do you hide your cheating from them? (My grandfather, for instance, would always move the ball around a bit, using the phrase "winter rules," but he assumed we would do the same thing and did not try to hide his rule-bending activity.) If you hide your cheating from others, do you at least acknowledge it to yourself, or do you try to justify and rationalize away your actions? Shapiro uses the answers to these sorts of questions as both a means of improving the golf game and as a means to understanding overall psychological health. I am not claiming that this is meant to be interpreted as mystical, but it does highlight the importance of freedom and responsibility. In fact, his correlation between taking responsibility and mental health could have been lifted straight out of Sartre, who famously said that we are, after all, "condemned to be free."[31] As for responsibility, the main concern is not so much the kind of cheating agreements of the sort I had with my grandpa, but the willingness, or not, to cheat as an individual when one can get away with it.

This point is illustrated in both *Golf in the Kingdom* and *The Legend of Bagger Vance.* Early on during his round of golf with Irons, Murphy plays a spectacularly awful hole. When MacIver asks him his score on the hole, he first responds by indignantly telling MacIver to just mark down an X, assuming the others would not count the hole. When MacIver and Irons balk at this, Murphy says with exasperation, "Oh, put down a ten." Again, MacIver and Irons are put off by this, and finally Irons says, "Michael, Ah think 'twas eliven."[32] This forces humility, even a little fear, and finally recognition of the importance of taking responsibility in much the way Sartre proposes.

In the second part of the book, the author Murphy looks more specifically at how Irons thinks of the rules (from the writings that the character Murphy received from Irons), which adds a further mystical element to the freedom to follow the rules, or not. One of the marks of the mystical mentioned earlier is that it is a paradoxical experience. Murphy reflects on Irons's keeping such a close watch on the score, while being such a "large spirit," as being paradoxical. The paradox stems from the fact that Irons is completely open to most experiences yet is quite narrow when it comes to rule following, something that initially seems unexpected given his general attitude. Murphy also writes of golf as "simultaneously a doorway and a prison," which he thinks is depicted in Irons's being bound to this world, most explicitly by linking himself to golf, yet also transforming, mystically, out of this world into a "luminous body."[33] Though I will not pretend to understand all of this, since by definition a paradox cannot be rationally understood, it should be at least clear enough that none of it would make any sense at all if there were not an extreme freedom to follow the rules more or less closely.[34]

    The Legend of Bagger Vance contains a similar illustrative moment. Toward the end of the match, when Junuh has a chance to win, he is examining his lie when he causes the ball to move ever so slightly. At that point he calls a penalty on himself, even over the protestations of Jones and Hagen. This is the final act that allows the audience to recognize that Junuh has had a fully transformative experience in a typically mystical fashion, and for emphasis Vance leaves immediately after this point. It is only upon recognizing the full range and capacity of his freedom that Junuh is finally able to carry over the lessons from the course back into his life. Earlier in the film Bagger Vance had helped Junuh find his "authentic swing," vividly represented in the film through a sweeping, tunnellike shot that indicates the beginnings of Junuh's mystical, unitive experience with his surroundings. Once he comes to recognize his full freedom and responsibility, his transformation is complete. Finding his "authentic swing" mirrors in many ways Sartre's notion of living an authentic life, in which freedom and responsibility are essential. Those elements, combined with the others discussed earlier, such as nature, work together nicely to explain why golf is chosen over many other sports when it comes to pop cultural mysticism. As a final point of interest, it should be noted that Bobby Jones did in fact once call just such a penalty on himself while playing Hagen, and it resulted in his losing by one stroke.

    Apart from the freedom to follow the explicit rules, there is also the issue of just how much to listen, or not, to one's teacher. In both *Golf in the Kingdom* and *The Legend of Bagger Vance* we have instances of mysterious teachers who teach *not* by explicit instruction, as teaching is typically understood, but through the use of oblique language and references that are used to get the student (i.e., Murphy, Junuh) to figure things out for himself. This student-teacher relationship is reflective of and informed by a more Eastern approach found in Zen Buddhism.

In one branch of Zen Buddhism a student is guided by a teacher, called a *roshi*. The *roshi* presents *koans* that are meant to lead the student to attain a *satori*, which is a kind of enlightenment.[35] *Koans* are riddles, stories, or dialogues that are often paradoxical in nature and sometimes even non-sensical. The point, however, is not to come to a logical understanding of the *koan* but, as Thomas Merton describes it, to "live" and "work through" the *koan*. And even though there are no clear-cut guidelines for approaching the *koan*, there is still great "discipline and procedure" involved. Again, as Merton writes, "Nothing is arbitrary or left to chance; one either hits the target or misses it entirely." This, by the way, sounds like a pretty good description of golf as well.[36]

Interestingly, Merton relates the trials of Saint John of the Cross and his self-described "dark night of the soul" to the attempts by the student of Zen to come to grips with such Zen concepts and ideas as giving up the ego and attaining "pure consciousness," which "will be in a sense 'unconscious.'" He points out that the "pure consciousness" of Zen is "the *freedom* of the consciousness that has no finite object," which parallels the "pure faith" that Saint John achieved through the travails of the dark night of the soul, which resulted in a greater "divine and personal *freedom* that is a gift of grace."[37]

Both Murphy and Junuh also achieve a kind of freedom that comes from this opening up and understanding that very much reflects these Zen ideas. In fact, Murphy even goes through an actual, not merely metaphorical, dark night. Murphy and Irons go, at around midnight, to try to find Seamus MacDuff, the even more mysterious and elusive teacher of Irons. They never find MacDuff, but they do find his lair after a dangerous trek. They also find golf balls of the sort used in the 1800s (called featheries) and MacDuff's golf club, which is made from an old shillelagh.[38] It is only upon returning from this harrowing night that Irons trusts Murphy enough to give him his own writings; enlightenment is thus achieved after a dark night of the soul, leading one to believe that this reflection of Saint John's metaphorical journey is not a mere accident.

Shivas Irons, as a teacher, also echoes Awa Kenzo, the famous archery teacher of Eugen Herrigel portrayed in Herrigel's book *Zen in the Art of Archery*.[39] So, for example, Kenzo famously said that "the bow and Zen are one," which reflects of Irons's teaching that the sweet spot of the club and the golf ball are "already joined" before the game is even played.[40]

There is one particularly famous moment when Awa Kenzo is practicing archery: upon the release of his arrow, "his self flew apart into infinite grains of dust, and, with his eyes dazzled by a myriad of colors, a great thunderous wave filled heaven and earth." This is much like the descriptions of true gravity and auras around the golf balls in *Golf in the Kingdom* and the tunnel effects used in *Bagger Vance* to illustrate those special moments when the golf shot is virtually perfect. Kenzo, in fact, goes so far as to say that one can "see *true nature* in the shot."[41] This could apply as easily to golf as it does to archery, and it nicely ties together the role of freedom and nature as I have been presenting them.

Individuality, time for contemplation, nature, and existential freedom are the combined elements, according to my proposed diagnosis, that help explain why popular representations of golf often have a mystical component. If golf in fact leads to more purported mystical experiences than other sports, I believe these elements provide an initial hypothesis with which to explain that as well. As it stands, though, these basic elements provide a natural jumping-off point and a lot of wiggle room for an artist who wants to explore mysticism through a sport, more so than with other sports. Even the brilliant comedy (and many would argue the best golf movie ever) *Caddyshack* has its mystical moments. I will leave you with just one of those moments, the words of Ty Webb, so that you may meditate on golf and mysticism yourself. Ty Webb (Chevy Chase) is putting in a way that is extraordinary as he is giving advice to Danny Noonan (Michael O'Keefe), who is holding the flag and listening bemusedly. Ty says that according to the Zen philosopher Basho, "a flute with no holes is not a flute and a donut with no holes is a danish."[42]

Notes

I would like to extend a special thanks to David Raguckas, Daryl Fisher, Alec Thomson, and especially James Tierney for very helpful discussion and comments.

1. Michael Murphy, *Golf in the Kingdom* (New York: Arkana, 1972). *The Legend of Bagger Vance* (2000), directed by Robert Redford, DVD (Culver City, Calif.: Dreamworks Video, 2001). The movie is based on Steven Pressfield's 1995 novel of the same title. I use the title to refer to the movie.

2. The Web site of the Shivas Irons Society is quite substantial. The society issues a literary journal, publishing the likes of the poet and golf writer Andy Brumer and the famous journalist Alistair Cooke, which one receives upon becoming a member in the society.

3. See Murphy, *Golf in the Kingdom*, 28–29, where the discussion of auras and true gravity begins.

4. Ibid., 51.

5. Jerome Gellman, "Mysticism," *Stanford Encyclopedia of Philosophy*, November 11, 2004; revised January 10, 2005, http://plato.stanford.edu/entries/mysticism/, 1.1.

6. Hal Bridges, *American Mysticism: From William James to Zen* (New York: Harper and Row, 1970), 4.

7. When I say "recognized mystics" I do not mean to imply that the states of the mystics are necessarily veridical, but only that they are acknowledged as mystics in the scholarly literature (e.g., Meister Eckhart in Christianity) owing either to their own self-recognition or to recognition by others.

8. Bertrand Russell, *Religion and Science* (1935; rept., Oxford: Oxford University Press, 1997), 179.

9. Ibid., 176.

10. William James, *The Varieties of Religious Experience: A Study in Human Nature* (1902; rept., New York: Barnes and Noble Classics, 2004), 328–30.

11. William James, "A Suggestion about Mysticism," *Journal of Philosophy, Psychology, and Scientific Methods* 7, no. 4 (1910): 85–92. The quote is from page 85; emphasis added.

12. James, *The Varieties of Religious Experience*, 329–30. Interestingly, James even gives a specific time frame for the "transience" of the experience: no more than two hours but usually only half an hour. It is never quite clear why he thinks this.

13. Gellman, "Mysticism," 1.1.

14. Here I am merely adapting the term the philosopher Wittgenstein used to indicate categorization by means of overlapping similarities (family resemblances) as opposed to categorization by virtue of individually necessary and jointly sufficient conditions.

15. For an interesting discussion of the last two, *revelatory* and *transformative*, see Anthony N. Perovich Jr., "Innate Mystical Capacities and the Nature of the Self," in *The Innate Capacity: Mysticism, Psychology, and Philosophy*, ed. Robert K. Forman (New York: Oxford University Press, 1998), 213–30. For a nice discussion of the role of para-doxicality, see Gellman, "Mysticism," 3.2.

16. It should be mentioned that Murphy is no mere poser on this front. In fact, he cofounded Esalen, the famous institute and retreat center, in California in the 1960s. Its main function is to blend various traditions and disciplines with the goal of gaining some insight into the world and ourselves.

17. For example, one of the main current debates is whether mystical states are completely constructed from cultural influence, an argument called "constructivism," or if they arise from some innate capacity of the individual, an argument called "decontextualism" or "perennialism." For a discussion of this debate see Gellman, "Mysticism," 6, and Forman, *Innate Capacity*.

18. *The Natural* (1984), directed by Barry Levinson, DVD (Sony Pictures Home Entertainment, 2007); *Field of Dreams* (1989), directed by Phil Alden Robinson, DVD (Universal Home Entertainment, 2006).

20. For an interesting, personal, mystical approach to golf, see Bruce Hoffman's essay

"Baseball Zen," April 2006, http://tpqonline.org/zen.html. Hoffman points out that "baseball is infinite"—that is, there is no clock; the field, in a sense, is endless. He contrasts baseball with other sports, including golf, in which he finds a rival for "a certain boundlessness in space and time." Unfortunately, he then proceeds to reject golf as a sport.

20. I recognize that this topic deserves a much more substantial treatment and defense; however, that treatment would take us too far afield, given the topic of this chapter.

21. I am not including "focus" or "being in the zone" because they are common to all sports; but for an interesting initial discussion on golf and the zone see Tom Ferraro, "The Zone and Golf," *Athletic Insight: The Online Journal of Sport Psychology* 1, no. 3 (November 1999), http://www.athleticinsight.com/Vol1|ss3/Golf_Zone.htm.

22. Of course, I am not counting doubles tennis in this case.

23. I recognize that there are other possibilities as well, such as running or fly fishing (if that should be considered a sport), but they also fail to have some of the other components.

24. Ralph Waldo Emerson, *Nature*, in *The Collected Works of Ralph Waldo Emerson Volume I: Nature, Addresses, and Lectures*, ed. Alfred R. Ferguson (Cambridge: Harvard University Press, 1971), 9–10. I have to admit I find it nearly impossible to pass up the opportunity of sharing a phrase such as "transparent eye-ball."

25. James, *The Varieties of Religious Experience*, 340.

26. Ibid., 368.

27. This is not to claim that we are necessarily free in any strong metaphysical sense. I am merely using some of Sartre's views as tools for analysis.

28. Jean-Paul Sartre, *Existentialism and Human Emotions* (New York: Philosophical Library, 1957), esp. 15–25.

29. Jean-Paul Sartre, *Being and Nothingness: An Essay on Phenomenological Ontology*, trans. Hazel E. Barnes (New York: Philosophical Library, 1956), 580.

30. Alan Shapiro, *Golf's Mental Hazards: Overcome Them and Put an End to the Self-Destructive Round* (New York: Simon and Schuster, 1996), 25–26.

31. Sartre, *Existentialism and Human Emotions*, 23.

32. Murphy, *Golf in the Kingdom*, 25.

33. Ibid., 161–65.

34. In fact, one might highlight one of the significant differences between philosophical and mystical attitudes in terms of paradox. If a paradox is understood as a logical contradiction, then it is the philosopher's job to try to resolve that paradox, whereas the mystical attitude is one that often embraces paradox.

35. Thomas Merton, *Mystics and Zen Masters* (New York: Farrar, Straus and Giroux, 1961). See esp. 235–37 for Merton's discussion of these various terms.

36. See ibid., esp. 236, for the key points about *koans*. As a brief example of an actual *koan* (apart from the one everyone is familiar with: What is the sound of one hand clapping?), Merton (241) relates a story of the *roshi* Joshu, who was asked by a student, "Does

the dog have Buddha nature or not?" Joshu's answer: "MU!" Or another example related by Merton (235), in which a student named Ho asks the famous *roshi* Basho: "What is it that transcends everything in the universe?" Basho responds: "I will tell you after you have drunk up all the waters of the West River in one gulp." Ho: "I have already drunk up all the waters of the West River in one gulp." Basho then responds: "Then I have already answered your question." I hope this gives some sense of the teacher-student relationship and the often paradoxical nature of their exchanges.

37. Ibid. The discussion of Saint John of the Cross occurs primarily on 240–42; emphasis added in both instances.

38. Murphy, *Golf in the Kingdom,* 76–80.

39. Herrigel's book was originally published in German in 1948. My primary source, however, is Yamada Shōji's article "The Myth of Zen in the Art of Archery," *Japanese Journal of Religious Studies* 28, nos. 1–2 (2001): 1–30.

40. Ibid., 27.

41. Ibid., 10; emphasis added.

42. *Caddyshack* (1980), directed by Harold Ramis, DVD (Warner Home Video, 2000).

Midround and Midlife Defining Moments

Andy Wible

Defining moments in golf are often thought to occur at the end of the game: Larry Mize chipping in to win the 1987 Masters; Paul Azinger holing a bunker shot on the final hole at the 1993 Memorial tournament; Roberto De Vincenzo signing an incorrect scorecard to lose his chance to win the 1968 Masters; Jean Van de Velde's final hole collapse at the 1999 British Open. These last-minute heroics and disasters identify these tournaments to this day.

Our lives are different from sports events in this respect. We rarely define someone by what happened at the end of his or her life. We might regret the tragic end of a person's life or rejoice that the end was peaceful, but it is the middle of that life that usually makes the person. Earning a prestigious degree, giving birth to a child, marrying one's spouse, beating a disease, fighting in war, and heroically saving a person's life are often life-changing and defining midlife moments. Good decisions boost confidence and bad experiences often haunt for a lifetime. On second thought, golf is not that much different from life. A perfect shot can give confidence to propel a round, and a single chili dip can ruin an entire year around the greens. No place exemplifies defining moments in the middle of a round more than the par-3 twelfth hole at Augusta National. Masters Tournaments are alleged often to be won or lost on the menacing twelfth, even though it is in the middle of the round. A birdie or par will often spur a player on to victory, and a water ball leading to bogey or worse deflates a person's chances. For those who have never graced Augusta National, the results are much the same: the countless midround shanks, slices, chili dips, chunks, yips, water balls, and skulls on hard and even easy holes often affect the rest of the round or, in my own case, a good five years of golf.

Why do certain events in our lives, more than others, make us who we are? The answer to this question may be best answered by looking at more general philosophical questions of personal identity, such as "Who am I?" and the related "How does this continuous self persist over time?" In other words, how is it that I am the same person I was five or ten years ago, even though I have changed? I have different qualities from the ones I had ten years ago (I'm smarter and better-looking), but I am still the person who earned a philosophy degree at that time. So personal identity is not about having exactly the same qualities as in the past (often called "qualitative identity"); it is whether a person is one and the same person he or she was in the past (often called "numerical identity"). Just as a shirt can survive the loss of a button and still be the same shirt, a person can undergo many changes and still be the same person. On the other hand, some people will say that after certain events they are no longer the same person they were. For example, a person in an accident who suffers severe brain damage is often thought not to be the same person anymore. The person has changed so much that she is a new person in the same way that a club that suddenly receives a new shaft and head but retains the same grip is now a new club. Figuring out which properties a person can and cannot lose while still surviving is at the heart of understanding personal identity. This chapter will examine various theories of personal identity to help us better understand ourselves and how we should handle defining moments both in life and on the course.

Who Am I?

There are several theories of what makes me who I am and why I am the same person who ten years ago shot even par (yes, it was for nine holes). One answer that might come readily to mind is that I am what I do, namely, my job.[1] After more than forty years of selling shoes, my father is known as "the Shoeman"; Tiger Woods is known as "the World's Greatest Golfer"; and Joe "the Plumber" dominated discussion in the 2008 presidential election. A loss of identity is a common problem when people retire. Retirees often ask, "Now that I don't work, who am I?" Jobs certainly do contribute to one's sense of self. But jobs don't seem to get at the essence or core of personal identity. I am still who I am even if I change jobs. I may decide to be a realtor next year rather than a philosophy teacher, but I am still the same Andy. Outside factors, such as a job or one's family, shape a person, but they do not get at the heart of who a person is or explain how someone can persist through change. In other words, a job gives one a sense of identity by giving one the ability to describe one's self to the world, but it does not provide numerical identity.

One traditional theory of personal identity is called the body theory, which says that I am the one who shanked the ball out-of-bounds on the last hole because the body that is standing here now shanked it out-of-bounds. The same body makes the same person. Common sense gives support for this theory. We identify people by their bodies. DNA and fingerprints identify suspects of a crime, and the rotund body of John Daly helps us distinguish him from the ripped and debonair Camilo Villegas. The body certainly changes as we age. Remember that Daly was relatively petite when he won the PGA. In fact, over seven years almost all the cells in our body die and are replaced (and expanded, in Daly's case). This kind of change is acceptable, however, because the change is consistent with the type of thing a body is. The slow, gradual process of normal cell replacement keeps the body essentially the same. The slow change is similar to updating a golf course. If it is done in small increments, the same course remains even though over many years every hole is substantially changed.

The body theory does have its own problems. The philosopher John Locke (1632–1704) points one out using his idea of body switches. He imagines that a prince and a cobbler change bodies. The thoughts, memories, and desires of the prince are now in the cobbler's body and vice versa. The prince is in the cobbler's body. The guy who married the princess last week and shot three over par on his honeymoon is the person in the cobbler's body. Other people will think he is the cobbler, but he rightly knows that he is the prince. Personal identity is internal, not external—like one's body or other people's perceptions of it. Golf is telling here, for one's identity is often found to be internal on the course. The problem with the shank on the last hole is that I cannot get it out of my mind. I am the person who hit the shank, even if I disguise myself from everyone around me. Golf becomes part of our identity because of the mental effect it has on us.

The soul theory of personal identity overcomes some of the problems of the body theory. The soul theory says that I am the same person who played the last hole if I have the same soul, and it handles the body switch by saying that the prince's soul is in the cobbler's body. This theory was held by the French philosopher René Descartes (1596–1650). Descartes thought that I could doubt that this was my body, since I could be dreaming that this is my body and I am sitting at this table. Nonetheless, I cannot doubt that even if I am dreaming, I exist and have these thoughts of sitting here. Descartes then concludes with the famous saying "I think, therefore I am."[2] I have these thoughts, so certainly I am here. The soul is who I am and it is the "I": the constant subject of experience. The soul theory is a popular theory and of course has religious connections. It is popular largely because it supports the possibility of an afterlife: the soul lives on, after the body dies. People then say things such as "Grandpa is probably playing golf in heaven" (bodiless, eternal golf).

Unfortunately, the soul theory has its own problems. One problem is an epistemological, or knowledge, problem. How do we identify souls? Souls are immaterial, so they cannot be seen, smelled, or touched. I cannot know that I always have had the same soul, and we cannot identify the souls of friends and family. Yet I seem to know that I am the same person, and others do as well. We tend not to identify people by their souls. For all I know, I get a new different soul every minute that I am sitting here. The soul theory also has problems with switches. Suppose somehow my soul gets switched with Tiger Woods's soul, but my thoughts, desires, body, and memories stay the same in my body. My soul may be in Woods's body, but I am still here in my body. If the soul theory is right, then I should go wherever my soul goes. But I am still the same poor me, even though I have Tiger's billion-dollar soul.

What does seem to be essential to my identity is my memory. If the person in Tiger Woods's body can remember doing the things I did, then I am that person. Even in everyday life, I know that I am to blame for doing something wrong if I remember doing it. I remember choking and losing my final high school golf match twenty years ago. No one else knows the exact feelings that I had. With the unique memory of what happened twenty years ago, I am the same person who choked. John Locke was a significant proponent of the memory view.[3] He thought that the prince and the cobbler switch and the soul-switching cases are easily handled by the memory theory. Wherever one's memories go, the person goes. Locke even claimed that if one's little finger were separated from the rest of the body and one's conscious memories went with the little finger, one would now be in the little finger. Locke says, "It is evident that the little finger would be the person, the same person; and self then would have nothing to do with the rest of the body." Another philosopher, Gottfried Wilhelm Leibniz (1646–1716), gives the following thought experiment to support the memory theory.[4] Suppose that you are offered the chance to become the richest person in the world (Bill Gates or Warren Buffett today; for Leibniz it was the king of China) on the condition that all your memories will be washed away on transfer. Would you do it? Most of us would say, "NO!" The person in Bill Gates's body would not be me. My soul might be in Bill Gates's body, but I am not. If my memories are washed away, then I am washed away. Memories seem to define who I am.

The memory theory can help us understand why midround and midlife defining moments happen. There are events that we cannot forget and that shape who we are for the rest of our round or our lives. The reason is that we cannot get these experiences out of our heads. I am the person who "duck-hooked" my drive on the second hole and have pushed it to the right ever since. I am the person who made this terrible shot, and although I don't like it, the act is at least temporarily central to who I am. The yips seem to have the same cause. Negative thoughts of past bad chips or putts come rushing through a person's mind, making a normally calm person shudder in his spikes. Many people experience tragedies in their lives that they cannot forget. Post-traumatic stress disorder (PTSD) from war or the death of a child causes constant depression. Such events are indelibly imprinted on who we are. We are our present experiences and memories. The more vivid the memory, the more clearly I realize it was I who did the past act, and it makes up who I am. When there is no memory of an event, it seems as if it happened to someone else or it never happened. The end-stage Alzheimer's patient or total amnesiac does not remember any past experiences. Thus, we usually consider such a patient to be a new person by saying such things as "that's not Grandma anymore."

The memory theory does have its problems. First, even without Alzheimer's we often forget things that we obviously did. I forget what I shot on the eighteenth hole last month, but I am the one who played the hole. This problem can be easily overcome by including indirect memories. Indirect memories are memories I don't currently have but a former self (that I do remember) had. So, I remember yesterday's experiences, that person remembers the day before that, and so on all the way back to last month or further. I am the person who double-bogeyed eighteen last month (I checked an old scorecard) because I have an indirect memory of it.

Another potential problem is that we are more than our memories. Some people consider themselves to be different persons, even though they retain memories of their former selves. "Born-again" Christians are an example. They maintain that they have changed so much that they are now new persons. They do not have the devilish desires and interests of the past. The days of pornography, sex, drugs, and late-night golfing are behind them. Because they now love God and value sobriety and monogamous relations, they are new persons. Of course, we might question whether this is really true. The born-again Christian often talks about what *he* did in the past. He will say, "I used to drink, I used to fool around, but no more!" Thus, he is referring to his old self as identical to his new self. He has changed, but he is the same person, albeit now reformed. The objection is certainly right that desires and interests affect who we are, but our memories seem to be more central.

A final potential problem with the memory theory is that I could remember doing something that I never did. These are called false memories. Many people claim to have been places where, there is good evidence, they never were. Often there are photos, stories of others, and news events that all sketch past events that we seem to remember but that we never experienced. Friends might talk about an occurrence so often that you can feel you were there. Someone might say, "I kind of remember going on the golf trip to Doral with my buddies in 1987, but records show I wasn't there." False memories have other potential causes as well. A hypnotist might put apparent memories of winning the Masters in my head. I now remember winning, but unfortunately I have never even played at Augusta National. Thus, as is, the memory theory cannot be correct. I cannot get out of the problem by saying that genuine memories are of the experiences that I had, for that would beg the question by assuming the "I" of identity. Thankfully, there is a way out of this problem. We can modify the theory by bringing in what the philosopher Sydney Shoemaker (b. 1931) calls quasi-memories.[5] Quasi-memories are experiences that I seem to remember (the memory seems real to me), that someone actually had (they cannot be fabricated, like my experience of winning the Masters), and that were caused in the right way by actual experiences (the memory cannot be put in a person's head by someone such as a hypnotist or by hearing stories and looking at photos after the fact). None of these three criteria contains an "I," and hence the modified memory theory does not beg the question by assuming identity. The memory theory still is not a perfect answer, however. Either quasi-memories are really sneaking in identity by using the phrase "caused in the right way" to mean experiences I had, or quasi-memories allow for multiple people to have the same quasi-memories. The first half of the disjunct brings us back to the problem we started with, and the second half would allow many people to be one and the same person, which is impossible. Thus, we cannot be simply our direct and indirect quasi-memories.

Nevertheless, with the use of indirect memories and quasi-memories we seem to be much closer to understanding what makes us who we are. I am the same person who played golf the last hole, last week, last month, and last year, largely because I have direct or indirect quasi-memories of those events. The memory of hitting the ball out-of-bounds on the previous hole causes me to block it right on the next hole. Memories are central to who we are and have a great effect on our behaviors.

Overcoming Yips, Shanks, and Other Disasters

How should this better understanding of who we are affect these midround and midlife moments? How should we handle a double bogey at the twelfth hole or PTSD from the evils of war or rape? From our earlier discussion, it certainly seems that if we control our memories, we in many ways control who we are. One radical solution is to deny that there is any personal identity or continuous self in the first place. Any change results in a new person. The idea of a continually existing self is simply an illusion of the mind. Buddhists and philosophers such as David Hume, William James, and even the ancient Greek Heraclitus supported such a view. Heraclitus believed that we are like a river. We never witness the same person. We are always changing, just as it is impossible to step into the same river twice. Our thoughts, memories, and perceptions are changing just as the water in a river is always changing. In this view, a continuous self is a chimera.

Such a position might have some initial plausibility. If we change, how can we be the same? The more we think about it, however, the less credible it sounds. If there is no persistent self, then life will change dramatically. The credit card with my name on it becomes useless, for I am not the same person who signed the contract when it was received. Strictly speaking, I own nothing, because someone else bought it all. I also could lie and kill with immunity, for when stopped, I could just say, "It wasn't me." I would also lose incentive to practice golf. Why practice to improve when I am not going to be around in the future? The idea of a continuous self is necessary to the lives we live.

The good news is that we can learn something about how to handle midlife moments from such a position. Buddhists believe that much of our suffering in life comes from the idea of a permanent self. We are greedy and constantly plotting for the future, wanting more and more money, better and better golf scores. This never-satisfied desire causes persistent suffering. Buddhists believe that if we are to achieve enlightenment (unification and bliss) we should get rid of our belief in a permanent self.[6] We should worry about the present and not the future. Such an approach might be helpful when we hit a bad shot in the middle of the round. We should somehow forget about the previous shot and focus on our current shot. The memory of the shank on the previous hole can overwhelm our thoughts. Yet if I don't believe in a permanent self, then I did not hit the shot on the last hole. So I should not worry about the shank that someone else hit and should just focus on the shot at hand. Such a mind-set can also help when trying to complete a good round. Rather than focusing on what you need to shoot in the last few holes, you should focus on the moment.

One problem with the Buddhist approach is that if I get completely rid of my memories and ideas of a permanent self, then it certainly seems I am no longer there. If all my thoughts, desires, and memories are gone, then I am gone. Overcoming greed is one thing; getting rid of all notions of the self is death. Additionally, even if getting rid of bad memories is a good idea, hearing the advice of Buddhism and acting on it are two different things. We often say, "I try to think it was someone else who hit the shank, but I know it was I. I cannot get the experience out of my mind." Buddhism understands how hard such a mind-set is and teaches us that most people are born over and over again thousands of times before being able to drop notions of a permanent self. Now, thanks to modern science, we may be able to speed the process up a little.

The drug Propranolol is a beta-blocker that was developed to reduce blood pressure. The drug also has been found to have an interesting side effect. By slowing down the heart, it helps musicians and others who have stage fright. The drug can also assist a golfer by calming a racing heart and expunging the bad memories of chili dips and shanks that flood the mind. The drug inhibits the stress hormones that influence stronger and longer memories. The reason we remember big events in our lives, such as the first time we met the love of our life or scored a dreaded 8 on a par 3, is that adrenaline is flowing in these circumstances. Early studies have shown that when people take Propranolol after a traumatic event, they don't develop lasting stressful reactions to these events. The drug also worked in some studies long after the event when participants were instructed to remember the event or watch similar events and then take the drug.[7] People who took the drug said that the event that had been hounding their lives now seemed distant and almost as if it had happened to someone else. The result is encouraging for people with PTSD and possibly for some golf players: now, after a hole where a player shanks two wedges into the water, she can take Propranolol and will not be shaking in her spikes the next time she plays.

The player can control who she is and what type of golfer she is by controlling her memories! Propranolol affects adrenaline, which affects memories fundamental to our identity as persons and golfers. The drug changes who one is by quickly disconnecting those past memories. The drug will not make a golfer totally forget a shank; rather, it dulls the memory, which tends to happen naturally over time. Propranolol is just speeding the process. Time is often said to heal these types of wounds, and Propranolol heals in minutes. In the near future every well-equipped golf bag may have clubs, balls, tees, energy bars, and Propranolol.

There are some serious ethical worries that such a drug poses. Ideally, the best advice for all golfers is to have a better mind-set. We are often told, "Be like Tiger and don't let the bad swings get to you." Because people *can* do it without drugs, they *should*. Drugs like Propranolol, though, still have a case for being prescribed, since most of us don't have the talent and willpower Woods has. We should remember that beta-blockers like Propranolol are taken for high blood pressure. Doctors encourage people to exercise and lose weight to control blood pressure, and then prescribe billions of dollars worth of beta-blockers like Propranolol when patients are not able or willing to control it by other means. Patients should not have to suffer if effective treatment is available. The USGA and other governing bodies might claim that the game of golf is not synonymous with health and ban the drugs because they provide an unfair advantage to those who take them. But anyone can take them, and beta-blockers do not seem less fair than the painkillers that Woods himself took when he won the 2008 U.S. Open.

A bigger worry is that the drug will dull not just the bad memories but also the good memories. The special night that brings a smile to my face every time I think of it may now vanish. Or perhaps equally important, the perfectly crisp four iron on the par-3 fourteenth hole at Tippecanoe Lake Country Club, which resulted in a hole in one, might be forgotten. I like the fact that it seems like yesterday. That four iron is my favorite club. Good memories keep me under 90 from time to time and in general enhance life immensely. We don't want to partially lobotomize ourselves trying to get rid of a bad memory.

Even if the drug or future ones could act only on the bad memories, some argue that we should still not take them. The President's Council on Bioethics rightly says that we learn from our bad experiences. We remember that a stove is hot and don't touch it again. Memories that trigger guilt and shame sometimes keep us from additional immoral behavior. With Propranolol, the worry is that we will no longer learn from these bad experiences. The President's Council holds that there is a normal process of recovery and that drugs like Propranolol will interfere with this recovery and personal development.[8] Most golf announcers have said that the person who blows an opportunity to win will learn from his or her mistakes. The loss is good for him or her. So, of course, the President's Council certainly is right that we learn from our mistakes as much as from our successes; but some traumatic experiences are so bad that people's lives are affected forever. For example, untrained airline employees were made to pick up body parts after the 1978 Pacific Southwest Airlines plane crash in San Diego; as a result they suffered from PTSD and were permanently disabled. Others who have been raped, beaten, or shot have never been the same. In golf, Jean Van de Velde has not exactly been a force on the course since falling apart at the 1999 British Open, and Greg Norman's classic stumbles perpetuate their own existence by continually coming to mind. Propranolol seems to be a miracle cure for these cases. In fact, even if general use is unacceptable, guidelines could be put in place to make sure Propranolol is used only in extreme circumstances, like the restriction on narcotics for extreme pain.

Though the President's Council concedes that Propranolol is good for many individuals, it recommends that the drug never be used for such purposes. It suggests that there is a social obligation for people to remember and discuss past events, such as the Holocaust. We are doomed to repeat history if there are not these first-person recollections. These harrowing stories make for a better society. The criticism of the President's Council's position is a Kantian one. By keeping Propranolol from certain people we are unjustly using them for the public good. There seems something terribly wrong about saying to a Holocaust survivor that because what she went through is so bad, we cannot help her. Van de Velde's experience cannot be compared to those of such survivors, but it also seems wrong not to help him just because his first-person account can help other golfers. His foibles were caught on air for all see. Let him be happy. Let him have Propranolol.

Where do we go from here? We have learned that we should learn from the good and bad in golf and in life. All those midlife and midround experiences shape our memories and make us who we are. As for the ball that just went into the water on the twelfth at Augusta, we need to be introspective and improve ourselves. We should strive to avoid bad events and remember we are lucky enough to be at Augusta. We can also learn from Propranolol. The reason some memories are so strong is that they were accompanied by an increase in adrenaline. If we can calm down and stop the adrenaline, then we can ease the long-term worries. Good reasoning can help us evaluate what is good and what is bad. If we are prepared to deal with the bad shots, then we won't get so upset and ruin the rest of the round. Beyond golf, the same lessons can be learned. The untrained desk clerks and baggage handlers who picked up body parts after the crash did not know what to expect and were traumatized. Experts who knew what to expect and were trained to control their emotions should have done the work. Of course, this is all easier said than done. Buddhism teaches us that it will take potentially thousands of lifetimes to learn the right way to live. With better understanding of why memories are so central to personal identity and of how they work, maybe we can have greater control of who we are in this lifetime.

Notes

1. Al Gini, author of our first chapter, argues for this position in his book *My Job, My Self* (London: Routledge, 2001).

2. René Descartes, *Meditations on First Philosophy*, trans. John Cottingham et al. (Cambridge: Cambridge University Press, 1988), 80.

3. John Locke, *An Essay Concerning Human Understanding*, ed. Alexander Campbell Fraser (Oxford: Clarendon Press, 1894), 445–68.

4. G. W. Leibniz, "Discourse on Metaphysics," in *Leibniz Selections*, ed. Philip P. Wiener (New York: Charles Scribner's Sons, 1951), 340.

5. Sydney Shoemaker, "Persons and Their Pasts," *American Philosophical Quarterly* 7 (1970): 269–85.

6. The Buddhist notion is the opposite of the Western Judaic-Christian-Islamic idea of enlightenment or an afterlife. The Western idea is of a permanent self living on forever in some type of eternal bliss.

7. Scott LaFee, "Blanks for the Memories: Someday You May Be Able to Take a Pill

to Forget Painful Recollections," *San Diego Union Tribune,* February 11, 2004, www
.cognitiveliberty.org/neuro/memory_drugs_sd.html (accessed October 26, 2008).

8. The President's Council on Bioethics, *Beyond Therapy: Biotechnology and the
Pursuit of Happiness,* October 2003, http://bioethics.gov/reports/beyondtherapy/index
.html (accessed August 15, 2008).

FREE AND EASY WANDERING ON THE GOLF COURSE

Swing Like a Taoist

Scott F. Parker

One of golf's old saws has it that in every round you will hit one shot just good enough to bring you back to the course another day. The good shot will stick with you as all the bad ones blend together. You will start to think how good a round you could play if only you could string a few of *those* shots together. Vexingly, this kind of thinking may be the source of your frustrations as you struggle through another round wondering why you aren't hitting the good shots that you know you're capable of. If you are like many amateur golfers, you have a tendency to begin your rounds in excitement and end up playing much of it in frustration. Eventually, though, you will forget about how badly you think you're playing, stop trying so hard, and finally hit the shot that you've been waiting for all day. At this point in the round there are a few ways you can go. You can say to yourself, "See, that's how I should have been shooting all day," and get upset with yourself that you haven't shot that way. You can say, "That was great. I'm going to make sure to hit the next one just as well," which, you know from experience, you will not. Or, you can ask yourself if on that shot you did anything differently from what you had done the rest of the round. And you might notice that you weren't trying to hit a great shot. You were just swinging your club. On your next shot, you wonder, how can you try to not try?

These kinds of contradictions are at the heart of golf and at the heart of Taoism. Though its naturalistic and mystic influences date back to Chinese antiquity, Taoism as we know it today was first recorded in the *Tao Te Ching*, written around the sixth century B.C.E. Authorship of the *Tao Te Ching* is ascribed to Lao Tzu, but the text was written and revised over centuries. So too was the other pillar of Taoism, the *Chuang Tzu*. The eponymic Chuang Tzu is said to have lived in the fourth century B.C.E. It is believed that he wrote the first seven chapters of the book, the "inner chapters," and that his students and followers wrote the following fifteen chapters, the "outer chapters," and the final eleven, the "miscellaneous chapters."[1] Similar in theme, the *Tao Te Ching* and the *Chuang Tzu* are disparate in style. The *Tao Te Ching* is pithy and poetic, whereas the *Chuang Tzu* overflows with parables, dialogues, and fantasies. These contrasting styles are apt complements in elucidating the essence of the Tao: flexibility, adaptability, nonattachment, humility, humor, and harmony, among others. The discussion of Taoism in this chapter will be limited to these two original texts.

The lessons from Taoism that I will present are nonattachment to results, doing without doing, and self-knowledge or self-acceptance. To draw these out I will discuss four different passages from the *Chuang Tzu* alongside examples from golf. The reason for this structure is that Taoism is a philosophy of application, not of abstraction. Knowing a lot about Taoism is not necessarily to have any particular understanding of its meaning or usefulness. Rather, understanding is expressed in living—or in activities such as golf. The golf is here to provide exegesis for the *Chuang Tzu*, so it can be better understood, which is to say so that it can be applied—to, say, golf. But as we learn in the opening line of the *Tao Te Ching*, "The Tao that can be told is not the eternal Tao."[2] This paradox of the ineffable nature of the Tao that befuddles the analytic mind can only be transcended—not solved—in effortless embodied action. If you take up Taoism with the goal of improving your handicap, you've already lost the Tao. So what then is the purpose of an essay on Taoism, and how can you understand Taoism if even to try to understand it is to fail? Hopefully, we'll get to that. First, the examples.

Nonattachment to Results

You have been having a good round. Your drives have been landing on the fairway; your irons have been landing on the greens. Your putting has been consistent too. You've played most of the holes in par, gotten one birdie and a few bogeys. You are aware that you are playing well but not thinking about it too much. Instead, you are enjoying one of the first warm days of spring and the company of your friends. Just as you're reaching the eighteenth, your friend who is keeping score tells you that you are having an excellent round and asks what your best score is. You tell him that on this course you once shot 4 over par for the round. He says, "You ready to beat your record? All you need is a par. Bogey to tie."

As you step into the tee box, you start to consider your friend's words. You congratulate yourself on how well you have been playing and ask yourself to please keep it up for just one more hole. This is one of your first rounds of the year, and you'd love to get the season off to such a strong start. Maybe by the end of the summer you could play the whole round at par—as long as you make par here, or at least a bogey to tie your personal best. The one thing you cannot do is screw up your whole round with one bad hole.

Your thoughts are becoming preoccupied with success and failure as you address the ball. You think to yourself, "Okay, come on. Just one more good drive. Put it on the fairway. You can do it from there. Don't mess up. Don't hook this one." This *don't hook this one* is running through your head on your backswing. It becomes "Damn it. You hooked it" as you watch your ball leave the fairway and disappear into the trees.

You punch your next shot back onto the fairway and are hoping to save bogey with a nice chip onto the green. A bogey would be okay, you think. At least that would tie your record. "Just make sure to put this one on the green. And not in that bunker." Four shots later, after blasting out of the bunker and 3-putting, your friend says to you, "Sorry. I hope I didn't jinx you on that one."

"No," you say, "I just lost my focus for a while." Of course, really, you blame him and think that if he hadn't said anything you would have made par and been quite proud of your round.

At this point, if you are familiar with the *Chuang Tzu*, you may wish to reflect on the parable of the archer: "When you're betting for tiles in an archery contest, you shoot with skill. When you're betting for fancy belt buckles, you worry about your aim. And when you're betting for real gold, you're a nervous wreck. Your skill is the same in all three cases—but because one prize means more to you than another, you let outside considerations weigh on your mind. He who looks too hard at the outside gets clumsy on the inside."[3]

The archer's ability never changes; neither does the target. All that changes are the archer's thoughts about the target. But suddenly the target becomes difficult for him to hit. So too the eighteenth hole became more difficult for you, not because of your skills as a golfer, but because your thoughts about the consequences of your actions changed. On the first seventeen holes, when you were playing well, you were still trying to hit the fairways and make greens in regulation, but you were not concerned with the consequences of not making it. You were playing free-and-easy golf. It was only when you began to worry about not making it that your game faltered.

The *Chuang Tzu* suggests that nonattachment to results is the way to the results we desire. Some readers may want to see the causal connection between thoughts and actions better elucidated, but the paradoxes that Taoism diagnoses are not to be solved; they are to be dismantled by first continuing to practice, and then by making par on eighteen the next time you play *by not worrying about making par.*

Doing without Doing

Still drawing on the above scenario, we can perceive the Taoist concept of *doing without doing.* For the first seventeen holes you played well without trying particularly hard to play well. This is not to say that you were goofing off or unfocused, just that you were loose and comfortable. As soon as you tried so hard on eighteen to have a strong hole, you lost it.

As Ursula Le Guin notes in her rendition of the *Tao Te Ching,* "Over and over Lao Tzu says *wei wu wei:* Do not do. Doing not-doing. To act without acting. Action by inaction. You do nothing yet it gets done."[4] This cryptic notion is illustrated in the *Chuang Tzu.* Cook Ting is explaining the source of his butchering skills to the impressed Lord Wen-hui:

> When I first began cutting up oxen, all I could see was the ox itself. After three years I no longer saw the whole ox. And now—now I go at it by spirit and don't look with my eyes. Perception and understanding have come to a stop and spirit moves where it wants. I go along with the natural makeup, strike in the big hollows, guide the knife through the big openings, and follow things as they are. So I never touch the smallest ligament or tendon, much less a main joint.
>
> A good cook changes his knife once a year—because he cuts. A mediocre cook changes his knife once a month—because he hacks. I've had this knife of mine for nineteen years and I've cut up thousands of oxen with it, and yet the blade is as good as though it had just come from the grindstone. There are spaces between the joints, and the blade of the knife has really no thickness. If you

insert what has no thickness into such spaces, then there's plenty of room—more than enough for the blade to play about in. That's why after nineteen years the blade of my knife is still as good as when it first came from the grindstone.[5]

Cook Ting's excellence as a butcher comes from the effortless way in which he wields his blade. He does not fight against the ox in front of him, trying to force it to come apart the way he thinks an ox should. Rather, he follows the contours of the particular ox and lets it come apart in its own way. The knife in this case allows the ox to come apart in the gentlest way. *Play,* Chuang Tzu says. The knife and the butcher are playing together with the ox, like it's a game. This is how butchery is done well.

Consider driving a car: though not necessarily play (depending on traffic) it's not usually work either—you expend little effort getting from here to there. You can extrapolate the same lesson from golf. As the butcher cuts without cutting, so too a good golfer swings without swinging. For a good golfer the game is play, is a *game.* It is only when it becomes for him a responsibility that must be handled that it ceases to be a success. As soon as a golfer tries to *do* something with his golf game, the play will be lost, and the game itself soon after. To be like Cook Ting a golfer must think of golf as an ox. If he focuses on the whole round at once, he will hack his way through it. If he focuses on each hole, he will do better. If he can focus on each shot, this will be best of all. A golfer still comes to tricky situations, which require patience and reflection. If he chooses the appropriate shot he will see the kind of result Cook Ting sees when he is challenged: "Whenever I come to a complicated place, I size up the difficulties, tell myself to watch out and be careful, keep my eyes on what I'm doing, work very slowly, and move the knife with the greatest subtlety, until—flop! the whole thing comes apart like a clod of earth crumbling to the ground."[6] To fail to adapt one's game to the course, the weather, the lie would be like a butcher unnecessarily chopping through bone.

"The sage goes about doing nothing."[7] The golfer goes about doing nothing, just hitting the shot that's before him.

Self-Knowledge, Self-Acceptance

Many golfers have had the following experience. You want to prove something to yourself or your playing partners by driving a particular green that is just beyond your normal reach. You take a quick breath, bring your club back as far as you can twist, swing through the ball as hard and fast as you can, and, often, pull out of your follow-through. All you can do is hope the ball goes straight, which maybe it does or maybe it doesn't. What is more interesting is that attitude you have about the shot. It could be that the distance is just about the end of your reach, and you think to yourself that you have nothing to lose, so why not go for it? In this case, when there is nothing (pride included) to lose, the shot is for fun. If you don't clear the water, or hook it wildly onto the fairway of the parallel hole, it doesn't matter. You can proceed in your round without regret.

But if you are playing a competitive round, or have a lot of pride riding on the shot, you're in trouble. If you miss the shot—which more often than not you will—you might end up in a prideful struggle, hitting ball after ball into the water. Golf requires you to have self-knowledge of your strengths and weaknesses. With self-knowledge can come self-acceptance. If 150 yards is as far as you can control your drive, then your best game is going to be based on hitting solid 150-yard drives, not straining for 200-yard shots that are not there for you. You might recall that in winning the 2007 Masters Zach Johnson played the par 5s better than anyone else in the field (eleven birdies, no bogeys) without once attempting to reach the green in two. The *Chuang Tzu* articulates the same kind of acceptance. We have, for example, Master Yu:

> Dragging himself haltingly to the well, he looked at his reflection and said, "My, my! So the creator is making me all crookedy like this!"
>
> "Do you resent it?" asked Master Yu.
>
> "Why no, what would I resent? If the process continues perhaps in time he'll transform my left arm into a rooster. In that case I'll keep watch on the night. Or perhaps in time he'll transform my right arm into a crossbow pellet and I'll shoot down an owl for roasting. Or perhaps in time he'll transform my buttocks into cartwheels. Then, with my spirit for a horse, I'll climb up and go for a ride. What need will I ever have for a carriage again?
>
> "I received life because the time had come; I will lose it because the order of things passes on. Be content with this time and dwell in this order and then neither sorrow nor joy can touch you."[8]

Master Yu does not try to live his life other than it is. If his arm becomes a rooster he will start his day by it. Presumably, if his arm became a putter, he would not drive with it. A game must be crafted around the skills that are available.

In America we like to say that you can be whatever you want to be. While this adage can be inspiring, it isn't true. To take some unambiguous examples: we can't all be scientists; we can't all be movie stars; we can't all be on the PGA Tour. We have different abilities in all aspects of life: intelligence, charisma, athleticism, and so on, and no amount of practice can ultimately compensate for those inequalities. No amount of practice can make *everyone* as good as the best. The trick is to realistically assess your capabilities and choose your goals accordingly.

In golf, as long as you fail to accept your limitations, your game will suffer. If you try to force your game to be what it is not by hitting shots that you can make only once in ten tries, you will fail. It is foolish to fight against the world. How often do you see Tiger Woods hit the ball as hard as he can? Rarely. And he's the best player in the world, good enough to be able to do it. Woods's game demonstrates the flexibility of the Tao:

> A man is born gentle and weak.
> At his death he is hard and stiff
> Green plants are tender and filled with sap.
> At their death they are withered and dry.
>
> Therefore the stiff and unbending is the disciple of death.
> The gentle and yielding is the disciple of life.
>
> Thus an army without flexibility never wins a battle.
> A tree that is unbending is easily broken.
>
> The hard and strong will fall.
> The soft and weak will overcome.[9]

Remaining flexible in body and strategy allows the golfer to respond appropriately to the unfolding game. Stiff bodies and stubborn minds are broken on placid links.

Now, say you get lucky and make the low-percentage shot; it could set you up for future failure that stems from overconfidence. Again from the *Chuang Tzu:* "Don't you know about the praying mantis that waved its arms angrily in front of an approaching carriage, unaware that they were incapable of stopping it? Such was the high opinion it had of its talents."[10]

The mantis, perhaps drunk off previous successes with insects, fails to see the present danger for what it is. It lacks the self-knowledge to accept the situation. The analogy with the golfer is clear but does not go far enough. Even if the mantis recognizes its powerlessness against the carriage, it will still be helpless to alter the outcome—all it can do is wait passively to be run over. As a golfer, however, you have an alternative. If you can recognize the vanity of attempting a shot that is beyond your ability, you can play a different shot. This is the danger in making a lucky shot—you will want to take credit for it. Success in golf requires knowing the difference between your lucky shots and your skillful shots—it requires self-knowledge.

In golf you must know and accept yourself. Playing without both self-knowledge and self-acceptance will lead to frustration and failure. Everyone's game has limits, even Tiger Woods's—inconceivable as they are. Woods knows as well as anyone how to pick his spots and when to be aggressive, attacking easier holes and playing a bit safer on more difficult ones. You must be like Woods and, knowing your skills intimately, play your game accordingly. There is a distinction here between acceptance and resignation. There is always room for improvement and extending your current limits, but this shouldn't come at the risk of overreaching—as we can divine from the birds:

> There is also a bird there, named P'eng, with a back like Mount T'ai and wings like clouds and mist, shouldering the blue sky. He beats the whirlwind, leaps into the air, and rises up ninety thousand li, cutting through the clouds and mist, shouldering the blue sky, and then he turns his eyes south and prepares to journey to the southern darkness.
>
> The little quail laughs at him, saying, "Where does he think *he's* going? I give a great leap and fly up, but I never get more than ten or twelve yards before I come down fluttering among the weeds and brambles. And that's the best kind of flying anyway!"[11]

Knowing when to push your limits and how far is integral to self-knowledge.

To some the "forget results to get results," "do without doing," and "control yourself to free yourself" of Taoism are shallow platitudes; to others they are meaningless contradictions—in either case not real philosophy. The *Tao Te*

Ching and the *Chuang Tzu* are short on ethical edicts. Their metaphysical speculations are readily subverted to the Tao, which is not a metaphysical entity, but just what is. There are no arguments. Instead, there are parables and insights. They offer practical advice about life—a trite subject, I guess, to some, but one in our constant proximity. You could do worse than to figure out from a game or from ancient texts how better to handle your work, your thinking, your emotions, your relationships: your life.

The pieces of advice that I have picked up here are not exhaustive of Taoism, just a few instances that I think are instructive with regard to golf. Golf, like any activity in life, I have tried to show, can be at once the source of profound Taoist insights and an opportunity to apply those insights. The test of whether any of this succeeds is not if a clever argument can be raised against it. Clever arguments can be raised against anything.[12] The test is whether this is useful. So: Is it?

To answer this you must experiment, you must try to be with the Tao. But to want to be with the Tao, you must be away from the Tao. "You may imagine that you are outside, or separate from, the Tao and thus able to follow it or not follow; but this very imagination is itself within the stream, for there is no way other than the Way."[13] There are no easy answers, and I'm sorry, but on its own this essay won't do much for your golf game. If you want to improve, you will need to continue practicing your swing so your body will know how to make shots. And you will have to practice focusing your attention.

One of the fundamentals of Taoism is that our minds can distract us from our tasks if we let them. This is why you make putts on the practice green and miss them on the course. So you want to quiet your mind before your next shot (you know you'll do better). So you try to try to not try. But you cannot quiet your mind with effort—it's self-defeating. Instead of trying to not try, you must just not try. You've done this before, of course. How did you do it?

When you figure that out, you can forget about anything called Tao. "When a man has had his feet amputated, he doesn't care much about shoes."[14] All of Taoism emanates from the first lines of the *Tao Te Ching:* "The Tao that can be told is not the eternal Tao," harmoniously iterated in the *Chuang Tzu:* "Words exist because of meaning; once you've gotten the meaning, you can forget the words. Where can I find a man who has forgotten words so I can have a word with him?"[15]

What exactly do you think as you hit those shots that keep bringing you back to the game?

Notes

My thanks to Andy Wible. His feedback has greatly improved this essay.

1. *Chuang Tzu: Basic Writings,* trans. Burton Watson (New York: Columbia University Press, 1996), 13.

2. Lao Tzu, *Tao Te Ching,* trans. Gia-Fu Feng and Jane English (New York: Knopf, 1972), chap. 1.

3. *Chuang Tzu,* 122.

4. Lao Tzu, *Tao Te Ching: A Book about the Way and the Power of the Way,* trans. Ursula K. Le Guin (Boston: Shambhala, 1997), 7.

5. *Chuang Tzu,* 46–47.

6. Ibid., 47.

7. Lao Tzu, *Tao Te Ching,* trans. Feng and English, chap. 2.

8. *Chuang Tzu,* 80–81.

9. Lao Tzu, *Tao Te Ching,* trans. Feng and English, chap. 76.

10. *Chuang Tzu,* 59.

11. *Chuang Tzu,* 25.

12. Cleverest of all in this case is that both *clever* and *not-clever* are part of the Tao, are equal. The Tao is what is, is tautology, is meaningless.

13. Alan Watts, *Tao: The Watercourse Way* (New York: Pantheon, 1975), 38.

14. *Chuang Tzu,* 69.

15. Ibid., 140.

VII. Golf and Idealism

PLATO AND CONFUCIUS ON THE FORM OF GOLF

From the Real to the Ideal

Stephen J. Laumakis

The Global Context

Unless you are a Luddite[1] or spend all your time on the driving range, it seems indisputable that in the twenty-first century the trend toward globalization will continue and accelerate. It is simply impossible to deny that the world as we know it continues to shrink. Events in distant corners of the world have the power to produce almost instantaneous consequences in just about every other part of the world. In short, it is becoming increasingly more difficult to deny that the proverbial butterfly of quantum physics that flaps its wings in China produces thunderstorms in the middle of your round of golf!

This same trend is producing new and exciting opportunities for dialogue and discussion in all areas of human interaction, including economics, politics, religion, philosophy, scientific research, technology—even sports. These cultural exchanges are especially evident in the growing field of comparative philosophy and the study of world religions. In fact, more and more philosophers are beginning to recognize the value of considering philosophical questions and problems from various multicultural and global points of view. As I have noted elsewhere, the growing interest in research and teaching about world philosophies and religions is confirmed by the ever-increasing number of books published on non-Western thought.[2] It simply goes without saying that our children and grandchildren will need to know more than our traditional Western ways of approaching the world in order to survive and flourish in the latter part of the twenty-first century. One way of creatively instantiating this practice is to consider, through a thought experiment, how two philosophical giants of Eastern and Western philosophy would advise us about how to live our lives and even play a game such as golf. It is just this kind of thought experiment that I will attempt in this chapter. What do Plato and Confucius have to say about the form of golf and living a good human life? Is it really better to develop a "perfect" swing, like Tiger Woods or Ernie Els (as Plato would insist), or is it more useful to develop your own unique swing (as Confucius would claim), like Lee Trevino or Jim Furyk?

Two Views of Reality and Golf

Although it may seem odd to those who have some knowledge of philosophy to suggest that Plato or Confucius would have anything of value to say to us about either the nature of the game of golf or how to play it (the former because of his chronic problem with offering practical advice about anything, and the latter because of his concerns with more dignified human arts and his focus on how to govern the masses), I suggest that despite their apparent shortcomings, both philosophers have profound, important, and even useful things to say about how to think about and play the game of golf—as one element in the pursuit of living a good human life. As a result, the purpose of this chapter is to present a double comparison between an Idealist (Plato) and a Realist or Pragmatist (Confucius), and an Eastern and Western view of reality—especially as these views are applied to the nature, practices, and aims of the game of golf.

For the purposes of this essay I will be treating Plato as an Idealist (i.e., someone who is committed to the view that the ultimately real is the World of the Forms—the realm of the timeless, eternal, and unchanging patterns or exemplars—and not the World of the Senses—the realm of particular material things). I will begin by presenting his arguments for the existence of two kinds of realms of existence, and his claims about how we know both. I will then apply his distinction between the two realms to the particulars of the game of golf (i.e., the Idea of the "perfect" golf swing and your own copy of it; the Idea of the "perfect" round of golf and your own approximation of it; the realm of mathematical objects, such as your score and the manipulation of it with the handicap system). The second part of the chapter will focus on Confucius as an example of a Realist or Pragmatic thinker. That part of the essay begins with the blueprint for Confucian philosophy and ethics— the *Great Learning.* After focusing on his notion of self-cultivation, I will shift my discussion to the *Analects.* In discussing the *Analects,* I will talk about specific sayings of Confucius that seem appropriately connected to both the mental and physical aspects of human action in general, and then I will imaginatively apply some of Confucius's advice to the playing of golf. I will end the essay by trying to show that to be successful at the game of golf, one must somehow combine both realism (the Confucian approach) and idealism (the Platonic approach) to fully realize both the mental and physical aspects of the sport.

Plato's Views about Reality and Golf

One of the easiest ways to make sense of Plato's philosophical views is to think about them as a series of answers to some basic questions in epistemology—the area of philosophy concerned with questions about the nature, origin, and limits of knowledge: Is knowledge different from opinion? In what way or ways are they different? What are their respective objects? And how does one "know" this is the way things really are? To help clarify Plato's responses to these questions, it may be helpful to sketch briefly the historical context from which these questions emerged.

One way to think about Plato's views about philosophy is to think of them as emerging from a series of transitions in the ancient Greek way of thinking about the fundamental nature of reality and how one ought to live one's life in response to that reality. The first attempts to understand and explain reality in the West were offered by Homer and Hesiod, who tried to explain the natural events happening around them (e.g., life and death, growth, nourishment, and reproduction, as well as such phenomena as drought and flood) by appealing to supernatural gods. This religious method of explanation was soon questioned by a group of thinkers later known as the pre-Socratics, who tried to offer natural explanations of the same natural events. These first philosophers and protoscientists claimed that they had a better explanation of reality because their views did not depend on myths and stories but rather on arguments and evidence that were available to anyone. These thinkers (including Thales, Anaximander, Anaximenes, Pythagoras, Heraclitus, Parmenides, Anaxagoras, Zeno, Empedocles, and

Democritus) spent nearly two hundred years trying to figure out whether reality was one or many, permanent or changing, and ultimately known by the senses or reason or some combination of both. Their basic problem was that they simply did not agree on the answers to these questions. As a result, a new and different group of thinkers, the Sophists, proposed a fresh approach to the problems.

The Sophists, whose name means "wise," were itinerant teachers of rhetoric who not only charged a fee for their "wisdom" but also argued that the ongoing two-hundred-year disagreement among the pre-Socratics clearly showed that there were in fact no real or final answers to the questions they were wrestling with—so they advocated a kind of skepticism about ever finding the ultimate truth about reality. In addition, their travels to various towns and cities inhabited by people who held differing beliefs and practices helped them realize that one's views about reality are more a function of where one is from than instances of some kind of universal absolutes—so they advocated a form of relativism and insisted that while in Rome one ought to do as the Romans do, but when in Athens it is better to do as the Athenians do. This combination of skepticism and relativism led the Sophists to reject the pre-Socratic view of philosophy as the search for answers to questions about reality; instead, they claimed that the aim or goal of philosophy was to help one be successful in life by living a good human life. As a result, they shifted the focus of philosophy away from cosmological speculation about the fundamental nature of reality to more practical concerns about human affairs and how one ought to live one's life in order to get ahead and be successful—which they claimed both the ability and the "wisdom" to teach. It was as a direct reaction to this account and pursuit of philosophy that Socrates raised his famous questions about the meaning and purpose of life (the examined life, as he called it), and it was his student Plato who later offered answers to his teacher's questions.

According to Socrates, the good human life and living it well focus on the pursuit of wisdom (i.e., philosophy—from "philo," meaning love of or concern for, and "sophia," meaning wisdom), knowledge about reality, and care of the soul precisely because "the unexamined life is not worth living."[3] The good human life is not, as the Sophists suggested, about getting ahead in society by acquiring money, power, fame, political office, and material possessions. Consequently, it is useful to think about Plato's answers to Socrates' questions as an answer to his teacher's queries but also as a response to and critique of the views of their predecessors.

Understood in this way, the Platonic answers to these questions begin with a basic distinction between knowledge and opinion. The former is unchanging, objective, and universal, whereas the latter is changing, subjective, and relative to a particular point of view. The most basic difference between the two is that knowledge is unchanging, and opinions are subject to revision and change. Given that the world of material objects around us is characterized by the obvious fact of change, Plato proposes the following argument for the existence of a different and separate realm corresponding to the objects in the world of the senses as the appropriate objects of knowledge:

P1. If knowledge of objects in the world of the senses is impossible, then either there is no knowledge at all or there must be some other realm of existence that consists of the objects of knowledge.

P2. It is not the case that there is no knowledge at all (because if one knows nothing, then one must at least know that one knows nothing, which is a piece of knowledge).

P3. Knowledge of objects in the world of the senses is impossible (because its objects are constantly changing).

C. So there must be some other realm of existence that consists of the objects of knowledge.

This other realm is the realm of the Forms, or the timeless, eternal, unchanging Ideas or patterns (e.g., the "perfect" golf swing) that are the originals from which copies in the world of the senses are made (e.g., everyone's unique, particular swing) or in which the particular objects in the world of the senses "participate," and it is the realm of the objects of knowledge precisely because they are unchanging. It was from this realm that one's soul came into one's body, causing it to forget its previous contact with the Forms, and it is to this realm that one's soul will return after death or the separation of the soul from the body, provided one has studied philosophy, purified one's soul, and prepared by means of a philosophical life for the return to the world of the Forms. Those, however, who are interested only in the goods and pleasures of the body, and have not pursued wisdom through the study of philosophy, will be reborn, perhaps as a human but more likely as an animal or insect, on the basis of the kind of life they have lived. Such an outline is Plato's response to his predecessors and the reason for his belief in a separate, unchanging realm of the Forms as the source of and anchor for their account of reality and knowledge.

Although a full analysis of his argument and response is beyond the scope of this chapter, I think it should be rather easy to see how Plato's view of reality and our knowledge of it can be applied to the game of golf.

First of all, according to the basic features of his account, each object in the world of the senses is a copy of an original, timeless, and unchanging Form of it that exists in the world of the Forms. So, for example, every golf ball in your golf bag, whether it is a Titleist, a Nike, a Precept, or even a scruffy old range ball, is an instance or copy of the one, timeless, eternal, and unchanging Form of Golf Ball or Golf Ball-ness that exists in the separate and immaterial realm of the Forms. The same is true of your swing, your golf clubs, your golf bag, your tees, and any other objects you use in playing the game. Each of them is a copy or rough approximation of the one, timeless, eternal, and unchanging pattern or Form of it that exists in the world of the Forms. And we know this, Plato says, because the existence of the Forms is the only plausible explanation for *both* the existence of any particular material thing and the ultimate account of how we know what kind of thing any particular thing really is.

As Plato sees things, the only way to explain *both* how things exist (or more precisely are copies or images of their Forms) and how we know them (through preexistence in the world of the Forms and through recollection or remembering that is triggered by sense experience of the copies) is to argue for the existence of two separate and distinct kinds or levels of reality (which are nevertheless also connected by the mysterious relationship called "participation"). According to this distinction, the objects that surround us in the world of the senses are simply copies or knockoffs of their original and unchanging blueprints or patterns—for example, your swing and its relationship to the "perfect" swing—and these same patterns not only make the copies be copies by way of "participation," but also serve as the ultimate anchor for or object of our knowledge about particular things such as golf balls, golf bags, golf clubs, and swings.

These same metaphysical and epistemological views can be extended to whatever other kinds of things are thought to exist, such as games or rules, and various kinds of actions or qualities as well. This position, though, is not uncontroversial, because of Aristotle's criticisms of the theory and Plato's own worries about whether "things" such as hair, mud, dirt, and other vile things have Forms of which they are copies—though interestingly enough he does claim in book 10 of the *Republic* that there is a Form for a bed and a table—so artifacts, such as golf balls, clubs, and tees seem to be covered.

In this reading of Plato's view, there are Forms or exemplars for the rules of the game of golf and golf etiquette in the same way that there are both laws of this world and laws of the underworld. There are also timeless and eternal Forms for the game of golf and the various actions that constitute the playing of the game. In other words, there is a Form of golf and there is a Form of the swing, and a Form of the drive, and a Form of the chip, and a Form of the putt as well. And, at the very same time, as is evidenced by my own often frustrating attempts at playing the game, there are particular actions aimed at trying to instantiate these Forms that have varying degrees of success and failure. So, in the same way that Charlie Brown's Christmas tree is a rather pitiful copy of the eternal and unchanging and perfect Form of Christmas tree, my own golf game is usually both a poor imitation of the Form of golf and my swing is closer in form to Charlie's tree than it is to the Platonic Form more perfectly copied in Tiger Woods's or Phil Mickelson's swings. That does not mean, however, that I am not at least instantiating in some way, fashion, or degree some other Form related to the Form of golf, say, being a hacker or a duffer, and my wife and the other members of my foursome are usually the first to point out how perfectly and often I have realized that rather ignominious distinction. Yet even these kinds of failure serve a useful epistemic purpose in Plato's view of reality and golf because they not only indicate how far removed my game and its parts are from the perfect Forms of the game of golf, but they also help me and those who happen to be playing with or near me on the course to remember just what the goal or target of playing the game of golf is: not par, but the perfection of the timeless, eternal, and unchanging Form of golf. It's about trying to measure up to the Ideal.

Confucius's Views about Reality and Golf

When we turn our attention to the East and the philosophical views of Confucius, we are not only entering a markedly different culture and worldview, but also considering a fundamentally different approach to questions about reality, values, knowledge—and even the game of golf. To make sense of Confucius's views about the nature of reality, how we know it, and the various ways in which we might play our roles in it, I suggest that whereas Plato and the Greeks in general were interested in figuring out just *what* something is, Confucius and the Taoists and the Chinese in general were more interested in *how* to get along with one another and the world and the forces at work in it. Instead of thinking about living one's life or playing the game of golf as the pursuit of certain scientific knowledge that is based on the kinds of things and their natures involved (such as building a bridge or laying pipe using the sciences of physics, engineering, metallurgy, etc.), from the Chinese perspective one is to think about how one lives one's life or plays a game using the model of art and aesthetics and following the pursuit of harmony and balance (e.g., making a painting or cooking a meal in such a way that one's artistic and aesthetic sensibilities about what to do and how to do it are the standard of good practice).

One of the easiest ways to make sense of Confucius's philosophical views is to think about them as a series of answers to some basic questions in ethics—the area of philosophy concerned with good and bad and right and wrong actions, and more generally with how one ought to live in order to be the best kind of human person: How ought one to live in order to flourish as a human being? What kinds of actions help a human being flourish? Is there a standard or standards for evaluating human flourishing? If so, what are the standards for human flourishing and how are they to be realized in this life? These are obviously fundamentally different kinds of questions from those pursued by Plato, and their differences should prepare us for a different and unique Confucian understanding of both reality and golf.

We can think about Confucius's views about philosophy as emerging from and within the context of the Warring States Period in Chinese history. According to Confucius, the Warring States Period was caused by the failure of the Chinese people to live up to the standards of the great Sage Kings of China's past, who he claimed were the social and political leaders ultimately responsible for elevating the people of what was to become known as China or the Central Kingdom from their state of quasi-animal existence to the heights of cultured human thriving. What Confucius meant by this is that the Sage Kings were responsible for helping their subjects realize that their lives could transcend purely biological and animalistic urges for food, sex, and basic survival, and instead achieve a culturally enriched life of human flourishing that transformed eating into a banquet, sex into marriage, grunting and noise into music, and animal markings into works of art. He claimed that the root cause of the Warring States Period was a failure on the part of Chinese citizens to live up to the lofty social and cultural standards created and enacted by their Sage Kings and their choice to follow instead a path of petty self-interest and personal gain.

As far as Confucius was concerned, the solution to the Warring States chaos was simply to return to the well-ordered days of the past, when citizens cultivated both themselves (through their personal excellences or virtues) and their communities (through harmonious and generous sharing) by engaging in the appropriate kinds of ritualized practices and following the Tao, or "Way," marked out for them by their great social and political organizers and leaders—the Sage Kings and China's other cultural heroes and icons. In this sense, it seems appropriate to think of Confucius as an example of a Realist (as opposed to Idealist) or Pragmatic thinker who is always and everywhere concerned with getting along in the *here and now* in response to the particular circumstances in which he finds himself.

To help highlight and clarify Confucius's Realism and Pragmatism I want to offer a reading of both his *Great Learning* and *Analects* that shows exactly why and how he was concerned with the eminently practical problem that all humans face of figuring out how to get along with one another and the world and the forces at work in it.

Confucius's *Great Learning,* which is actually a short chapter from the *Li Chi* or *Book of Rites,* is best thought of as a programmatic outline of Confucian ethical advice. Its basic teaching is that self-cultivation—in conformity with the rites and rituals (*li*) enacted by the Sage Kings—"the ancients of illustrious virtue and excellence"—is the foundation for a flourishing and harmonious community and "the root of everything else besides." In fact, the teaching of the *Great Learning* moves from a macroscopic consideration of virtuous living at the level of the kingdom down through the state and the family (i.e., social morality), and ends at the microscopic level of the individual person who cultivates his or her excellence in his or her own heart, mind, and thoughts (i.e., personal ethics).

Confucius's *Analects,* on the other hand, is best thought of as a hodgepodge collection of practical sayings about how he and his immediate followers tried to live out the program outlined in the *Great Learning.* Earlier in this volume I presented the basic ideas of the *Analects—xiao,* filial piety or family values; *li,* rites and rituals; *yi,* moral appropriateness; and *ren,* the exemplary moral person and his or her morally praiseworthy actions—see the section "The *Analects* and Golf" in the chapter "Finding the (Fair)Way with Confucius and Ben Hogan."

According to Confucius, fully realized persons are filial (1.2), do their utmost, make good on their word (1.8), do no wrong (4.4), deal with difficulties (6.22), establish others in seeking to establish themselves, and promote others in seeking to promote themselves—that is, they correlate their conduct with that of those near at hand (6.30).[4] They also set their sights on the Tao, sustain themselves with excellence, and practice the arts (7.6). They do what needs to be done (7.30), and they continue to study without respite and instruct others without growing weary (7.34). They are self-disciplined and observe ritual propriety, or *li* (12.1); they do not do to others what they do not want done to themselves (12.2); and they are slow to speak and unrelenting in action (12.4). They not only love others (12.22), but are also firm, resolute, honest (13.27), bold (14.4), and not anxious (14.28). They study broadly yet are focused in their purposes; and they inquire with urgency yet reflect closely on the question at hand (19.6).

Given this description, is there any wonder why even Confucius himself did not think that he had made much progress in trying to live the life of an exemplary person (7.33), let alone consider himself a sage, or *ren* (7.34)? In fact, the key for Confucius was not so much the achievement of these states but the unrelenting commitment to pursue them—in the same way that excellence in any activity, and especially in a sport as difficult as golf, begins, continues, and is ultimately achieved only with the kind of unrelenting perseverance that Confucius himself and perhaps few others are able to maintain.

If we try to apply these Confucian ideas to the playing of the game of golf, I think we get a fundamentally different picture of the game from that suggested by Plato and his conception of reality. Instead of a clear yet more abstract model of a person who is concerned with living and playing up to an ideal standard of excellence and success that we get with Plato, with Confucius we have a richer portrait of a more down-to-earth, context-dependent, and situation-sensitive person, not so much one who is concerned with living and playing up to a transcendent absolute, but one who is a practical and pragmatic realist who knows through years of unrelenting practice and effort (and presumably failure as well) what is called for in the particular situations and circumstances in which he finds not only himself but also the others with whom he is playing the game and living his life. Such a person and golfer is clearly driven not by the goal of achieving some standard of perfection that is off in another world (e.g., playing the perfect round of golf), but by a desire to achieve harmoniously flourishing relationships that are both sensitive to all the nuances of the particular situation in which she finds herself and the result of the flexible yet unwavering pursuit of the Tao of excellence (e.g., a golfer who knows when to go for it and when to lay up and accept the consequences of a bad shot or less-than-perfect lie).

The basic difference between these two conceptions of reality and golf is that with Plato we get a crisp and clear picture of a philosopher-king as a golfer—one who looks to the eternal Forms as a guide to life and play, but also one who seems far removed from the muck and mud of divots and sand traps—like Tiger Woods when he is playing flawlessly. With Confucius, on the other hand, we get a more fine-grained portrait of a Sage as a golfer—one who is skillfully able to negotiate the changing and often unpredictable situations and circumstances he meets with the skill of a practiced virtuoso, or at least with the skill of a journeyman grinder—like Phil Mickelson when he finds himself in a trap with a terrible lie and is forced to try one of his unbelievable flop shots. The contrast could not be starker precisely because we have, in essence, what amounts to a rational, abstract, and pure consideration from the point of view of reason alone (Plato and the perfect swing) in comparison to a sensible, concrete, and mixed consideration from the point of view of lived experience (Confucius and those less-than-perfect lies). Though both points of view have their strengths and weaknesses, the question I want to consider now is whether it is possible to join them in a way that preserves the truth of each while simultaneously addressing their shortcomings. In other words, how does one join the pursuit of perfection with the necessity of playing your ball where it lies?

Integrating Plato's and Confucius's Views about Reality and Golf

One of the easiest ways to consider the possibility of integrating Plato's and Confucius's views is to remember that Plato and the later followers of Confucius already recognized the need to balance their respective Idealism and Realism or Pragmatism with some practical know-how (in Plato) and some stability in the face of ongoing change and unpredictability (in the Neo-Confucians).

Plato seems to have been aware of the obvious shortcomings of his Idealism because in the *Republic* he insists on practical training for those who eventually will become philosopher-rulers. Even though such people tend to want to spend their time in philosophical contemplation of the timeless, eternal, and unchanging Forms, Plato was wise enough to maintain that good leaders must also have some practical experience under their belts.

The later Confucian tradition also seems to have realized that the decidedly practical, real-world advice of Confucius needs to be balanced and anchored with the stability, reliability, and predictability of the timeless, eternal, and unchanging *li* in order to avoid the charges of relativism, and also to prevent the real possibility of abuse by leaders who could seek to justify any course of action simply by virtue of their presumed past experience.

Each of these responses, whether considered individually or together, seems to indicate both the recognition and necessity for balancing Idealism with Realism or Pragmatism, and practical know-how with theoretical insight and understanding.

Realizing the Ideal of Golf in an Ordinary, Everyday Round

When we extend this same integration to the game of golf, I suggest that it offers us a balanced, harmonious, and realizable form of advice about how to go about both thinking about and playing the game. On the one hand, there is clearly an Idealist or Platonic strain in the game of golf (with its rules and etiquette and its conception of par—which allows one to measure oneself against the golf course architect's vision of what one ought to be able to shoot on a particular course—as well as its handicap system that allows one to measure one's game, at least in theory, against anyone else's), and all those who have ever tried to play it know how much of a mind game it truly is. On the other hand, and quite naturally, playing the game also involves lots of practical know-how about what one ought to do in the face of changing circumstances throughout the course of any given round (e.g., Should I lay up or go for it on a par-5 hole? Should I use an iron for control and accuracy or the driver for distance and show?) as one tirelessly pursues the ideal of the perfect round of golf.

It seems fundamentally correct to suggest that one's pursuit of the Form of perfection and the perfect round of golf must be checked with the often painfully acquired yet eminently practical knowledge that the pursuit of perfection is and must be tempered with wisdom about the "rub of the green" and prudence about how bogeys, double bogeys, and the dreaded "others" are lurking just around the corner in the yet-to-be-realized context of one's very next shot. Such theoretical wisdom and practical knowledge, however, ought not make one shrink from the pursuit of excellence, as both Plato and Confucius remind, advise, and encourage us. So perhaps the best advice is to combine the wisdom of the West and the East. After all, the best way to play the game according to these two masters of the real and ideal is with an unrelenting commitment to the pursuit of perfection and the prudential wisdom that helps one recognize when one ought to go for it and when one ought to lay up and accept the consequences of an errant shot. In fact, as experience often teaches, sometimes the best shot is the result of a less-than-perfect swing—and if it gets the job done, that's all that really matters. Hit away!

Notes

1. Possibly named after Ned Ludd, an eighteenth-century Leicestershire workman who destroyed knitting frames, the name refers more broadly to anyone who is opposed to technology and technological change.

2. Stephen J. Laumakis, *An Introduction to Buddhist Philosophy* (Cambridge: Cambridge University Press, 2008), xiii.

3. Socrates, *Apology*, 38a (my translation).

4. All citations are from *The Analects of Confucius: A Philosophical Translation*, trans. Roger T. Ames (New York: Ballantine Books, 1999).

THE "IDEAL" SWING, THE "IDEAL" BODY

Myths of Optimization

Jason Holt and Laurence E. Holt

Movement is fascinating, especially when it is highly skilled, and most particularly in domains in which excellence in skilled performance is highly prized and even glorified. Golf, for better or worse, is one such domain. For the unfortunate masses—most of us—the golf swing is one of the most frustratingly complex and difficult maneuvers to master in all of sport. Wanting to improve one's golf swing, while hardly a desire common to all members of our species, is ubiquitous among those who play. The pursuit of optimal performance, making your good better and your better best, in such a game as golf is a natural and, within certain limits at least, laudable one.

So how do you begin the quest? You play, yes, and you practice, lots. Beyond that, you seek advice: lessons, books, magazines, those with the best "links cred." Their credibility aside, these sources rely, often implicitly, on a theory of skilled movement, a vision of what the ideal is and how best to bring your play as close to it as possible—in a phrase, how to optimize your swing. Ironically, optimization models currently in vogue in golf culture tend not to improve performance but to hamstring it, setting objectives that are irrelevant, or even detrimental, to golf performance and its enhancement. The ideal is a false one, and it derives from a naive theory of physical skills generally and the golf swing in particular. To uncover this false ideal and correct for it, we must engage in what may be called the *philosophy of kinesiology*, where kinesiology is the study of movement, and philosophy informs, as is the case with any discipline, its conceptual foundations.

Here we will focus on two not only incorrect but self-defeating applications of the concept of optimization to golf performance: the averaging model of the golf swing and the athlete model of the golfer, both of which are prevalent in golf culture despite a lack of sound support for either and a wealth of evidence against them. The averaging model presupposes, roughly, that the optimum swing to strive for can be found by taking a mean score of mathematical models of the swing characteristics among elite golfers, along with the corresponding goal of shaping all golfers' swings to that supposed ideal. The athlete model presupposes that, all else being equal, the better the athlete is, the better the golfer will be, and so prescribes various kinds of cross-training and general fitness conditioning intended to maximize the athleticism of the golfer. Underlying the simplicity of teaching and analyzing the golf swing in terms of a single ideal, not to mention the presumed need to legitimize golf as a real sport by athleticizing its competitors, is what appears to be an aesthetic bias against quirky swings and unathletic players, regardless of how successful either is even at the most elite levels of competition.

Against the averaging model we will argue for a multiple realizability view: that there is no such thing as *the* perfect swing for everyone, and different techniques will be suitable for different people largely on the basis of particular body characteristics (including neuromusculature). Against the athlete model we will argue that the moderate physical demands of golf make a general athleticism in golf of negligible if any benefit, whereas certain cross-training regimens can interfere with much more important factors and so detract from rather than enhance golf performance. We will diagnose the problem as arising from certain aesthetic biases, and then show how our perspective applies more broadly by examining the question of whether golf is really a sport.

Homogenized Technique

We all have some understanding of what a great golf swing is or at any rate what it looks like. We know it when we see it, however difficult if not impossible it might seem for us to achieve, and however unaware we are of the very complex physiological mechanisms involved. We know that the majority of professionals approximate this ideal swing to varying degrees, and the presumption is that those who are the better players, those who have better swings, are the ones who most closely approximate if not outright instantiate the elusive ideal: the fixed head position, the slightly inside-the-line backswing that stops parallel to the ground at the top and in line with the target, the inside-out path of the clubhead during acceleration, the path of the clubhead in direct line with the target toward the end of the down-swing, the smooth follow-through dissipating all unused kinetic energy, all in perfect tempo. We think we know, and observations of excellent players seem to confirm this. But beyond conveniently unschooled and, in both senses, partial observation, which tends to help us ignore or explain away recalcitrant evidence, what is the justification for this alleged knowledge of this alleged ideal?

Biomechanics is the subdiscipline of kinesiology that uses physics to ana-lyze and explain human movement. One of the key objectives of this and all branches of science is to formulate general principles that apply universally. This type of thinking continues to be the objective of many biomechanists when it comes to human physical expression in the panoply of many and varied sports. From this perspective there should be an optimal model for accomplishing the objective of each type of movement. A simple way to start the process is to observe and measure one or two examples of golfers who are agreed to have the best swing (the classic swing of, say, Ben Hogan or Trevor Immelman). Another way is to scientifically analyze a large number of top performers, and then average their scores on selected movements, angles, positions, speeds, and so on, and create an optimization model for everyone to follow.

As persuasive as many find such an averaging model to be when applied to golf, the unquestioned assumption of a single ideal swing, the perfect swing, is unwarranted. First of all, it is easy to underestimate the extent to which elite players depart, and with successful results, from the ideal, and these departures are not always easy to spot, and sometimes they cannot be spotted with the unaided eye or even with an unschooled eye with all the advantages of the latest slow-motion digital video technology. Elite players often depart significantly from the ideal, and their success level does not correlate with the extent that such departures are minimized. Take the fol-lowing artificial and abstract but illustrative example. Suppose that in per-forming some component of the golf swing, tour players achieve some angle of body parts between ten and twenty degrees. This does not mean that there is an ideal angle of fifteen degrees that players should aim for. Reasoning that such a statistical average, even among the best players, is the ideal for everyone, is simply fallacious. In this case, perhaps two very different but equally viable techniques are involved, perhaps warranted by two very different types of bodies. Given the varieties of elite players' swings and all-too-apparent variations in their body characteristics (unlike those in many other sports, in which elite play often mandates specific body types), we should expect to find greater variety than a single ideal would comfortably admit.

And we do. It turns out that the essential elements of a great golf swing are in fact rather minimal, though by no means easy to achieve reliably. Variations among swings are due not only to huge variances in body tissues, but also to the fact that many different types of actual ball contacts can result in the ball arriving at the desired target. Straight shots, fades, and draws of different paths from the same lie can all result in an excellent shot. The requirements are that all must be struck solidly, near the sweet spot, with the appropriate clubhead speed and contact angle of the face necessary for each type of shot. Slight variations in club path and clubface angle can, when applied correctly, be part of a repeatable and successful golf swing.

It is inescapable that so many of the world's greatest players on the professional tours do not have ideal golf swings. The great Bobby Jones had a sweeping backswing that at its top crossed far beyond parallel and past the intended line of aim. Most experts characterize this swing as old-fashioned, useful only because of the era of play and the equipment then available. But there is every reason to believe that modern clubs and balls would only enhance the effectiveness of Jones's swing, which would be helpful in any case to those with limited thoracic flexibility or lower back pain, for it minimizes torque of the thoracic-pelvic interaction. Walter Hagen was similarly successful with a wide stance coupled with a short, fast swing, a completely different approach from Jones's, and yet a very effective one. Ben Hogan's classic swing can be contrasted with Byron Nelson's shorter, more abbreviated swing with the noticeable downward-forward initiation of the striking movement. Both differ greatly from the Miller Barber swing, an upright, unusual series of movements and positions. The list of "deviant" swings would also have to include Doug Sanders, Lee Trevino, Craig Stadler, Jim Furyk, Jim Thorpe, Kenny Perry, Tom Lehman, Duffy Waldorf, and many others. The same type of thing has occurred on the women's tour, where many variations in rhythm, positions, and patterns can be observed. Of particular interest is the fact that these swings are unique to each golfer, and many who have tried to adopt the "ideal" swing have had difficulties.

Successful golfers have learned or fallen into a pattern of movement that works for their anatomies, kinesiological predispositions, and neuromuscular systems.[1] There are very few cases of elite golfers completely altering their already successful swings and equaling or surpassing their previous achievements. The hoopla surrounding Tiger Woods's allegedly new swing is particularly overblown. The alterations might feel like major changes to Woods himself, but analysis reveals that his full swing is basically the same as it was a decade ago.

The notion that there is more than one way to perform a certain type of action (more than one way to skin a cat) is a familiar one. The philosophical term for this, one that originated in cognitive science and the philosophy of mind, is *multiple realizability.*[2] To say that the optimal golf swing is multiply realizable means that there is no one physical manifestation, no single type of swing, that constitutes the optimum across the board. A Hogan-style swing might be optimal for Hogan himself but be an inferior option for Jones, who lacked Hogan's trunk flexibility, and for whom a Jones-style swing is far more suitable. The optimum, if it makes sense to speak of one at all, is nontransferable. The quirky, even bizarre variations among elite swings, as we mentioned, and the appreciable success of these players, given how far they stray from the alleged ideal, are perhaps all the evidence we need to discard the ideal as false. Of course, most swings are ineffective, so it is not the case that anything goes; but all swings that meet the speed, path, and clubface requirements for a given shot can be counted as being on equal footing, regardless of the movement patterns producing them. The important thing for golfers is to discover a swing that works for them given their particular body characteristics.

The Athleticized Golfer

Golf is no different from many sports that have seen a strikingly radical and potentially disturbing increase, almost to the point of fanaticism at professional and other elite levels, of extreme cross-training and general fitness conditioning that have little if anything to do with performance enhancement in the specific sport and sometimes actually compromise performance. In the best-case scenario one's performance is relatively unaffected, whereas in other cases one might well enhance some capacities at the expense of others that are as crucial, if not more so, to excellent performance in the sport. At worst, such conditioning, either inappropriate in itself or untowardly extreme, can directly cause or predispose body tissues to unnecessary injuries, whether unfortunate and temporary or distressingly chronic.

A number of fallacious inferences, betraying a sometimes merely superficial and sometimes hopelessly flawed understanding of the body and how to improve its skilled performance, are lurking in the background. One such fallacious inference is to reason that a certain outcome (say, driving distance) will be improved by increasing a certain basic physical capacity (say, strength), even though the athlete may already have an optimal level for that particular skill, that is, a level beyond which performance will not be further enhanced by increasing the capacity. Another fallacy is reasoning that other desirable capacities (say, flexibility) or outcomes (say, accuracy) will remain unaffected if not enhanced by increasing other capacities in certain ways (say, strength by lifting heavy weights). Yet another fallacy is to reason that an increase in one's general fitness will yield better performance in an activity like golf. One more fallacy can be captured by the slogan "More is better": if some conditioning is good, then more frequent, longer, and more demanding conditioning is presumably better, and the more demanding the better, even though there is clearly a point of diminishing returns beyond which tissues, worked harder and harder still, eventually break down.

The physical requirements necessary to play golf at a very high level are modest indeed. A player has to be able to walk a few miles at a slow to moderate pace, stop to strike the ball, and wait for others to do the same. The most vigorous part of any round is ball striking (propulsive phase, the downswing), which takes about half a second each time. For elite players this means about thirty-six strokes and eighteen seconds of dynamic movement per round. Strokes like putting and chipping require precision and very little energy. Each round is also played without the burden of carrying one's clubs, since this is not mandated by the rules. Elite players and wealthy amateurs have caddies who not only carry the clubs, bag, umbrellas, and other paraphernalia, but also keep the players covered when it rains and clean the equipment as needed. The rank and file often uses either golf carts, which carry both the players and their equipment, or power or push caddies, which eliminate the need to carry the clubs and continually pick up the bag and put it down for each shot.

To function effectively, golfers need to maintain a walking regimen, preferably on mixed terrain to mimic most traditional courses, and swing golf clubs enough to maintain the dynamic flexibility of their musculoskeletal systems. Running, cycling, or other forms of aerobic training are not necessary, and excessive amounts might be detrimental, as they can result in diminished flexibility, particularly in the hip and knee joints, which can alter the full golf swing by placing tension on the shortened muscles earlier in the movement pattern, thereby altering the swing mechanics. Another problem associated with running (though not cycling) is the possibility of injuring the lower limbs as a result of excessive accumulative forces being absorbed during each landing. An interesting interaction can occur when one puts together a heavy weight-training program with a running program, in that the added upper-body muscle bulk compounds the loading problem at foot contact and may lead to ankle, knee, or hip joint injuries or, in the case of Tiger Woods, stress fractures in the tibia.

The world's most famous athlete, who has taken the "cult of conditioning" to extremes, might be the best example of why concentrating on this aspect of preparation for golf is unnecessary.[3] Tiger Woods was a superb golfer at age twenty, capable of taking on and beating the best players in the world. At six-foot-two and 160 pounds, he could generate 120-mile-per-hour clubhead speeds and hit drives of great length, and he had the other subtle golf skills that make for great play. He won his first Masters title by twelve strokes, and he did it with a basically lean (ectomorphic) and relatively unconditioned body. He continued to win at an astounding rate, even as he experimented with stroke adjustments, changed caddies, and then embarked on his extensive nonspecific exercise program. The reason for his successes lies in his nervous system; he has the right neuromuscular circuitry to run great golf programs, and he can call them up when needed. But over the past few years, although Tiger's fitness scores have been high, he has not produced his "A" game as often as he did in the past; his wins are often accomplished by struggling against various opponents, and his margins of victory have been narrow. Arguably, rather than improving Tiger's game, excessive concentration on fitness and conditioning has actually detracted from it, even though he has continued to win.[4] Woods missed half the 2008 season owing to injuries suffered preparing for and exacerbated during the U.S. Open, as he had to recover from anterior cruciate ligament (ACL) surgery on his knee and heal his stress fractures. There is no plausible way to attribute these injuries to playing golf.

The further benefits that are touted to accrue from adding a vigorous fitness and conditioning program to one's preparation did not seem to be realized when Woods met Darren Clarke for the finals in match play a few years ago (before any fitness efforts by Clarke). Instead of the unconditioned

Clarke's gradually becoming less effective as the thirty-six-hole match progressed, and Woods's finely tuned athletic body keeping up the pace and wearing down his opponent, Clarke went on to win the match rather easily. Of course, the reason is that Clarke hit better shots on that day, and that is what counts. On any given day, heavyset tour players like John Daly, Tim Herron, Jason Gore, and Rocco Mediate, or lighter, thinner players like Charles Howell, Jeff Sluman, and Sean O'Hair, can outplay Woods and the rest of the field. Even that player whom Woods is chasing, Jack Nicklaus, won most of his titles with what may be labeled by fitness gurus as a less-than-athletic physique. No matter: his skills, physical and mental, were unmatched during his competitive period. Nicklaus winning the Masters at age forty-six and Tom Watson missing winning the Open in his *sixtieth* year by *one putt* illustrate this point to a tee. The capacity to play top-level golf thus seems to be related more to having the high level of skills needed to stroke the ball effectively, a capacity to execute these skills under pressure, and the ability to deal with interferences (bad weather, play stoppages, and the like) that are par for the course in the beautiful game of golf.

Aesthetic Biases

There is nothing wrong with aesthetic preferences, in liking some things more than others because they are more beautiful, elegant, graceful, and so on. Indeed, it is hard to imagine how we could even begin to go about uprooting aesthetic preferences from our thinking, so interwoven are they with our choices, motives, judgments, and values. There is nothing wrong with making aesthetic judgments about a wide variety of things. In matters of purely personal taste, for instance, it seems that anything goes; you find something lovely and I do not: *chacun à son goût*, to each his own. In other domains, however, there seem to be more objective standards for what counts as exhibiting some aesthetic property. In such aesthetic sports as figure skating, diving, and gymnastics there are judicable facts of the matter about, for example, whether athletes maintain or break form and so achieve or fail to achieve the requisite aesthetic standard. In fact, the meeting of such standards is an integral part of the scoring of such events.

Even in purposive sports, where the scoring is in no way based on or affected by aesthetic achievements, praising graceful or stylish performance is often appropriate and perhaps even unavoidable. How else did Ernie Els earn the nickname "The Big Easy" but with a swing that few would hesitate to call beautiful? Generally speaking, great players in purposive sports often exhibit aesthetic properties like grace, elegance, and style, and nothing is amiss in our praising them for it. Something is amiss, however, when we blame a successful player in a sport like golf, even subtly by innuendo or lightheartedly by joke, for failing to perform with the sort of grace or style exhibited by other players, and this is not just because such performative beauty is supererogatory, above and beyond the call of duty. Such criticism is also amiss because it smuggles in the questionable concept of the ideal swing. Put the other way round, part of the implicit justification for and lingering appeal of the false ideal of the perfect swing appears to be a latent, unnecessary, potentially misleading, and decidedly aesthetic bias. Without question, the averaging model provides an attractive simplicity when it comes to commentary, criticism, and teaching of the golf swing. But this does not warrant negative judgments about the quirky or "ugly" swings of a Trevino or Furyk. We should at least bracket our traditionally minded aesthetic judgments about such departures from the norm of the alleged ideal so that these judgments do not infect truly germane discussion. (Sometimes aesthetic discussions are relevant, sometimes not.) Or better still, we should guide our aesthetic sensibilities toward a more pragmatic, pluralistic outlook, so as to be able to recognize the functional beauty in the quirky and the classic swings alike.

There seems to be a similar though differently motivated aesthetic bias underlying the athlete model of the golfer, and here the bias's aesthetic nature might be more readily apparent. Athletic-looking bodies are attractive, aesthetically pleasing. Most of us want such bodies, and many of us feel a need to see athletes not only *be* athletic but also *look* athletic. We tend, *à la* the ancient Greeks, to associate the physical excellence we admire in athletes with the physical beauty we want them to have, a sort of virtue by association. From this viewpoint, the phenomenon of a Babe Ruth in baseball or a John Daly in golf is difficult to take. The motivation for this aesthetic bias in golf is plausibly and in part a perceived need, from the perspective of players who want to be regarded as genuine athletes or fans or others who want them to be so regarded, to cement the status of the game as a legitimate, bona fide, fully fledged sport. The odd presumption seems to be that the more closely golfers resemble athletes in other sports (the classically athletic bodies prevalent in decathlon and gymnastics, defensive backs in football, and the lighter weight classes in boxing), the more we will be drawn toward admitting golf as a real sport.

Other Sports

Tendencies toward homogenized technique, undue athleticization, and aesthetic biases are often also found in other sports. Wider application of our multiple-realizability and activity-specific perspective on physical skill is more significant than its narrower if still important application to the domain of golf alone. Thus, to move from what we have said about golf and generalize to other sporting domains, it will be useful to examine briefly the essential nature of sport.

By drawing on and modifying various definitions of sport that already exist in the philosophy of sport literature, we may define sports, provisionally, as *competitive games of inclusively gross physical skill*.[5] Qualifying sports as competitive games distinguishes them from activities, even vigorous physical activities, that intuitively do not count as sport by virtue of being noncompetitive; outdoor team-building activities, for instance, and so-called cooperative games are not sports. Sports are games in that they consist in what Bernard Suits describes as "the voluntary attempt to overcome unnecessary obstacles," these obstacles, like the games themselves, being defined by the rules.[6] We include the requirement that sports must involve not only physical skill but, crucially, gross physical skill to distinguish them from contests that require merely fine motor skills, that is, those that do not involve the movement or control of the entire body. Games of pickup sticks and guitar duels are not sports, because although they do require physical skills, they involve not gross motor skills but fine motor skills. Sports, by contrast, necessarily involve skilled movement or control of the entire body.[7]

Although it differs from many other sports in important ways, golf meets such a definition of sport, since it is a competitive game of inclusively gross physical skill, the skill required involving the movement and control of the entire body to participate in the activity. Those who would resist classifying golf as a sport no doubt at least implicitly think that all sports require, as many indeed do, great degrees of bodily strength, speed, or endurance. Though such basic physical capacities, in isolation or in combination, are required for many sports, this frequency should not mislead one into thinking that it is a necessary condition for sport that a game place extreme physical demands on those who play it. Counterexamples abound, including bowling, billiards, croquet, darts, shooting competitions of all types, archery—and golf. With the exception of a few moments of sprinting, baseball and softball players also have few physical demands placed on them (pitchers and catchers excepted); the same is true of cricket. Despite the selective importance of strength, speed, and endurance in many sports, what counts most of all in classifying a game like golf as a sport is the presence or absence of gross physical skill.

Because golf and certain other activities count as low-demand sports, we cannot generalize from the mild physical demands of golf to the physical requirements of high-demand sports. We can, however, generalize from the multiple realizability of the golf swing to the nature of skills in other sports, especially those that involve very complex movements like the golf swing. We can also make the reasonably confident claim that sport-specific conditioning should always take priority over general conditioning or cross-training when the goal is improved performance in that particular sport and not, among other possible goals, overall fitness or athleticism. Even in the latter case, it should be noted, extreme training is rarely if ever warranted—and excessive training, never.

As the physical demands in a sporting activity diminish, the potential for variations in bodies increases, as does the opportunity for different patterns of movement. Interestingly, more variations of movement patterns exist when striking or throwing light objects, and less when throwing heavier objects. The idea of multiple realizability, of the possibility for success in a sport resulting from diverse approaches to technique, is based on obvious differences that have evolved in the form and function of individuals within our species. Where a sport both involves the performance of a required set of skills and is judged on its aesthetic qualities, multiple realizability is possible, although judging attitudes often place constraints on the diversity of patterns that will be acceptable, as is true in figure skating, gymnastics, diving, and dance.

A philosophy of skilled human movement must be sensitive to the various ways in which skills can be performed, what the performance of those skills actually requires, and variations among the bodies performing those skills. Pursuing optimal performance must not gloss over these varieties, from body characteristics to skills types and means of execution. At the same time, attempts to optimize performance should not be infected by overtraining or inappropriate cross-training or general fitness conditioning, which will at best leave performance unaffected and at worst be extremely counterproductive. False theories of skilled movement, together with the fallacies that subtend them, must be abandoned on pain of undermining the very goal at which they aim. Achieving the optimum, in golf as in life, requires an awareness of what really matters, hand in glove with a sensitivity to differences among people and ways of getting things done.

Notes

Special thanks to Andy Wible for patient encouragement and helpful suggestions. Thanks also to two anonymous reviewers for useful questions.

1. An anonymous reviewer has suggested the possibility that elite players with unorthodox swings have managed to develop compensatory skills for departing from fundamentals, whereas this would not be practical for golf instructors teaching players who lack the time required to develop such mechanisms. We, however, are offering an alternative account of what the fundamentals are. And as for practicality, approximately 80 percent of the population lacks sufficient thoracic flexibility for anything like the ideal backswing.

2. For an earlier application of the concept of multiple realizability to golf, see Laurence E. Holt, *An Experimenter's Guide to the Full Golf Swing* (Lantz, N.S.: Aljalar, 2004), 9–11.

3. Lorne Rubenstein, "Are Tiger's Injuries Self-Inflicted?" *Globe and Mail*, July 12, 2008, S5.

4. Note the irony of the apparent decrease in clubhead velocity generated by tour players, including Tiger Woods, despite recent significant strength gains. For discussion of Dick Rugge's study, see Thomas Maier, "Golf Players Stronger, but Swing Speeds Down?" *Newsday*, June 20, 2009.

5. Elements of this formula may be found in John W. Loy Jr., "The Nature of Sport: A Definitional Effort"; Bernard Suits, "Tricky Triad: Games, Play, and Sport"; and Klaus V. Meier, "Triad Trickery: Playing with Sports and Games," all in *Philosophy of Sport: Critical Readings, Crucial Issues,* ed. M. Andrew Holowchak (Upper Saddle River, N.J.: Prentice-Hall, 2002), 20, 30, and 40, respectively.

6. Bernard Suits, *The Grasshopper: Games, Life and Utopia* (1978; rept., Peterborough, Ont.: Broadview, 2005), 55.

7. An anonymous reviewer has suggested that the game Twister might be a counterexample to our definition of sport, since intuitively Twister is not a sport, and yet it seems to meet our conditions for sport (as a game involving gross physical skill). Twister involves positioning of the body and requires some flexibility, but gross physical skill implies dynamic motion to achieve a specific outcome, not merely holding a contorted position. Likewise, in Twister chance figures too largely in the determination of outcomes—it is more a game of chance involving skill than a game of skill per se. Sports, by contrast, are games *of* gross physical skill, in which chance may figure not too prominently. The *inclusively* in our definition is meant to allow other outcome determiners, such as strategy and fine motor skills, so long as these do not unseat gross physical skill from its privileged position.

VIII. Golf and Meaning

GOLF AND THE MEANING OF LIFE

Randy Lunsford

In May 2008, at the age of thirty-seven, Annika Sorenstam stunned the golf-ing world by announcing her retirement from the LPGA Tour. Even some of the players close to her were surprised at the news, as the announce-ment came in the prime of her golfing career. In just the previous weekend, at the Michelob Ultra Open in Williamsburg, Virginia, she finished play at 19 under par, winning the tournament by 7 strokes. Her list of career achievements is impressive. The seventy-two career tournament victories are third on the all-time list behind Kathy Whitworth and Mickey Wright, and her ten career majors place her fourth. She was named player of the year a record eight times, five of those from 2001 through 2005. During that five-year stretch she dominated women's golf, posting forty-three tournament victories and finishing in the top three nearly 70 percent of the time. In 2001, in the second round of the Standard Register Ping in Phoenix, she shot the lowest round in LPGA history, a 13-under-par 59. Upon hearing of her decision to retire, Tiger Woods was moved to call her the greatest female golfer of all time, adding that it was sad to see her walk away from the game. This invites the question, "What caused Soren-stam to walk away from golf?" Her initial response provides some clues: "You start thinking, 'What else is more important in life, and what else do I want to achieve on the golf course?'"[1] For her, playing competitive golf was apparently no longer a meaningful activity. This quite naturally leads one to wonder, "What is it that makes playing golf meaningful?" As it turns out, answering this question takes us a long way toward answering the age-old philosophical question "What is the meaning of life?" In this chapter I discuss some of the meaning-conferring attributes of the game of golf and in the process draw parallels to corresponding characteristics that make for a meaningful life.

What, then, is the meaning of golf? At first blush it might seem a bit odd to ask such a question. It should be fairly obvious. Golf is a game, and as such it is an activity that is designed to be engaged in with others for the purpose of entertainment. It is also a competitive endeavor: the goal is to win. Players compete against themselves or against others by following a given set of rules. Using special clubs with long shafts, players attempt to sink a very small ball into a distant, very small hole, in as few strokes as possible. This type of answer speaks to the nature and purpose of golf. The same kind of answer could be given in response to questions regarding the meaning of life, such as "Where did we come from?" or "Why are we here?" Unlike the single purpose of the game of golf, however, there are at least two possible answers to the question of life's purpose: one is provided by Western religion, and one is provided by science.

The Western religious answer goes something like this. Human beings were created by God, and our purpose is to love God, to accept the teachings of scripture as the word of God, and to conduct our lives in a way that is consistent with the prescriptions in those teachings. The ultimate aim of our earthly existence is to prepare ourselves for spending eternity with God. This answer aims to provide objective meaning because meaning and purpose are supposed to exist independent of us, having been assigned to us by God.

The scientific answer goes something like this. The universe was created some 14 billion years ago in an initial event known as the "Big Bang." In the aftermath of this original occurrence, the universe began to expand and cool, forming dense clumps of matter that eventually became the galaxies, the stars, and the planets. On our particular planet, the primordial seas responded to energy from the sun to create the building blocks of life. Eventually, through the processes of mutation and natural selection, ever more complex organisms developed, culminating in the life forms present on the planet today. Since the universe was apparently not designed with some ultimate purpose in mind, this answer offers no objective meaning to life.

Because of this deficiency, many have found the scientific answer impossible to accept. The author Leo Tolstoy became suicidal at around age fifty when he came to believe that, without meaning in the objective sense, life is not worth living. He found himself faced with a dilemma: to accept religious faith would have amounted to a denial of reason; on the other hand, to reject religious faith would have meant for him a denial of life. His final solution was to choose faith. But for many the denial of reason represents far too great a sacrifice.

Tolstoy's predicament notwithstanding, many are able to find meaning in life whether or not it includes the objective meaning or purpose that religion claims to provide. Whether in the absence of religion or as complement to it, we are able to find meaning in many values we hold in common. We value interesting work, being helpful to others, fostering enduring relationships with family and friends, appreciating beauty and art, engaging in entertaining pastimes, and so on. So whether we choose to adopt the constraints of the religious framework or not, our lives may be made more meaningful or less meaningful depending on how we choose to live.

Golf tends to work the same way. The game may be said to be objectively meaningful simply because it was designed for a particular purpose. All who play the game by the rules fulfill this objective purpose. But there is much more to the game of golf than just following the rules. For example, one thing that makes golf meaningful is that it is an activity that we *desire* to do. Obviously, those who have no desire to play will find the activity much less meaningful than those who freely choose to play because it is something they want to do. I remember one occasion when I was having a terrible time on the course; I wasn't focused on the game, was playing terribly, and subsequently became frustrated and angry. I had not yet learned to cope with my emotions on the golf course. Consequently, neither I nor the rest of my foursome were enjoying my presence on the course. Once I stepped back and took stock of the situation, I realized that I had completely lost my desire to play on that particular day, and that I wasn't doing myself or anyone else any good by remaining on the course. The game, at least on that particular day, had lost all meaning for me because I no longer had the desire to play.

The same is true in life in general. For the most part, we find our lives meaningful if we are doing, within certain limits, what we want to do. Obviously, we are not free to do as we wish if it involves a careless disregard for the well-being of others. But within the framework of societal constraints, our present set of desires would seem to serve as the foundation for the pursuit of a meaningful life. Our task is only to recognize those desires and then to work to satisfy them. In this instance meaning is subjective, in the sense that it will vary from one person to the next depending on a person's existing set of desires.

But is the satisfaction of desire really all there is to living a meaningful life? The philosopher E. J. Bond takes exception to this idea:

I remember being puzzled, as an undergraduate, when my professor and my fellow students all seemed to accept without question that only moral considerations stood in the way of doing what one pleased, and that otherwise there was nothing problematic about the pursuit of ends. One simply had desires for certain things. . . . I was certainly the odd-man-out, for I did not have any such set of wants (except the obvious appetites of course) and did not know what to do with my life. I wanted to find out what was of value, what goals were genuinely worth pursuing, before I could formulate a "rational life plan," and that required something more than consultation of my already existing desires or "concerns" or speculation about any future ones.[2]

For Bond the object of one's desires makes all the difference. What is important is to discover those things that are *worth* desiring. He argues that there are certain objects in the world that have value whether or not there is anyone who actually values them. The idea is that meaning is not subjective; it is not relative to each of us as individuals, depending on our own particular set of preferences or wants. It is the case, rather, that there are things in the world that have meaning for anyone because of their *inherent* value. Such things are said to have objective value because their value exists not by virtue of the fact that someone actually has a desire for them or takes an interest in them, but rather because that value may be arrived at via rational argument. This opens up the possibility that life has objective meaning distinct from that which religion claims to provide. Our task then becomes to identify through rational reflection those things that are objectively valuable and to pursue them as ends. This is what provides our lives with meaning and purpose. As we shall see, meaning in this sense may be applied to the game of golf as well. Finding meaning in both the game of golf and in life then becomes a process of discovery.

　　Objective meaning doesn't mean our mental states don't matter. On the contrary, it's not enough to discover through rational inquiry what is valuable, and then simply to pursue that as an end. For it to be meaningful it must also be something we want to do. For instance, the philosopher John Stuart Mill (1806–1873) spent a good deal of his early life trying to devise for himself a rational life plan. Ultimately he decided that he wanted to be a "reformer of the world." And though he knew his chosen life's work to be morally virtuous, at some later point he suddenly lost interest in it. It no longer mattered to him. The work didn't satisfy him and no longer contributed to his happiness. This may be in large part the reason for Sorenstam's decision to retire from golf. Without subjective satisfaction, a pursuit becomes a burden and loses its meaning.

Subjective satisfaction is typically not a problem for recreational golfers. Most of us play the game because we enjoy it. It isn't just *that* you play and enjoy the game that matters, however. The way in which you approach the game can make it more or less meaningful. The same is true in life. There is an approach to life that can make it more meaningful, above and beyond subjective satisfaction. But before getting to that, let's explore the limitations of subjective satisfaction.

Hedonism

In an ancient myth, the character Sisyphus divulges divine secrets to mere mortals. His behavior angers the gods, who subsequently punish him for this transgression: he is condemned to roll a large boulder up one side of a hill, only to watch it roll to the bottom on the other side. His fate is to repeat this process throughout eternity. This is perhaps the epitome of meaningless existence. There is no purpose, no point, no ultimate objective beyond the activity itself. Yet, even Sisyphus's life can be made meaningful. The philosopher Richard Taylor suggests that if the gods were to inject a chemical into Sisyphus's veins that made rolling the rock up the hill the thing that he desired most, then his life would become instantly worthwhile. Sisyphus would then love to rise every morning, because he would be doing exactly what he wanted to do, and this love would make his life meaningful.[3]

There is obviously some truth to this. For many of us the ultimate aim in life is simply to be happy. But it can be difficult to discover what it is that truly makes us happy. One school of thought, called Hedonism, maintains that a happy life is one that includes the greatest amount of pleasure and the least amount of pain. The ancient philosopher Epicurus is probably the most famous spokesperson for this philosophy. "Pleasure is our first and kindred good," he writes. "It is the starting point of every aversion, and to it we come back and make feeling the rule by which to judge every good thing."[4]

But Epicurus also understood that the immediate experience of pleasure is not by itself sufficient for happiness. The application of wisdom is essential. Wisdom leads us to accept temporary pains that lead to future pleasures, and to pass on temporary pleasures that would lead to future pains. In the absence of wisdom, we allow our pleasures to control us and in the process sacrifice long-term good for short-term gratification. In an example from the game of golf, a player may not enjoy spending endless hours on the driving range perfecting her swing. Her short-term discomfort will pay dividends in the future, however, when things go well on the golf course. The long-term result is less frustration and greater satisfaction in well-played golf.

It is certainly true that one of the reasons golfers devote so much time to the game is subjective satisfaction. Playing golf can be extremely pleasurable. Take, for instance, the drive from the tee. When a golfer has the mechanics of the swing down, and the ball is properly struck on the sweet spot of the clubface, there is a familiar sound that is music to every player's ears. And the long flight of a well-struck ball as it soars across the fairway is itself a beautiful thing to behold. The satisfaction from this grand feat is intense.

Another example of the pleasure of golf is the appreciation for the beauty of a golf course, its aesthetic appeal. Golf courses are some of the most beautiful places on earth, coming close to matching the human conception of paradise: sweeping vistas of closely manicured fairways, colorful flowers and foliage, scattered groupings of green trees, ponds with aquatic vegetation, beautifully designed bridges crossing over streams, and, on some courses like Pebble Beach, magnificent ocean views.

On rare occasions, what happens on the golf course can result in the ultimate in gratification. Imagine the following scene. You are playing on a very famous and difficult golf course, one that you have wanted to play all your life. You are accompanied by your favorite playing companions, it is an absolutely gorgeous day, and you are hitting the ball better than you have in your entire life. You complete the front nine with an eagle and finish with an incredible score of 32. Your phenomenal success continues on the back nine, culminating in a hole in one on the par-3 eighteenth. Your final score for the entire round is 62, a new course record! As you and the rest of your foursome enter the clubhouse to celebrate, you joke about whether there is any prospect that Tiger Woods would be up for some match play today. You are then stopped by a journalist who says he wants to do a feature on you for the next edition of *Golf* magazine!

Well, then you wake up from your dream. Sort of. In reality, it's no dream—you've been taking a ride in a virtual reality experience machine. It wasn't *you* who beat the course record. You only experienced what it would be like to accomplish this feat. A similar device has been described by the philosopher Robert Nozick. In an experience machine, neuropsychologists stimulate your brain so that you believe you are doing something you always wanted to do—writing a great novel, parachuting from the clouds, . . . or playing a spectacular round of golf. But all the while you are floating in a tank with electrodes connected to your brain. Nozick poses the following question: "Would you plug in? What else can matter to us, other than how our lives feel from the inside?"[5]

Why are most people reluctant to plug in and live out their dreams? Nozick provides three possible reasons:

(1) We want to actually do things, not just have the experience of doing them.
(2) We want to be a certain type of person, not an "indeterminate blob" floating in a tank.
(3) We don't want our experiences to be limited to a manufactured reality, to a world no deeper or more important than that which people can construct.

What is missing from life in the experience machine is truth. Part of what makes an experience valuable is that it is based on true beliefs about the world. For example, it may make me feel good to believe that I had won the lottery or had discovered a cure for cancer. But if my euphoria is based on false beliefs, then the value of the experience is greatly diminished. In the example of shooting a record score on a difficult golf course, I don't want just to experience what it would *feel like* to accomplish it. I want it to be the case that it was *I* who actually scored well. That is something I could never achieve in an experience machine.

The Pursuit of Perfection

Taking pleasure in playing golf is undoubtedly essential to its being a meaningful activity. And for a few golfers, this is the only reason to play. But golf is a game, and as such involves a competition with others or oneself. To play for fun and pleasure alone, without trying to improve, is to miss the point of the game. The object is to get the ball into the hole in the fewest number of strokes that you can manage, not to get it there in as many strokes as it takes. That is why the final score matters so much to golfers: The game of golf involves the pursuit of perfection.

A golfer accepts this challenge, however, in full knowledge that perfection is not really attainable. As Bobby Jones once said: "Golf is assuredly a mystifying game. It would seem that if a person has hit a golf ball correctly a thousand times, he should be able to duplicate the performance at will. But such is certainly not the case."[6] On top of this, there is much about the game that is beyond a player's control: sudden changes in wind direction, rain, background noise, unlucky bounces, and uneven lies are just a few examples. So, rather than reaching perfection, the best a golfer can hope to achieve is some level of excellence. To borrow a line from the movie *The Legend of Bagger Vance:* "It's a game that can't be won, only played."

In life, as in golf, pursuit of excellence is an essential component. According to E. J. Bond:

> A vital ingredient that is missing from the hedonistic picture . . . is the kind of value that commands or merits *respect* in addition to constituting a reward or pay-off. If a person has a lot of what she likes and little of what she dislikes over a long period of time, we may say that she is well off and we may envy her, but there is nothing about her yet which gives her any special worth as a person, which commands, inspires, or indeed merits special respect, including self-respect. And this is to ignore a dimension of value which simply cannot be ignored. In the most general, and the most ancient, sense of the term, what is missing is virtue, or excellence.[7]

Professional golfers competing on the PGA and LPGA Tours pursue and achieve the highest degree of excellence. For these players golf is a way of life. They work on their games year-round and play in tournaments almost weekly. This level of achievement is not open to the vast majority of players. It requires not only endless practice, but also a special talent that only a very few possess. That, of course, doesn't mean that the pursuit of excellence is not open to other players. Success on the golf course may be measured in terms of both *absolute* and *relative* excellence. The level of success achieved by pro golfers may be categorized as excellence in an absolute sense. Here success is gauged in comparison to what the best golfers in the world have achieved or may reasonably be expected to achieve. In the relative sense, the level of excellence is measured against how an individual has himself played in the past. Any improvement in one's game is a move in the direction of heightened excellence. As an example, a golfer's goal may be only to improve to the point where he consistently shoots in the 80s, or reduces his handicap to 10. Depending on the player's level of talent and physical condition, this might be a reasonable goal. The point is that, in the game of golf, everyone is capable of achieving excellence. Excellence could perhaps be referred to as a process of "self-actualization," and there are many opportunities in life in which to seek it. It might be pursued in the workplace, or in following one's passion. Approaching these endeavors creatively, and with a determined focus on trying to perfect one's performance, enhances meaning in life.

But excellence is not limited to performing some activity well. Excellence may also be pursued in terms of trying to become a certain kind of person. As Bond points out, being the type of person who inspires both respect from others and from himself is important to living a meaningful life. This requires adopting the moral point of view, which includes the recognition that *everyone* has the right to pursue a meaningful life. Since my actions can have either negative or positive effects on others, I must take into account how my actions affect others in the pursuit of their life's plan. The philosopher John Kekes recognizes the importance of morality:

> The form social life takes is the establishment of some authority, the emergence of institutions and conventional practices, the slow development and deliberate formulation of rules, and all these demand conformity from members of a society. This imposes restrictions on what we can do and provides forms for doing what we want and what society allows. Different societies have different authorities, institutions, conventions, and rules. But no society can do without them and no human being can do without some participation in social life, provided he seeks satisfaction and a meaningful life.[8]

Important moral questions surround the activity of golf itself, and the pursuit of excellence requires that they be given thoughtful consideration. Some examples:

- The game of golf is an expensive pursuit, from the high price of equipment and apparel to exorbitant greens fees. Since this money could be used to address more pressing social needs, an important moral question is how much one may rightly invest in the game.
- The construction and maintenance of golf courses can have an adverse effect on our environment. It is therefore critical that we reflect on the

need to promote and support eco-friendly golf courses that protect the environment and conserve natural resources.

- Some private golf clubs have a history of excluding certain groups from their membership on the basis of race, religion, or gender. It is therefore essential that we reflect on the importance of diversity within our golf clubs, and boycott those clubs that we suspect of discriminatory practices.

Once the decisions about whether, where, and when to golf have been made, the ethics of play must be considered. Like all games, golf is constituted by its own unique set of rules. These rules, because they allow for competition and the pursuit of excellence, are part of what make golf a meaningful activity. The rules not only place constraints on what a player may and may not do in pursuing the objective of putting the ball into the hole (thereby defining the game itself), but are also in place to ensure that everyone is given the same fair chance to succeed. These include refraining from speaking while another player is making a shot, raking sand trap footprints, repairing ball marks on greens, being aware of one's shadow on the greens, and so on. Rules of conduct, whether they are the rules of a game or the moral rules of society, necessarily place limitations on our freedom. But they are an important component in playing meaningful golf and in leading a meaningful life.

Some might object that though playing within the rules is perhaps a necessary condition for playing fully meaningful golf, it is not as clear that it is necessary for leading a meaningful life. For example, imagine the case of the "Happy Hitman." Even though his work involves taking the lives of others, he takes great pleasure in his chosen profession, happens to be very good at it, and earns the kind of money that permits him to enjoy the finer things in life (including playing some of the best golf courses in the world). What's more, he never suffers pangs of guilt and is forever able to elude the authorities. Wouldn't this life, albeit immoral, be meaningful for him?

As difficult as it is to acknowledge, we must admit that this is indeed a possibility. There are examples of individuals who lead immoral lives and yet appear to be happy and fulfilled. But genuine instances of this are undoubtedly quite rare. It is much more often the case that an individual pays a price for immoral behavior, from relatively minor penalties such as personal guilt or social ostracism, to more serious punishments such as imprisonment by society. So it is generally in our best interests to lead moral lives, and doing things that are in our best interests is conducive to living a meaningful life. In life, as in the game of golf, we are typically better off when we choose to play by the rules.

Within the broader context of social concerns are those special relationships we have with friends and family members. These are important above and beyond our general concern for others because they are characterized by deeper intimacy and mutual caring. The importance of these special relationships goes beyond the pleasure and happiness they bring. It is the nature of the relationships themselves that enhances meaning in life.

An indispensable part of these close relationships is the sharing of activities together. Not only is it more enjoyable to engage in joint pursuits with those with whom we are close, but it also serves to nurture and deepen the relationships. The game of golf can serve as a wonderful vehicle in this capacity. Since it is an exceedingly difficult game to master, it provides us with a great opportunity to learn from everything involved in playing the game well. On the golf course we are able to discover a great deal about one another: how patient we are, how we handle adversity, how we cope with frustration, and how we respond to success. By way of this process we are able to enrich the special relationships that are so central to our lives.

Potential Sources of Meaninglessness

Golf presents us with a wonderful opportunity to reach for perfection, but its pursuit does not come without a price. One famous quote is "If frustration is your aim, then golf is your game." The sources of frustration are numerous. For golfers new to the sport, the initial excitement in playing their first few rounds is often blunted by subsequent periods of mediocrity and stagnation. Even after becoming reasonably competent, players must still endure periods of suffering on the course. When things are going well, golfers will often start to focus too much on their final score and end up playing poorly. And when things are not going well, the frustration often continues to mount as the day wears on, gradually making a bad situation even worse. These negative aspects of golf have caused a few to "hang up their spikes," deciding that the costs of playing the game are just too high.

Some philosophers have adopted a similar perspective on life in general. Schopenhauer is perhaps the most famous philosopher espousing this point of view, which has come to be known as Pessimism. He believed that all evidence indicates that any perceived contentment in life is doomed to frustration, or is ultimately determined to be illusory. He argues that life lacks meaning because people are perpetually dissatisfied, because of the constant inability to satisfy their desires. This is an important point because, as we discovered in the discussion of the myth of Sisyphus, satisfaction of desire is a key aspect in living a meaningful life. Schopenhauer goes on to point out that in the rare instances in which individuals are able to achieve their aims, they discover in the end that they are a complete disappointment: a temporary euphoria is replaced by dissatisfaction and in some cases even boredom. Once it is discovered that achieving a particular aim is not really satisfying, a new aim takes its place and the same absurd pursuit begins all over again. In a gloomy, final indictment of human existence, Schopenhauer pronounces that "all good things are vanity, the world in all its ends bankrupt, and life a business which does not cover its expenses."[9]

There are some days on the golf course when Schopenhauer's account seems to sum up the situation quite accurately. Golfers must contend with such emotions as the fear of failure and humiliation, frustration over hazards or uneven lies, and anger with slow players up ahead. Then there are the myriad painful miss-hits of which all golfers are capable: hooks, slices, scruffs, chili dips, skulls, skyballs, and shanks are just a few examples. Every golfer experiences moments when the game seems more a curse than a blessing.

There is no doubt that the game of golf is a roller coaster of emotion. But part of the challenge of golf is mastering the mental aspect of the game. A key to this is to acknowledge the negative emotions as they occur, but not to allow them to interfere with the actual playing of the game. Controlling emotion and simply being open to whatever happens on the course provide an opportunity to learn. Rather than blaming a poor shot on changing conditions or on some distraction, the golfer must take responsibility for the shot. Only then is the player in a proper mental state to learn what the game of golf has to teach, and then to respond accordingly.

Coping with the emotional highs and lows of the game of golf offers us lessons on how to approach life. When we take responsibility for what happens to us, which includes the recognition that our lives are something that we create—not something that happens to us—then life becomes less frustrating and more satisfying. Taking responsibility affords us the opportunity to open ourselves to the events of life and to learn from them, and it goes a long way toward helping us to achieve our objectives. As Schopenhauer rightly points out, often the achievement of our goals leaves us feeling empty and dissatisfied. But the importance of goals lies not only in their achievement, but also in the process itself. This is really what makes setting goals worthwhile. If it were merely their attainment, then as soon the major goals in life were achieved, meaning would necessarily be lost. It is in the very act of seeking to achieve that our lives take on enhanced meaning.

Sometimes the joy we take in playing a great round of golf is mitigated by the fact that play must come to an end after the regulation eighteen holes have been played. When the drives have been long and straight, chipping has been clean and precise, and the putts all found their way to the hole, we often wish that play could continue. But the game must come to an end, as each life must come to an end. Philosophers writing on the absurd, such as Schopenhauer and Albert Camus, have put forth the claim that life is made meaningless just because of the fact that there is no afterlife and hence life must come to an end.

It is certainly true that, for many of us, the prospect of death and the inevitable end of the world is difficult to contemplate. Scientists tell us that in another five billion years or so our sun will come to the end of its life, exploding into a giant supernova that will engulf the entire solar system. As the philosopher Bertrand Russell writes, "All the labors of the ages, all the devotion, all the inspiration, all the noonday brightness of human genius, are destined to extinction in the vast death of the solar system, and the whole temple of man's achievement must inevitably be buried beneath the debris of a universe in ruins."[10]

Many find the prospect of individual and societal death alarming. But does it make sense to say that life is meaningless just because it is finite? It is certainly not the case with the activities that occur within a life. The knowledge that a particular endeavor is finite does not prevent people from finding it valuable and engaging in it. The game of golf is not rendered meaningless just because it is finite in duration. In fact, quite the opposite is true: golf is meaningful *because* it is finite. Because a round of golf is only eighteen holes, we cannot afford to take a hole off and decide that we'll put forth a more concerted effort on the next hole. The fact that a round of golf is short means that we have to make every shot count. Similarly, because life is short, we must ensure that we make every day count. In golf we are often sad to see a well-played round come to an end. When a life has been good, it is saddening to acknowledge that one day it too must come to an end. We know, of course, that in all likelihood we will have an opportunity to golf another day. Though it cannot similarly be said that we will probably have a second shot at life, this does not render life meaningless. In fact, if this is all there is, if this is all we get, then we must make wise use of the time we do have.

Another reason that a finite duration gives golf meaning is that it would become tedious if it were to go on indefinitely. It would turn from an enjoyable pastime into something that would be virtually unbearable. Perhaps the same is true of life. An endless life, like an endless game of golf, might over time make us less appreciative of it. It might become not only tedious but perhaps monotonous as well. When considering the prospect that death marks the end of existence, the philosopher Walter Kauffman wrote: "It is possible that this is wrong. There may be surprises in store for us, however improbable it seems and however little evidence suggests it. But I do not hope for that. . . . The life I want to live I could not endure in eternity. It is a life of love, intensity, suffering and creation that makes life worthwhile and death welcome. There is no other life I should prefer."[11]

Meaningful Golf, Meaningful Life

Some people believe that sports such as the game of golf are a waste of time. On a certain level this feeling is understandable. Playing a round of golf will not solve the problem of world hunger; it will not put an end to military conflicts; it will not save our environment; it will not help us to address any of the pressing social issues confronting us today. But, if approached in the proper way, the game of golf can be much more than a diversion. It can teach us something about how to live. What we learn from golf is that life is more than just "one damned thing after another." In golf, it is not just that we play, but how we play that matters. Our approach will determine what meaning and value the game holds for us. Similarly, in life what matters is *how* we live, not just *that* we live. In drawing parallels to the game of golf, what we discover to be important in living a meaningful life is this: to pursue excellence in both what we do and how we live, to spend time with those who matter to us most, and to simply enjoy the passage of time.

Notes

1. "Citing Other Priorities, Sorenstam to Retire at End of Season," May 14, 2008, http://sports.espn.go.com/golf/news/story?id=3394086 (accessed February 7, 2009).
2. E. J. Bond, *Reason and Value* (Cambridge: Cambridge University Press, 1983), vii.
3. Richard Taylor, *Good and Evil* (New York: Macmillan, 1970), 259–60.

4. Epicurus, "Letter to Menoeceus," in *Greek and Roman Philosophy after Aristotle,* ed. Jason L. Saunders (New York: Free Press, 1966), 51.

5. Robert Nozick, *Anarchy, State, and Utopia* (New York: Basic Books, 1974), 42–43.

6. "Bobby Jones Quotes," http://en.thinkexist.com/quotes/Bobby_Jones/ (accessed February 3, 2009).

7. Bond, *Reason and Value,* 121.

8. John Kekes, "The Informed Will and the Meaning of Life," in *Philosophy and Phenomenological Research* 47, no. 1 (September 1986): 85.

9. Arthur Schopenhauer, *The World as Will and Idea,* trans. R. B. Haldane and J. Kemp (London: Kegan Paul, Trench, Trübner, 1883), 383.

10. Bertrand Russell, "A Free Man's Worship," in *Why I Am Not a Christian* (New York: Simon and Schuster, 1957), 107.

11. Walter Kauffman, *Existentialism, Religion, and Death* (New York: Meridian Books, 1976), 214.

More Than a Playing Partner

Golf and Friendship

Andy Wible

The angel Clarence in the movie *It's a Wonderful Life* may have said it correctly when he observed, "No man is a failure who has friends." Humans love others, and family and friends are what make life special. Golf, on the other hand, is often thought to be the ultimate lonely and solitary sport—an individual alone against the course. Winning or losing is totally dependent on the player and no one else. Nonetheless, much of the joy and attraction of the sport seems to come from the friendships that one develops playing golf. Few of us would play much golf if we always had to play alone. The intent of golf is not to create friendship, but, more than most other sports, golf has the virtuous side effect of nurturing enduring friendships. Whether it is the closeness of a regular foursome or the fun-loving friendships of a golf retirement community, golf brings people together. Why is golf so good at fostering friendships? First we need to look at what friendships are.

What Is Friendship?

Every day we call someone a friend. But if someone were to ask us, "What is a friend?" we might have trouble coming up with an answer. A friend is obviously someone whom you like to be around. The opposite of friends is enemies, and enemies are people whom one does not like. Saying much beyond this becomes difficult because there are different kinds of friends. For example, there are many types of "special-purpose" friends. We have fitness friends, political friends, work friends, golf friends, tennis friends, and so on. These are friends because of a shared vision and interest. The ancient philosopher Aristotle called these friendships "friendships based on utility." These people are friends because they derive benefit from one another. Aristotle sees such friends as impermanent and limited, because, for example, when a golf friend quits playing golf, he is no longer a friend. Thankfully, many playing partners in golf become more then golfing buddies; they become unqualified friends.

It is this type of friendship proper that this chapter will focus on. Yes, we like to be around friends, and they are often useful to us, but this is not the reason we like them. The reason we spend time with a friend, according to Aristotle, is the person's good character. A change in one's favorite sport, job, or political party does not affect these stronger friendships. A friendship lasts through these changes. A friend is given up only if the person is thought to be immoral. As Aristotle's theory illuminates, it is hard to maintain a friendship with someone who lies to you and causes you harm.[1]

There is much more to be said about the nature of friendships. We know that if friendships are special, then everyone we think highly of cannot be our friend. I think highly of Barack Obama; unfortunately, he is not my friend. Sometimes people overuse the word and call everyone they have met and admire a friend. Real friendships take time. Even playing eighteen holes with someone is not enough to form a friendship. On the other hand, time is not sufficient for friendship. We might spend hours with someone at work and yet not consider him or her a friend. He or she is just someone with whom we are forced to work.

Friendship takes at least two additional features: intimate knowledge and care. We must know something more about the person than we know of strangers or acquaintances. The more we know about the person's thoughts, values, and desires, the stronger the friendship. The coworker is just a work friend because we often don't know much about the person other than work-related details about him or her. This inside information is what makes for strong personal bonds. A friend wants to know about these intimate matters, because a friend also cares about the other's welfare. Of course, there are persons who tell you intimate details of their lives, such as a parent's impending death, when they first meet you. This does not make the person a friend, for we don't care as much as if this were happening to a friend. Friends are people we care about more than strangers. When a friend is distraught, we are distraught, even if often on a lesser level. We want what is good for the friend and are hurt when this does not occur. In essence, there is love between two friends.

The philosopher Laurence Thomas suggests that there are three additional salient features of friendships. The first is that friendship involves a choice. Friends are people we choose to be with and are not like parents or siblings whom we care about and love. Our parents will almost always be our parents, but friendships often change because of the choices we make. The choice is limited in many ways. We might want to be friends with Tiger Woods or Jack Nicklaus, but the feeling is not likely to be reciprocated. Also, friendships often occur owing to happenstance. Lifelong friendships often begin in golf when a single is randomly paired with a threesome for eighteen holes. The second feature is that no one is under the authority of another in a friendship. There is some level of equality in a friendship. One person cannot force the other person to be his friend, nor can one party avoid self-disclosure, as is the case with a therapist.[2] If I paid people to play golf with me and they could only listen, then these people would not be my friends.

Thomas's final feature of friendship is mutual trust. Friends are moved by caring to help one another and trust that the other will also be there to lend an ear or hand. Friends share personal information because they trust that the other person will keep it secret. Friends want to help each other and depend on each other. Friends who lie or don't show up in times of need eventually fail to be friends. These features help show that a friend is a chosen and trustworthy equal whom you enjoy.

The Foursome Fostering Friendship

All sports encourage friendship because of mutual interest in the activity. With the exception of children who are often forced to play sports and professional athletes who need to make a living, people play sports for the love and enjoyment that the sport provides. This is not to say that all sports are the same when it comes to nurturing friendships.

Golf is fairly distinctive among sports in that there is plenty of time for conversation during play. Walking or riding to the next shot and waiting to putt or tee off over several hours allows for plenty of conversation to take place between playing partners. Friendships take time and golf takes time. Baseball allows for conversation when in the dugout, but such conversation is limited to those on the same team. Other sports, such as tennis, basketball, and football, allow for conversation only during breaks or between games.

Golf conversations often carry over to the nineteenth hole, but the sport facilitates conversations among all participants during the competition itself.

Golf friendships tend to last because golf is a sport that can be played from ages 3 (2 in the case of Tiger Woods) to 103. Many sports, such as football, kite surfing, or even basketball, are often played only during one's peak physical years or are too grinding on the body to play for extended periods. It is not likely that Michael Jordan will be competing with the best in basketball at 59, as Tom Watson did at the 2009 Open. Uniquely, golf participation tends to increase with age rather than decline. The shared love of this beguiling game builds intimacy from the junior leagues to the super-seniors.

Golfers become so close that they tend to build their lives around the friendships golf fosters. People often join private golf clubs, where they socialize at dinner or the pool as much as they play golf. Also, increasingly popular is the golf retirement community. Retirement communities such as the Villages in Florida or Sun City Communities in Arizona and elsewhere attract thousands of people who want to spend their time around golf. The joy is not so much in the reasonably priced golf that is available in these communities. The real beauty of such places is the time spent with good people at a similar stage in their lives who have common interests and values. Golf is the draw, and the friendships are the glue that keeps them there.

Golf also promotes equality. Golf has a handicap system that creates greater equality in competition by allowing golfers of most abilities to compete and play with one another without diminishing the enjoyment of the other players. In other sports, such as tennis and baseball, it is just not much fun for people to play with competitors who are much better or worse. In golf even Tiger Woods can enjoy competing against and possibly be beaten by a 15 handicapper when scores are adjusted by this system.

Our struggles against the course or opponents enhance friendship because of the shared intimacy that golf provides. Golf exposes physical and mental weaknesses, opening up one's inner vulnerabilities. Strong wills and good bodies rise to the top, and those who are weak or who choke in competition languish at the bottom. (Yes, I am a bottom feeder.) From the almost orgasmic elation derived from a perfectly struck five iron to the agony of missing a two-foot putt, golf exposes each of us to those revealing high- and lowlights in time. No one can be blamed or rewarded but ourselves.

Significantly, golf, like other sports, provides moments of shared activity that only a few can remember together. The hole in one, the winding fifty-foot putt to win a dollar Nassau, and even the shank into a passing car's windshield are special times that bind playing partners. Memorable moments foster memorable friendships.

I know what you are probably thinking. Doesn't competition get in the way of friendship? Friendship is present when there is mutual caring or goodwill between two people. In competition, beating the other person in order to win is the goal: the opposite of mutual goodwill. Competition brings out selfish rather than cooperative behavior. True friendships might be better enhanced in a club (like Rotary or Kiwanis) or a religious setting where there is no overt competition. Golf is especially troublesome as an individual sport. Participants in team sports have the advantage of being able to bond together in an attempt to beat the competition. Team competitive sports are particularly good because there is a common enemy, and nothing brings people together like a common enemy (think of the United States after 9/11).

Golf, of course, does have some team competition. Professional golfers who play in the Ryder Cup and President's Cup often tell about how close they became to their teammates when they played against the Europeans or international contingent. Amateurs as well often have team events in which partners form special bonds. In addition, golf fosters mutual trust even when being played by individuals. Since players are required to call their own penalties, each player must trust that the other person will be honest and forthright. Further trust is needed because scores are kept by fellow players rather than officials. This trust explains why golf is great for business development or for promoting close friendship. If a player is honest on the course, it is likely that he or she will be honest in other areas of life (and the converse is true as well). Also, a common enemy is present on a golf course and probably is a morally better target than the one in team sports. The common enemy is the course. Golfers often threaten to do things such as cut down a tree that is frequently in the way of their shots. Fortunately, most people don't carry a chainsaw in their bags, and the comment is just a joke. Yet notice how much worse it is to say such things against human beings. When Carl (Bill Murray) in *Caddyshack* talks of cutting the tendon in Judge Smails's leg to help Ty Webb win, even though he means it as a joke, it makes one quiver a little and think Carl is crazy.

Finally, competition in golf can, when properly understood, encourage close bonds. Competition provides mutual interest in winning that often adds to the fun of the game. People enjoy competition against one another and seek it out by choice. This competition is what the philosopher and golfer Robert Simon calls "a mutual quest for excellence." Simon believes competition within the rules of the game and within moral guidelines brings people closer. Competition is not about winning at all costs. Rather, "good competition presupposes a *cooperative* effort by competitors to generate the best possible challenge for each other. Although one wins the contest and the other loses, each gains by trying to meet the challenge."[3] Sportsmanship is required for this effort to be cooperative. Thus, while trying to beat one's opponent, one should also respect and wish one's opponent well. We hope that our friends play well. I might want to beat a friend, but I also should wish that he or she plays well and that I play even better. A player who has a win-at-all-costs attitude might win the battle of the day, but he or she will lose the long-term war for friendship and mutual moral excellence.

Why Is Friendship So Important?

The enjoyment found in mutual competition and excellence brings us to the next reason that friendships are important. Descriptively, we obviously value friendship, as can be seen in our desire to play golf with people we know. Good golf is playing with anyone; great golf is playing with close friends. Another interesting way to see how much we value friendship is to see how we view and interact with sports stars. Many of us have gone to PGA and LPGA Tour events to watch the game's best players compete. We love the good shots, but we also enjoy the personalities. In the back of our minds, one reason we want to see Woods, Nicklaus, Palmer, or Ochoa play is that we want to interact with them and become their friends. Imagine one of these players saying, "Hey, you seem really cool, do you want to have dinner after I am done competing?" Most of us would feel like we had won the lottery: this god likes me and sees me as an equal. The sports writer John Feinstein believes the allure of Arnold Palmer comes from his ability to connect as a friend with fans. Feinstein writes of Palmer, "When people call his name, he does not give them the Papal Wave the way most players do, he searches them out, makes eye contact—every time—and says something."[4] Palmer had a way of making nearly all in attendance feel that he was touched by their comments or sheer presence. Arnie's Army is Arnie's Friends.

So we obviously value friendship, but why do we value it, and is it always good for us? Aristotle says we value friendship because humans are social creatures. We enjoy the company of others and can fully realize ourselves only in friendship. Aristotle holds that a person cannot be happy without friends any more than a person can be happy while sleeping his or her life away. We enjoy loving others, and even more, we love being loved.[5] There is nothing better than someone you care about caring about you, too. The affection cannot be just for advantage. The friend must care about you as a person. It is nice when a playing partner cares when you are teamed with him or her; your playing partner is a true friend when he or she cares about you intrinsically as an end. According to Aristotle, this highest level of friendship or care is reached because each side sees that the other is a virtuous person. It is this type of friendship that is ideal, for it is one that endures. The friendship will last as long as both parties remain virtuous. The bad person takes no pleasure in another person unless there is something of benefit. The good person likes a virtuous friend through thick and thin.

Aristotle clearly thought that to be virtuous and fully achieve one's human potential, one must have friends. Most activities, even contemplation, are better when the process is cooperative.[6] Friends are able to bounce ideas off one another. We all know that ideas can seem great in our head and then when subjected to a friend's analysis can sound wacky indeed. Friends let friends know to hit a layup shot and not try to drive the ball three hundred yards over water. All humans have a tendency to self-deceive. Friends are mirrors that help counter the deception that occurs. Friends help us assess our lives more accurately and give us greater self-knowledge. Also, since friendship is based on virtue, a friend supports the other person's being virtuous, which provides happiness. A friend is a rational confidant and someone we have emotional ties to. A way to be moral is to be with moral people. One honest person in a foursome encourages her friends to be honest as well.

Aristotle also points out that the shared values and time spent together increases one's enjoyment of an activity itself. Activities ranging from playing golf to watching movies to performing grunt labor are much more enjoyable when done with friends. Yet the unqualified friend is not a friend for pleasure's sake alone. We care about a friend's well-being and think of him as a good person. The pleasure from such a friendship is secondary. The intent of the friendship is not to gain pleasure, but the care and common interests we have with such a person often result in it. In fact, there is paradox. We get deeper pleasure from friends we don't seek pleasure from. We receive more pleasure playing golf with a friend we respect and love than from one we seek out because he or she will be fun.

It is this understanding of friendship, then, that helps us see the value of friendship to the community. In essence, the idea is that society benefits from honest, courageous, and temperate people. Friends are persons who can be trusted to help out when we are in need and to tell the truth. The virtuous person is a good citizen, because he or she is the type of person we want as a friend. Lawrence Blum points out that one of the clearest ways that friendship causes a moral citizenry is through the mutual goodwill of caring for each other. Friendship is important because it involves acting for the sake of the friend. Care and concern are moral virtues. These moral emotions cause friends to take care of each other, which is essential for individual flourishing and a well-run society.

Blum believes that rational emotions of care, compassion, and sympathy are a good counter to the universal detached moral theories that dominate modern moral thought, such as utilitarian (following what brings maximal overall happiness to society) and Kantian (following universal moral duties such as don't kill, don't lie, etc.) moral thought.[7] The mutual well-wishing of friends seems to have greater moral value or at least counters moral theories such as utilitarianism and Kantianism, which imply that caring should be the same for both strangers and confidants. An example might help here. Suppose you are in the hospital and a friend comes to visit. You say to your friend, "Thanks for stopping by; it is nice to know you care." A utilitarian "friend" might say, "Well, I just stopped by because I know that visiting you will bring more overall happiness, and I wanted to do the right thing." A Kantian "friend" might say, "Well, I know that I have a moral duty to visit you, so I visited." Each person in this scenario did the right action but acted in a cold way for misplaced reasons. The good friend comes by because he or she cares about you and is worried about your well-being. The personal care at the core of friendships is morally advantageous to society. Thus, it is clear that friendships have the potential to make individuals and society better.

Evil Friendships and Unjustified Exclusions

One should not feel automatically righteous because one has friends. Just having a friend or friends does not mean that one is living a moral and fulfilling life. Here I will look at two potential pitfalls of friendships that need to be considered and avoided. The first comes from C. S. Lewis. He holds, unlike Aristotle, that evil people can be and often are friends. Mobsters and gang members as depicted in shows like *The Sopranos* come to mind. Tony Soprano seemed to have several friends who were evil and vicious people. They often did not bring the best out in Tony; rather, they often encouraged him to seek revenge and helped him cover up misdeeds. On the golf course, we all probably know groups who lack virtue. Far too common are people who play together because they love to be rude, lie, and make fun of others. Other groups enjoy supporting one another's prejudices and callous attitudes. Friendships among those who lack moral integrity seem to be based on evil over good.

Lewis certainly is right that evil people form close relationships. Yet this should not mean friendships are worse than previously thought. The friendship represents the good part of these evil people. The care for the well-being of a friend, even if the friend is vicious, is still an admirable trait. A person who feels bad about a friend's illness has an emotional goodness—even if these two friends regularly inflate their handicaps to win club events. Aristotle might have been wrong that only virtuous persons can be friends, but the care for another is a good character trait even in an otherwise bad person. Of course, not all close relations among evil people are friendships; a person who does not care about his "friend" and lies that he cannot help get him to the hospital because his car is broken down (when really he has a tee time he does not want to miss) certainly does not seem like a friend at all. Similarly, a so-called friend who borrows money from another friend with no intent of repaying is not really a friend.

A second and more serious problem with friendship is the partiality of friendship. Friendships are inherently exclusionary. Not just anyone can be a person's friend, for friendships take time and are based on mutual interests and values. The care we have for friends is different and deeper than the care we have for strangers. Caring for friends comes naturally. Caring for strangers in most cases is more strained. We are more likely to help a friend by buying him or her a nice but unneeded present than to give that money to a stranger who lacks basic necessities. The greater good of helping those most in need (the right thing to do) appears to be skewed by friendship. Friendships also can run counter to justice. An owner of a business might give an internship to a friend's daughter rather than to a more qualified stranger, or a teacher might give a better grade to a friend. The partiality of friendships also causes segregation. Sometimes the segregation is intentional (e.g., purposely having friends only of one's religious background) and at other times it is not. People just tend to have friends who are like themselves. Fundamental moral principles such as bringing overall happiness to society, doing what is fair or just, and promoting openness and diversity can seem to go against the ideals of friendship.

Golf certainly is not immune to these problems inherent in friendship. Great strides have been made (as pointed out in Gray's chapter, "Playing Through?"), yet many country clubs are often openly exclusionary on the basis of class, sex, or race, and are quietly exclusionary on the basis of sexual orientation, ethnicity, and religion. Feminists in particular have argued against the values of traditional communities for their disregard of gender-related problems.[8] Private clubs require that a prospective member have a sponsor to join those clubs. If a person is outside the inner circle, membership is unavailable. Businesspeople often join golf clubs to make business connections. These connections give the prospective member special priority because of the friendships that have developed. A person unconnected to such a friendship does not have those same opportunities. Even if a club is public and not explicitly exclusionary, the friends who play there can be. Sometimes groups of friends are known by their exclusivity. There are African American groups, Jewish groups, gay groups, and of course, the ever-popular groups of rich white men.

This exclusion does raise serious problems for friendship. Seemingly counter to what Aristotle suggests, exclusion allows friendships to be immoral. Fortunately, there are several ways to avoid these problems. One response is to treat everyone the same and never fall prey to the partiality of friendship. As I mentioned above, modern moral theory and some laws seem to promote this by focusing only on such concepts as overall societal happiness or abstract justice. Everyone should be treated equally. Presents should be given to friends only when equally given to strangers, and business dealings should never take friendship into account. Government and business certainly seem to be encouraging this approach; each has serious legal and self-imposed restrictions on entertaining and gift giving (to the detriment of struggling private golf clubs). In business, where profits and apparent fairness are central, such an approach may be appropriate (even though a loss of friendship and hence trust between clients now seems to be a general complaint in business). On a personal level such an approach seems to be going overboard. In our personal lives friendships make life more worth living. Happiness is increased when you have friends you enjoy and can trust. A moral society is one that includes friendships.

The feminist philosopher Marilyn Friedman gives another way of countering exclusionary friendships. Friedman recognizes the importance of communities for self-identity and societal flourishing, but she realizes that people are often born into families and communities that are sexist or racist.

This discrimination often goes unnoticed. Consider that even the angel Clarence said no "man" is a failure who has friends. Friedman's response is to recognize the equal importance of what she calls "modern voluntary friendship communities." She believes these communities are important antidotes to such traditional communities as families and neighborhoods. Political action groups, support groups, and associations of co-hobbyists are assemblies of voluntary friends that should be recognized as important parts of public and personal fulfillment.[9] Women's groups, African American societies, and gay political groups are examples of such voluntary friendship communities. In golf the LPGA might be a professional example of such a community. The LPGA was formed by women and for women to have the opportunity to have their own competitions, to fulfill their potential and achieve equality. It is more successful now than ever and is the longest-running independent professional women's sports organization. The LPGA and women's sports in general should not be thought of as inferior, but simply as a different type of competition. The alternative open community of the LPGA even provides an avenue for a fuller expression of individuality and fulfillment, as can be seen through a few openly lesbian players and a substantial lesbian fan base. At the recreational level, there are many voluntary friendship communities such as women's, Jewish, African American, and gay golf groups that have allowed these traditionally excluded groups to flourish.

The worry is that this continued segregation does not in fact offer real equality. If we learned anything from *Brown v. Board of Education,* which eliminated segregation in public schools, it is that separate is not equal. The answer is clear that segregation on the basis of religion, race, ethnicity, and sexual orientation is wrong, but the answer is not so easy when it comes to segregation based on sex. Some argue that the LPGA is not like the African American baseball leagues of the past, which gave black ballplayers a chance to compete, but were inherently unjust. Annika Sorenstam is not the equivalent of Jackie Robinson. Consider that no woman has even made the cut on the PGA Tour since Babe Zaharias at the 1945 Tucson Open. The argument is that it is not political or economic power that prohibits women from competing; it is physical power. *The LPGA might have cute players to watch, but the competition is third-rate.* Simple integration of men and women at highly competitive levels will leave most women destined for the mini-tours.[10] The LPGA and women's golf in general give women greater opportunities than integration would allow.

I think that there are at least three replies to the argument that women's sports should be segregated. First, integrated competition starting in the junior ranks might result in more equal competition and friendship in higher ranks. Michelle Wie might not be a powerful exception but a prototype of what could happen if boys and girls are integrated from the beginning. Second, golf courses could be set up to benefit the skills of women golfers. Courses could be played that offer tight fairways, shorter yardage, and small, fast greens. Such configurations would probably bring men and women into more equal competition. Finally, even if men and women are not physically equal, segregation does not follow as a logical consequence. Asians tend to be smaller than those of other ethnicities, but this does not justify having a professional league that allows only Asians. African Americans dominate professional basketball, but this does not justify a white-only basketball league.

At the recreational level golf clubs should have open memberships. For example, men's-only clubs and men's-only grills should be a part of our discriminatory past, and women's days should be considered only temporary solace until true societal justice takes place. Blum is correct that sympathy, care, and compassion are important aspects of a moral life, but a moral life includes other important values. The compassion, sympathy, and care of friendships must be balanced against other moral values, such as increasing overall happiness, justice, diversity, and rights. Unlike denying membership to someone who has a bad character, denying membership on the basis of the irrelevant characteristics of race, sex, religion, sexual orientation, and ethnicity is unjust. Further actions should be taken by clubs and courses to have wide-ranging antidiscrimination policies (as most Fortune 500 companies have) that include prohibiting discrimination on the basis of these and other irrelevant factors. These policies would encourage, for example, gay and lesbian couples to become club members, since they would be getting the same rights and benefits as heterosexual couples. Amateur and professional golfers probably would feel more comfortable being openly gay or lesbian if the PGA Tour, European Tour, and USGA also had such policies.

Individual friendships should also be more open in valuing acceptance and diversity. Friendships are based on choice, and many people are hesitant to criticize any friendship, because, after all, "it's a choice." Yet some choices are better than others. Excluding someone as a friend because she lied, stole, or harmed someone is justified. Excluding someone as a friend because of her race, sex, sexual orientation, religion, or ethnicity has no moral basis. Rarely does anyone admit racism. Often people say, "I am not racist" (or sexist, or prejudiced), and yet they have only friends of the same ethnicity, sex, race, or sexual orientation. Realizing our tendencies (which good friends help us do) and the importance of such values as acceptance and diversity is important to living a moral life. Diverse friendships can enhance our lives by making us ethically and intellectually more robust persons.

Making adjustments in our personal lives and in our institutions to avoid unjust exclusion, while maintaining the care and loyalty of friendship, is central to a good life on and off the course. One of the reasons golf is a wonderful sport is that, under the right conditions, it causes those friendships to flourish—so much so that Clarence might say in a summer remake of *It's a Wonderful Life,* "No person who plays golf is without good friends."

Notes

1. Aristotle, *Nicomachean Ethics,* trans. J. A. K. Thomson (London: Penguin Books, 1953), 1156a16–1157a9.

2. Laurence Thomas, "Friendship and Other Loves," in *Friendship: A Philosophical Reader,* ed. Neera Kapur Badhwar (Ithaca: Cornell University Press, 1993), 56.

3. Robert Simon, *Fair Play: The Ethics of Sport,* 2nd ed. (Boulder, Colo.: Westview Press, 2004), 27. Chapter 2 provides Simon's full defense of competition as a quest for mutual excellence.

4. John Feinstein, *A Good Walk Spoiled: Days and Nights on the PGA Tour* (Boston: Little, Brown, 1995), 254.

5. Aristotle, *Nicomachean Ethics,* 1159a9.

6. Ibid., 1177a34.

7. Lawrence Blum, "Friendship as a Moral Phenomenon," in Badhwar, *Friendship: A Philosophical Reader,* 192–210.

8. Particularly see Marilyn Friedman, "Feminism and Modern Friendship: Dislocating the Community," Badhwar, *Friendship: A Philosophical Reader,* 285–302. Friedman does not argue against traditional country clubs in particular, but in her assessment communities, families, and religious organizations certainly seem analogous to traditional communities in golf.

9. Ibid., 298–99.

10. For a fuller discussion of men and women in sports, see chapter 5 of Simon's *Fair Play,* and Betsy Postow, "Women and Masculine Sports," *Journal of the Philosophy of Sport* 7 (1980): 54.

IX. Parting Shots

SWING THOUGHTS

Tough Questions for a Tough Game

Andy Wible

The philosophical analyses in the previous chapters are just the beginning of the connection between golf and philosophy. Below are several additional (yet related) philosophical questions applied to golf. They are intended to provoke further thought, reflection, and discussion of the game, its players, and the world. You might try to answer one or more per round and then create your own list. As Albert Einstein said, "The important thing is to never stop questioning."

1. Philosophers have traditionally favored the rational over the emotional. Plato and Aristotle thought that for a person to be good and successful, his or her rational part should rule the emotional part. Golf certainly seems more rational than other sports. This can be seen in the fans of golf. Golf fans tend to clap politely and remain quiet. Their emotions are subdued and rarely result in unruly behavior. Should all sports follow this model? Is golf morally superior because of the quiet respect of its fans and participants? Are arenas that encourage cheers such as those heard at the Ryder Cup and the sixteenth hole at the Phoenix Open morally improper?
2. Many people pray to God before a big round or a big shot. Are such golfers asking that God cheat for him or her? If God interfered and kept the ball from going into the water, such interference would go against the rules of the game. If God just tinkered with the player internally, wouldn't that be similar to the taking of a performance-

enhancing drug? If it is just the thought of God that helps the player calm down, then it seems important that God just listen and not do what the player actually requests.

3. Saint Augustine once said that "an unjust law is no law at all." His belief inspired people to practice civil disobedience to protest unjust laws. Should similar protests be made in golf for some of its allegedly unfair internal rules? For example, should casual golfers commit acts of civil disobedience and tap down spike marks that are in their way? The previous player did not have the interference of the mark and the current player did nothing to cause the unnatural intrusion. Should the USGA have a court for amateur and professional golfers to hear their rules grievances?

4. Most professional and amateur golfers have played in a charity golf event. Many communities have one or more every weekend to help fund local charities. PGA Tour events have donated more than a billion dollars to charity through the years. Golfing for charity is thought to showcase one of the best aspects of the sport. Yet if golfers and fans really want to help society, shouldn't they just give a donation straight to the charity, rather than taking up a large part of the donation to pay for the golf, lunch, prizes, and so on? Is it justified because the charities get income from people who would not normally give? Should I demand entertainment for my charity dollars?

5. In Plato's famous book *The Republic* the story of the ring of Gyges is used to propose that everyone would be unjust if he could get away with it. The shepherd Gyges finds the ring and then realizes that it renders him invisible. Gyges uses this invisibility to seduce the queen, kill the king, and take over the kingdom. Did Tiger Woods have the ring of Gyges during his first thirteen years as a professional? Would you have committed similar injustices in Woods's invisible shoes? Do you move your golf ball when no one is looking? Glaucon, the character in *The Republic* who presents the story, says the person who would not do wrong when possessing such a ring is an idiot. Does the idea that God is always watching often prevent people from committing these invisible misdeeds? Or does the wise person gain sufficient inner peace simply from knowing that she is just?

6. Bishop Berkeley argued against one of our most common beliefs: that there is a material world. All the trees, bunkers, and other bodies that we perceive are perceptions only. There is no material world

out there independent of our observation. He asks us to try to conceive of objects independently of our perception. He says, "To make out this, it is necessary that you conceive them existing unconceived or unthought of, which is a manifest repugnancy."[1] Is Berkeley right that the material world does not exist beyond our perception? The philosopher Bertrand Russell argued against him by saying that the continuity of our observations is best explained by the existence of a material world. When we see our golf ball go in the pond, close our eyes, and then open them hoping the water is not there, the pond always remains. You might think that such a discussion does not matter, but if in the end you found out that all your clubs, balls, and playing partners were really just perceptions and not real, would it matter? Would the friendships developed and all that practice have been for naught?

7. Does the morality of something affect the beauty of it? There is great controversy in philosophy about whether a piece of art (say, a beautiful building) is less beautiful if it is morally bereft (it was made by slave labor or has words engraved on it that support slavery). In golf, for example, if a player has a beautiful swing but is a terrible person, is her swing less beautiful? Is a course less beautiful if it uses lots of chemicals that harm the local environment, or should we say that it is equally beautiful but the proprietors of the course are immoral?

8. Golf courses are on some of the most beautiful pieces of property in the world. Yet they also use thousands of pounds of pesticides and fertilizers, destroy natural habitats, reduce the quantity of affordable housing, contribute to suburban sprawl, and use millions of gallons of precious water. Is it wrong to cause these environmental problems simply for the middle and upper classes to be entertained? Are efforts to use less water and fertilizers simply trying to paper over the fundamental problem of the courses' sheer existence? Should golfers think outside the tee box with ideas such as developing virtual golf as an eco-friendly alternative?

9. The ball is going farther and farther, and for professionals courses are getting longer and longer. Should professional golfers be required to play with old-fashioned persimmon-wood drivers and balata balls, in the way that traditional wooden bats and uniform balls are used in professional baseball? Would such an action infringe on the players' quest for excellence and some of the fans' fun? Should such unifor-

mity be encouraged for amateurs as well to encourage fairness and the development of shorter, eco-friendly courses?

10. Would the world be a better place if everyone played golf? The USGA and PGA seem to suggest that societal problems such as poverty and racism could be lessened if more people played golf. Do you think this is the case? Can an expensive and exclusionary sport such as golf really have a beneficial effect on such social ills? Do programs such as the First Tee help children by providing moral structure? If they are helped, is it due to the access that they gain to wealthier social networks rather than the game itself? Have many courses forgotten their duty to promote civic justice by eliminating caddy programs that give social access to the lower classes?

11. We have often heard the phrase "What doesn't kill us makes us stronger." The general idea is that the more evil or pain that we experience in life, the better persons we are. Does that mean we should always play harder courses from the back tees? Should we encourage the managers of our home course to add more bunkers and water? Should we wear the spikes on the inside of our shoes rather than on the outside?

12. Casey Martin won his court battle to ride a cart on the PGA Tour because of his disability. That was a tough case, but walking does not seem to have the same importance to the game as running to make a tackle in football does. Allowing a football safety to use a cart to chase down a wide receiver would ruin the game. In golf, many of us ride carts almost every time we play. But should carts be available only for those truly handicapped even at the amateur level? Walking is eco-friendly, good for one's health, and often brings one more in tune with the course. Are such reasons sufficient to require handicap stickers for the use of carts, or are the harms of using carts so small and the enjoyment so high that everyone should be allowed to use them?

13. If aliens invaded the Earth, should they be allowed to play on the PGA Tour? Does it matter if they are made of different material from humans? Does it matter if they are stronger, weaker, or more flexible than most humans? Is such a consideration similar to whether men and women should play together? After all, men are from Mars and women are from Venus.

14. Virtual golf is commonly avoided because it is not "real" golf. Hitting into a screen is not real. But if technology improves and virtual golf is able to perfectly reflect the results of a person's swing, should it be

considered "real golf"? The swings are the same and the results are the same; isn't that what matters, or are we losing part of the game by playing virtually? Also, if the software were able to eliminate all luck from the game, such as sudden gusts of wind or a ball bouncing off a cart, would it be a truer and fairer test of one's golf game?

Now you are on the tee. Think away!

Note

1. George Berkeley, "A Treatise Concerning the Principles of Human Knowledge," in *Principles, Dialogues, and Philosophical Correspondence,* ed. Colin Murray Turbayne (Indianapolis: Bobbs-Merrill, 1965), 32.

THE FIELD

Jennifer M. Beller is associate professor of educational psychology at Washington State University. She is internationally recognized as a measurement specialist of moral reasoning and moral development and has coauthored five instruments on moral reasoning in competitive populations. She coauthored *Sports Ethics: Issues for Fair Play* with Angela Lumpkin and Sharon Kay Stoll, and has authored or coauthored more than sixty-five articles on a variety of topics. She is or has been a consultant for the U.S. Air Force, the U.S. Military Academy, the Idaho State Supreme Court, and the American Bar Association, as well as various sports organizations, including the NCAA, the National Youth Sport Coaches' Association, and the National Federation of High School Activities Association. She has been featured on CNN, *Nightline*, BBC TV, and ESPN, and in many newspapers throughout the country. She is known for playing a hit-and-giggle game of golf and dodging most golf balls hit by her colleague.

Robert Fudge is assistant professor of philosophy at Weber State University in Ogden, Utah. His areas of research include ethics and aesthetics, and he has published in such periodicals as the *Journal of Aesthetics* and *Art Criticism and Philosophical Papers*. In a possible world very distant from this one, he once almost shot par.

Al Gini is professor of business ethics and chair of the Department of Management in the School of Business Administration at Loyola University Chicago. He is also the cofounder and associate editor of *Business Ethics Quarterly*, the journal of the Society of Business Ethics. He can regularly be heard on National Public Radio's Chicago affiliate, WBEZ-FM. His books include *My Job, My Self: Work and the Creation of the Modern Individual* (2000), *The Importance of Being Lazy: In Praise of Play, Leisure and Vacations* (2003), and *Why It's Hard to Be Good* (2006); and he has written and produced two plays—*Working Ourselves to Death* and *Letters of a Consumaholic*. The best advice he ever got from a professional instructor on his game completely changed his life. He told him: "Take two weeks off and then quit!"

John Scott Gray is assistant professor of humanities at Ferris State University in Big Rapids, Michigan. He earned his Ph.D. in philosophy at Southern Illinois University at Carbondale. His interests focus on the various areas of applied philosophy, including bioethics, environmental ethics, and business ethics, as well political and social philosophy. His hobbies include playing or watching hockey as well as collecting vintage sports cards. His golf game is nothing worth bragging about (double-bogey golf), although he has not yet actually killed anyone on the course with his errant drives.

Jason Holt is assistant professor in the School of Recreation Management and Kinesiology at Acadia University, where he teaches courses in communication and philosophy of sport and physical activity. He is author of *Blindsight and the Nature of Consciousness* (2003), which was shortlisted for the 2005 Canadian Philosophical Association Book Prize; editor of The Daily Show *and Philosophy: Moments of Zen in the Art of Fake News* (2007); and coauthor (with L. E. Holt and T. W. Pelham) of *Flexibility: A Concise Guide* (2008). He has also published many essays on philosophy and popular culture, most recently on film noir, Alfred Hitchcock, Stanley Kubrick, *The Daily Show, Twin Peaks,* and *The Terminator.* He lost his mashie years ago.

Laurence E. Holt is professor of kinesiology (retired) in the School of Health and Human Performance at Dalhousie University. He is the author of *Scientific Stretching for Sport (3S)* (1974), the first sport-specific practical application of PNF (proprioceptive neuromuscular facilitation) stretching principles and techniques; *An Experimenter's Guide to the Full Golf Swing* (2004); and coauthor (with T. W. Pelham and J. Holt) of *Flexibility: A Concise Guide* (2008). He has published more than 150 research articles in the sport sciences, is past president of the International Society for Biomechanics in Sport (ISBS), and has served as a consultant for a number of professional sports teams. As a golfer he has enjoyed three holes in one—unfortunately, all shot by his wife.

Mark Huston is assistant professor of philosophy at Schoolcraft College in Livonia, Michigan. His primary areas of interest are epistemology, mind, language, and philosophy of film. He has had publications in *Ratio* and *Philosophy Now* magazines. Though his golf skills are minimal, his visual skills are quite sharp, and he has actually seen people who play golf well.

Stephen J. Laumakis is professor of philosophy at the University of St. Thomas in St. Paul, Minnesota. He received his doctorate from the University of Notre Dame. Recently his research, presentations, and upper-level teaching have focused on Chinese philosophy and Buddhism. His publications include "Confucius and ZHONG/'Doing One's Utmost,'" *East-West Connections: Review of Asian Studies* 4 (Spring 2004); "The Sensus Communis Reconsidered," *American Catholic Philosophical Quarterly* 82, no. 3 (2008); and a book, *An Introduction to Buddhist Philosophy*

(2008). He is an avid golfer. In fact, he has stood on the first tee box at St. Andrews and been on the eighteenth green at Pebble Beach; unfortunately, most of his golf balls are at other unknown locations around the planet.

Angela Lumpkin is professor of health, sport, and exercise sciences at the University of Kansas, where she served as dean of the School of Education. She previously served as dean of the College of Education at State University of West Georgia; department chair at North Carolina State University, as well as chair of North Carolina State's faculty; and professor of physical education at the University of North Carolina at Chapel Hill. She holds a Ph.D. from Ohio State University and an M.B.A. from the University of North Carolina at Chapel Hill. She is the author of twenty books and more than forty scholarly publications and has delivered more than 170 professional presentations. She has served as president of the National Association for Sport and Physical Education. A friend who had played professional golf was right when she told her: never take this game too seriously.

Randy Lunsford is adjunct instructor of philosophy at Muskegon Community College in Muskegon, Michigan. His main areas of interest include philosophy of mind, applied philosophy, and Eastern philosophy. He is an avid fan of sport in general and of the game of golf in particular. He first began to contemplate the meaning and value of golf when, on a warm summer afternoon, he asked his young son to accompany him to the driving range to practice their swings. His son's perplexing response: "I'm not interested in improving my game!"

F. Scott McElreath is assistant professor of philosophy at Peace College, a small liberal arts college for women in Raleigh, North Carolina. He has published papers in ethical theory and is currently working on papers on virtue ethics and action-guiding objections, the morality of hunting, and the value of ethics courses. He received his Ph.D. in philosophy from the University of Rochester and his M.A. in philosophy from the University of Maryland at College Park. He prides himself on having been taught how to play golf by Fred Funk at a twelve-and-under camp.

David L. McNaron is associate professor of philosophy at Nova Southeastern University in Fort Lauderdale, Florida. His areas of interest include philosophy of science, philosophy of mind, and ethics. He thinks of golf and philosophy as much alike: high-end, frustrating activities that offer dramatic highs and lows that are physically safe—except for when the snowbirds invade Florida golf courses in winter.

Scott F. Parker is a graduate of Portland State University and currently lives in Minneapolis. He is a contributor to *Lost and Philosophy* and *Football and Philosophy*.

While golfing, he always hopes to wake up, like Chuang Tzu's butterfly, and discover that he is really Tiger Woods dreaming he's Scott Parker.

Tom Regan is emeritus professor of philosophy, North Carolina State University. He has published more than a score of books and hundreds of essays and has lectured throughout the world on a variety of topics, animal rights in particular. Upon his retirement in 2001, he was awarded the William Quarles Holliday Medal, the highest honor his university can bestow on one of its faculty. He is a member of Wildwood Green Golf Club, in Raleigh. In early winter, when the ball is running, he has been known to play to a single-digit handicap.

David Shier is an associate professor and chair of the Philosophy Department at Washington State University. He received his Ph.D. in philosophy from Wayne State University. His research specializations are the philosophy of language and the history of analytic philosophy. Other research and teaching interests include philosophy of mind, logic, epistemology, and the philosophy of sport. His work has appeared in several journals and edited volumes, including *Analysis, British Journal of Aesthetics, Behavior and Philosophy, Pacific Philosophical Quarterly,* and *Medicine, Health Care, and Philosophy.* He comes from a long line of golfers—not to be confused with the long line of golfers behind him on the course.

Sharon Kay Stoll serves as the director of the Center for Ethics at the University of Idaho. She is considered one of the leading authorities on competitive moral education intervention techniques for college-aged students in America. She is a Professor of Physical Education, Distinguished Faculty Member, and winner of prestigious University of Idaho Outreach and Teaching Awards. A former public school teacher, coach, and athlete, she holds a Ph.D. in Sport Philosophy from Kent State University and is the creator and director of one of the few programs in America that is directed toward the moral education of competitive populations. She is or has been a consultant for the U.S. Navy, U.S. Air Force, the Idaho Bar Association and Idaho Supreme Court, the American Bar Association, and various sports organizations, including the President's Commission of the NCAA, the National Youth Sport Coaches' Association, and the National Federation of High School Activities Association. In 2005 she was featured in more than fifty major U.S. and international newspapers describing the center's project working with the Atlanta Braves. Like her coauthor Jennifer Beller, she plays a hit-and-giggle game of golf and generally hits more people and trees than pins.

Joseph Ulatowski is assistant professor of philosophy at the University of Nevada, Las Vegas. His philosophical interest focuses on naturalistic understandings of mind and action. Besides advanced degrees in philosophy, he holds a bachelor's degree in professional golf management from Methodist University, and he has worked for the Carolinas Section of the PGA, the Country Club of North Carolina, Norwood Country Club, and Walpole Country Club (the last two in Massachusetts). Joe's pursuit of a professional golf career was cut short by an incessant desire to ask questions about the nature of reality.

Andy Wible is instructor of philosophy at Muskegon Community College in Michigan. He received his Ph.D. in philosophy from Wayne State University. His areas of interest, research, and publication are business ethics, gay and lesbian rights, personal identity, and theoretical ethics. An avid golfer from an early age, he was often told that with just better putting, chipping, driving, and iron play, he could have been a contender.

INDEX